Stories Behind the Street Names of Albuquerque, Santa Fe, and Taos

Donald A. Gill, Ph.D.

Bonus Books, Inc., Chicago

98 97 96 95 94 5 4 3 2 1

Library of Congress Catalog Card Number: 93-74136

International Standard Book Number: 1-56625-004-8

Bonus Books, Inc.
160 East Illinois Street
Chicago, Illinois 60611

First Edition

Printed in the United States of America

This book is dedicated to the memory
of the late Clyde Allen Benn,
my father-in-law and my friend.

Contents

Acknowledgments

For all the help that I have received from numerous sources, I am grateful and appreciative. First, I would like to thank my family, especially my wife, Suzan, who graciously understood when I was too busy to do something or to go somewhere. Also I am thankful for the watercolor that she painted for the cover of the book. I am grateful to Bonus Books, Inc., who asked me to write this book after they had published my *Stories Behind New Orleans Street Names.*

My gratitude goes to Martha Benn, my wife's aunt who lives in Albuquerque; Martha was willing to give up her bedroom for us for a part of the summer and was always willing to share what was on her table. My appreciation goes to Dr. and Mrs. Hugh Witemeyer, who kindly permitted us the occupancy of their home in Albuquerque for one month while I did research, and to their two cats, David and Magnus, who made sure that I was out of bed early every morning so that I would have an early start on my research (and feed them first). I am also thankful to Suzan's cousin, Gary Benn, and his wife, Celia, who gave her the use of one of their automobiles while we were in New Mexico during the summer.

Gratitude and appreciation also go to many others who helped to make this book a reality: Allen Vigil, Taos Town Planning Commissioner, and Fayne Lutz, of Taos, who helped me a great deal with the street names of Taos; Skip Miller, archivist at the Kit Carson Memorial Museum in Taos, who permitted me to take virtually priceless photographs from the archives to Albuquerque for reproduction and who seemed apologetic at asking me to sign a release stating that I had taken the photographs into my possession; Al Regensberg, archivist at the New Mexico State Records and Archives in Santa Fé, for providing numerous photographs from all three of the cities at reasonable prices; Mo Palmer, archivist at the Museum of Albuquerque, for research assistance; the librarians, for all their special help, at Albuquerque Public Library, at the downtown branch and at the Special Collections on Edith, and librarians at the Museum of New Mexico History Library in Santa Fé and at the Harson Memorial Library in Taos; Renée Matthews, an Albuquerque real estate agent who helped tremendously in my initial planning; Mary Davis, Albuquerque City Planning Department, who also helped me to formulate my plans for this work when I first began thinking of it; Tom Burlison, of Bernalillo County Planning Department, who gave me much information on origins of street names; the many builders and citizens of Taos, Santa Fé, and Albuquerque who provided information; and, finally, all the many people who have given moral support, who have seemed genuinely excited over this project, and who have indicated that they are eagerly awaiting its publication.

And I extend my thanks also to the many Mexican food restaurants in the three cities for sustaining me through the summer. How I wish I could have some of that food at this moment!

THANK YOU, ALL; *GRACIAS!*

Author's Note

The intent of this work is to share the background stories, the origins, of some of the street names of three communities—Albuquerque, Santa Fé, and Taos. Because of space restrictions, there was no way that all street names of the three cities could be included; therefore, I am sharing some of the more interesting stories, most of which are historical.

Since the work deals with stories, I thought that an image of a storyteller and the two children learning the information would be appropriate on the cover. However, with these stories now recorded on paper, the children can concentrate on other tales to pass on to their children.

Some people may object to my use of the word *Indians* to refer to the people who lived in New Mexico before the coming of the Europeans. I am aware that it is politically correct to use the term *Native Americans;* however, most of the Native Americans with whom I have spoken have indicated to me that they prefer *Indians.* During my two-month sojourn in Taos, Santa Fé, and Albuquerque this past summer, I frequently had occasion to visit with native peoples. I heard very commonly, "And that's the way it is with us Indians." When I purchased a ring from a Hopi silversmith in Santa Fé, he explained that one of its symbols represents strength and the other represents harmony. He continued, "And if you have those, that's all you really need—at least, that's the way it is with us Indians."

Therefore, I have chosen to use the term *Indians.* If I have offended anyone with my choice of words, the offense was not intentional.

Introduction

New Mexico, *Nuevo México, Nuevo Méjico,* the Land of Enchantment—whatever one calls this space of earth set off by geographical boundaries, it is a land of beauty and excitement. Contrary to what some people may think, one does not need a passport to visit New Mexico, the forty-seventh state in the United States of America, which was granted statehood on January 6, 1912. Though the name of the state seems to derail some people whose senses of geography and history are not very acute, New Mexico lies between Texas and Arizona, and the borders between those states are always open.

Recently, when I told a cashier at a grocery store that I had spent the summer in New Mexico doing research for a book, she said, "Oh, I wouldn't want to go down there. Isn't it dangerous? Isn't that where the children are starving? My sister and some of her friends took a bus tour down there to buy prescription drugs at a cheaper price, but I don't think I would want to take those."

Having grown up in New Mexico myself, I was really quite offended at her ignorance.

The story of European discovery of the land that was to become New Mexico goes back to around 1528, when Nuño de Guzmán, governor of New Spain, who had heard stories of cities whose streets were lined with silversmiths and gold, set out in 1529 to find those cities. However, he was unsuccessful. Others, attracted by the tales of the cities of gold and silver, searched as well.

In 1539, Antonio de Mendoza, first viceroy of New Spain, planned an expedition into the northern lands. He first sent out a small exploring party, with Marcos de

Ninza, a Franciscan friar, as its leader. Ultimately, Fray Marcos discovered the Zuni pueblo, which he observed from the top of a mesa; he erected a cross on that mesa, claimed the land, and took formal possession of the land for the king of Spain. He returned to Mexico City to report his claim.

In 1540 Mendoza sent Francisco Vásquez Coronado and an expedition to conquer the land. Coronado eventually pressed as far north and east as present-day Kansas, where he discovered the Quivira Indians, but no cities of gold.

Forty years later, Agustín Rodríguez led an expedition, consisting of a small number of men, for missionary purposes. The soldiers returned to Mexico, but Agustín and Captain Francisco Chamuscado remained and were slain not long afterward.

In 1582–83, Antonio de Espejo and Bernardino Beltrán went to New Mexico to determine what had happened to Agustín and Chamuscado. After learning of the deaths of Agustín and Chamuscado, they explored much of Pueblo country and then returned to New Spain.

In the early 1590s, two attempts at colonization of the land were made, but both were unauthorized and both failed. Then in 1595, Don Juan de Oñate, a wealthy mine owner from Zacatecas, offered to equip an expedition at his own expense and to lead it into the new land. He was appointed governor of the area. On April 30, 1598, Oñate took formal possession of New Mexico at a point on the Río Grande below El Paso del Norte.

On July 11, 1598, he established the first Spanish capital in New Mexico at a Tewa village on the west bank of the Río Grande and named it *San Juan de los Caballeros,* "Saint John of the Gentlemen." This name was given to the pueblo across the river from where he founded his community because the Indians moved out of their houses in order to give shelter to the Spanish guests. The colony was referred to as *San Juan Bautista,* however, with the pueblo being called *San Juan de los Caballeros.* The main body of colonists arrived at San Juan five weeks later; thus, the first permanent colony in New Mexico and the second in the United States was founded. (St. Augustine, Florida, had been founded in 1565.)

In 1601, the name was changed to San Gabriel del Yunque. The capital remained in this place until it was moved to Santa Fé when that town was founded in the winter of 1609–1610. (See introductory section to Santa Fé.)

It is believed that the name *New Mexico* was first applied by Francisco de Ibarra in 1565. He called this land *un otro Méjico* or *Nuevo Méjico.* The name has been used ever since.

Albuquerque

Albuquerque is not one of the oldest communities in New Mexico; Santa Fé was settled almost one hundred years prior to the founding of Albuquerque, and some others precede Albuquerque as well. The city traces its lineage to the action of Francisco Cuervo y Valdés, who was appointed governor by the viceroy, on condition that the king approve. He arrived in New Mexico on March 10, 1705, taking over the leadership of the government in Santa Fé and acting as twenty-eighth governor. (Unfortunately for him, he was not approved as governor by the king, who sold the position instead to Don Joseph Chacón, the Marqués de la Peñuela.)

In 1706, Cuervo ostensibly moved thirty-five families from Bernalillo, a small town to the north of present-day Albuquerque, and settled them on the Río Bravo del Norte, now known as the Río Grande. According to Marc Simmons (*Albuquerque: A Narrative History*), an investigation later revealed that Cuervo y Valdés had founded the city illegally by not following the Spanish law exactly. He had reported to Spain that thirty-five families, with a total of 212 people, had settled in the new *villa*. In reality, as the subsequent investigation revealed, only slightly more than half that number actually settled at that place. When the illegality of the founding of the town was discovered, however, the town had already been created. Apparently most of the homes of the early settlers were spread out along the river rather than being concentrated in the small area that is now known as Old Town, although it appears that many of the residents of

the area constructed weekend homes near the church once it was erected.

Cuervo y Valdés, apparently in an effort at currying favor, named the new town in honor of the viceroy, the Duke of Alburquerque (with an *r* in the second syllable as well as in the third, though that *r* has been dropped from the name of the town in New Mexico). Located near the Portuguese border, the town of Alburquerque, in the province of Badajoz, Spain, is the home of the Dukes of Alburquerque. (In Lisbon, Portugal, the author visited a marble memorial erected to a Duke of Alburquerque in a church.)

Cuervo y Valdés named the new little *villa* along the river for his patron saint, Francisco Xavier, and the Duke of Alburquerque by calling it San Francisco de Alburquerque. Don Francisco Fernández de la Cueva Enríquez, who served as viceroy of New Spain from 1701 to 1708, was the particular Duke of Alburquerque for whom the town was named. And because of this name choice, Albuquerque is known today as the Duke City and the baseball team is known as the Dukes.

Shortly after the founding of Albuquerque, a royal decree was issued and arrived in Mexico City, ordering that the next *villa* established in the viceroyalty should be named San Felipe in honor of King Felipe V, who had recently been crowned. So it was determined by a council of advisors to la Cueva that the name of the town be changed to San Felipe de Alburquerque. With such a name, both the king and the viceroy were honored.

The council also decided on San Felipe as the patron saint, although the people of Albuquerque continued to honor San Francisco as their patron saint. In 1776, according to Marc Simmons, when Fray Francisco Domínguez arrived in Albuquerque to conduct an inspection of the church, he found an oil canvas of San Felipe de Nerí and had it mounted over the altar. From that time on, Albuquerqueans have recognized San Felipe de Nerí as the patron saint of the town.

A plaza was laid out, and the church was built on the north side of the plaza. This area is what is now called *La Plaza Vieja*, or Old Town.

Conflicting information regarding the number of original families exists. Some sources say as many as nineteen families settled the town; others say there were

as few as twelve. However, it is known that the original families had the following names: Barela, Candelaria, del Castillo, Jaramillo, Lucero, Romero, Sedillo, Guitérrez, and Trujillo. Some of these names were represented by more than one family.

Albuquerque soon became a place of considerable importance in trade routes, and the town grew slowly but steadily. By 1790 it had a population of 5,959. It was an important military post during the Spanish and Mexican regimes, though not quite so important as Santa Fé and El Paso del Norte.

Following the American occupation in 1846, Albuquerque became one of the the important outposts of the United States military. At one time an arsenal occupied the plaza.

The telegraph first came to Albuquerque in 1875, and the completion of the railroad in 1881 and the arrival of the Atchison, Topeka, and the Santa Fé Railway gave new growth to the town. It was the advent of the railroad, however, that sounded a virtual death knell to *La Plaza Vieja,* as the railroad came through the area two miles east of the old town.

Three businessmen—William Hazeldine, Franz Huning, and Elias Stover—purchased land for the railroad, then turned it over to New Mexico Town Company, which was owned by the railroad. Colonel Walter Marmon was employed to lay out the new town, and lots were sold, with Hazeldine, Huning, and Stover earning a share of the profits.

The new town was called New Albuquerque, but there were problems with the name. Marc Simmons, in his *Albuquerque: A Narrative History,* treats this story in depth, and that book is strongly recommended reading for the history of Albuquerque. In time, New Albuquerque was granted the exclusive use of the name, and *La Plaza Vieja* or Old Town was, for a time, called Armijo, for the family who built a large home on the plaza, the building that now houses La Placita Restaurant. Eventually, New Albuquerque grew to meet Old Town, and the two merged to become one Albuquerque.

Railroad repair shops were located in Albuquerque, so many workers moved to the town.

In the early 1900s, tuberculosis was the primary cause of death in the United States, and Albuquerque's beautiful, sunshine-bathed days recommended the city as a place for tuberculosis patients to come to seek the cure. By 1910, the town had a population of 13,000, and of that population, three thousand were tuberculosis patients.

Little by little, the Duke City grew along the Río Grande, which provided an oasis in the middle of the desert. Subdivisions were added over the years, and the town pushed eastward toward the Sandias, northward toward Bernalillo, and, in recent years, westward toward the escarpment.

It is ironic that when Colonel Marmon was platting the town, the officials of the New Mexico Town Company told him to stop creating streets when he platted High Street, as they felt that the town would never sprawl out that far!

By 1940, the population had grown to 35,449. But with the completion, on August 8, 1941, of Albuquerque Army Air Base (which became Kirtland Field in 1942), the town really began to grow. By 1950, it had ballooned to a population of 96,815. By 1960, it had more than doubled again, to 201,189. And it has continued to grow: 1970, 244,501; 1980, 332,336; 1989, 384,700. It is projected that by the year 2,000, there will be a population of 581,800. However, in the spring of 1993, Bernalillo County already boasted a population of 480,577. During the summer of 1993, local news indicated that approximately 1,200 people were moving to the Albuquerque area each week, thus increasing the population by almost 5,000 per month.

ABO AVENUE and STREET

Abo Street is located in southwestern Albuquerque, and Abo Avenue is farther south. Both remember the seventeenth-century mission of Abó, built near the old Abó Pueblo.

According to T.M. Pearce (*New Mexico Place Names*), the name is a Piro Indian word that was used for the pueblo at least as early as 1598. The mission there was not established until some thirty years later.

ACADEMY

The street was named for its proximity to the Albuquerque Academy located in northeast Albuquerque. Several streets take their names from the Albuquerque Academy, including Academy Hills, Academy Knolls, Academy North, Academy South, and Academy Parkway (East, West, and South).

Albuquerque Academy was founded in 1955 and was begun in the basement of St. Michael's and All Angels' Episcopal Church with twelve boys in grades seven and eight. It was incorporated in 1956 as a non-profit organization and was moved to a twenty-seven acre campus on North Edith.

In 1964, the academy moved to its current campus in northeast Albuquerque on property that had been donated to the academy by Albert Simms.

According to Walter Daub, assistant headmaster, the campus sits on approximately four hundred acres of land, and the school enrollment is approximately one thousand students.

ACADEMY RIDGE

One of the streets in Academy Place, platted by Home Planning Corporation in the early 1970s, this street takes its name from the Albuquerque Academy, which owned the land on which the development was created. The land had originally been a part of the Elena Gallegos Grant but was later acquired by Albert Simms, who donated much of the land in northeast Albuquerque to the Albuquerque Academy.

ÁCOMA

This Keresan-speaking pueblo is often called Sky City because of its location atop a 357-foot-high butte. Its name is Keresan *ako ma,* "people of the white rock." It is located about sixty miles west of Albuquerque.

The pueblo and Acomita and Santa María de Ácoma have about 3,200 residents and 245,672 acres. The people are primarily farmers and stockmen, though some produce some fine pottery and jewelry.

Ácoma Pueblo, or Sky City, is located atop a 357-foot-high butte. (Photo courtesy New Mexico State Records Center and Archives, McNitt Collection #5752)

Tours of the pueblo are offered, and visitors are driven up onto the mesa on a bus. Previously, however, the only entrance to the place was a series of steps carved into the butte. Certainly, its location served as a natural defense of the pueblo.

ADMIRAL DEWEY

In Academy Estates, Gary Swearingen of Academy Developing Company chose admirals' names for the street names.

George Dewey (1837–1917) was born in Montpelier, Vermont, and studied at Norwick Academy and the United States Naval Academy. As a lieutenant, he was executive officer of the U.S.S. *Mississippi* in David Farragut's fleet in 1861 and took part in the famous fall of New Orleans.

When war broke out between Spain and the United States in 1898, Dewey was in Hong Kong in command of the Asiatic Squadron. He went to the Philippines with orders to destroy or capture the Spanish fleet. His six ships destroyed the Spanish fleet of ten cruisers and gunboats at Manila Bay. As a result, Dewey won fame as the hero of Manila.

Upon his return to the United States in 1900, he became president of the General Board of the Navy Department. He served as an honored adviser on naval matters until his death in 1917. In 1925 his body was placed in the Washington Cathedral in Washington, D. C.

ADMIRAL HALSEY

This Academy Estates street is named for William Frederick "Bull" Halsey, Jr. (1882–1959), one of the leading naval commanders in World War II.

Born in Elizabeth, New Jersey, in 1882, Halsey was graduated from the United States Naval Academy in 1904.

He became vice-admiral in command of a Pacific carrier division and commanded that division in attacks on the Gilbert Islands and Marshall Islands and on Wake Island and Marcus Island in 1942. Also in 1942, he became commander of United States naval forces in the South Pacific. His forces defeated the Japanese in the Solomon Islands. As a result, American land forces were able to occupy the entire island chain.

Halsey took command of the Third Fleet on June 15, 1944. In October 1944, his fleet and Admiral Thomas Kincaid's Seventh Fleet crushed the Japanese navy and essentially eliminated it from the war.

It was on Halsey's flagship, the battleship U.S.S. *Missouri,* that the Japanese signed the surrender.

ADMIRAL NIMITZ

In Academy Estates, this street name was chosen in honor of Admiral Nimitz.

Chester William Nimitz (1885–1966) was born at Fredericksburg, Texas, and was graduated from the United States Naval Academy in 1905.

Nimitz served as commander-in-chief of the U.S. Pacific Fleet during World War II. He took command shortly after the fleet had been almost totally disabled by the Japanese attack on Pearl Harbor, and under him the U.S. fleet in the Pacific was rebuilt.

Nimitz led the U.S. fleet through victory after victory in the Pacific until the Japanese were forced back to

Japan. In 1944 he was promoted to fleet admiral. It was he who represented the United States at the Japanese surrender ceremonies in Tokyo Bay.

After the war, he became chief of naval operations. He left active duty in 1947 and became special assistant to the secretary of the Navy.

ADMIRAL RICKOVER

Located in Academy Estates, this street was also named for an admiral.

Hyman George Rickover (1900–1986) was born in Makow, Russian Poland, on January 27, 1900. In 1906 he and his mother came to the United States to be with his father, who was already working in Chicago.

He graduated from the United States Naval Academy, then earned a master's degree in electrical engineering from Columbia University in 1929. He became a qualified submariner in 1930 and served three years on submarines. During World War II, he was head of the electrical section of the Bureau of Ships.

In 1947 Rickover became convinced that a nuclear-powered submarine was possible, and the Navy approved his plans. He became head of the naval-power branch of the United States Atomic Energy Commission, and he took charge of designing and building the new nuclear-powered submarine, the U.S.S. *Nautilus,* which underwent sea trials on January 17, 1955. This was the first time that nuclear power had been used to propel a vehicle.

Rickover was retired from his post as Director of Naval Reactors by President Reagan in 1982. He died on July 8, 1986.

ALAMEDA

Alameda community, originally an Indian pueblo called San Carlos de Alameda, also known as Sandia Pueblo, was established in 1710 when a land grant was given to Francisco Montes Vigil for his military service.

This street in north Albuquerque was named for its proximity to the pueblo community.

ADONIS

Near Don Juan Onate Park lies a subdivision of streets named for Shakespearean characters.

In Shakespeare's "Venus and Adonis," Venus, the goddess of love, falls in love with Adonis, a handsome mortal youth who goes out to hunt the wild boar. The boar sinks his tusk into the youth's "soft groin," and Adonis dies. Where his blood has spilled upon the earth, a beautiful purple flower checkered with white, the anemone, springs up in Adonis' honor.

ALAMO AVENUE, ALAMO ROAD, ALAMOSA ROAD

These names derive from the Spanish for "poplar" or "cottonwood" and were given for the many cottonwood trees which grow in northern New Mexico, especially along waterways.

ALVARADO

In the summer of 1540, Captain Hernando de Alvarado led a reconnaissance party, sent by Coronado from his main camp at Zuni Pueblo. Alvarado was in charge of the mule-powered artillery in Coronado's expedition. He was one of the first Europeans to see Taos Pueblo.

AMIGANTE WAY

In a portion of Academy Estates, four streets were named with Spanish words denoting friendship. Apparently, the term *amigante* is a variant in New Mexico Spanish for "friendly."

AMIGO WAY

Near Amigante Way lies Amigo Way, from the Spanish for "friend."

AMISTAD

Near Amigante Way and Amigo Way lies Amistad, from the Spanish *la amistad*, "friendship."

ANAYA STREET

Anaya is a relatively common surname in New Mexico. According to Marc Simmons (*Albuquerque: A Narrative History*), one of the first references to this name states that an Anaya family were among the early settlers in an area called The Narrows of Bernalillo in 1605. Cristóbal de Anaya was born in New Mexico in the late 1620s. In his mid-thirties, he became involved in some factional squabbles of colonial New Mexico against some of the missionary fathers. He was arrested in 1661 by Inquisition agents and taken to Mexico City, where he was imprisoned for four years. He was finally released after being forced to march in a procession of penitents through the city.

During the Pueblo Revolt of August 10, 1680, the Pueblo Indians killed 380 men, women, and children among the Spanish settlers and twenty-one missionaries. Among those slain were Cristóbal de Anaya, his wife, six children, and servants. Their naked bodies were discovered scattered near the main door of the Anaya *estancia*.

The street name may memorialize this family, or it may have been named for another Anaya family who came to the area later.

ANDERSON

Senator Clinton Presba Anderson was a prominent man in Albuquerque, the State of New Mexico, and the United States.

Anderson was born in Centerville, South Dakota, on October 23, 1895. He earned a degree from Dakota Wesleyan University, then attended law school at the University of Michigan in 1915–1916.

He relocated to New Mexico because of tuberculosis and remained there. After his release from the hospital, he secured a job as editor with the old Albuquerque *Herald*, then with the *Journal*.

He returned to South Dakota to marry Henrietta McCartney. In 1923 he founded the Clinton P. Anderson Insurance Agency in Albuquerque.

In 1925 he lost a bid for the Bernalillo County Commission but never lost another political race.

During the Franklin D. Roosevelt administration, Anderson was appointed to head up the New Mexico Works Project Administration and National Youth Organization.

Anderson served as secretary of agriculture during the first administration of President Harry Truman. He also served nearly three terms in the House of Representatives and four terms in the Senate.

He died in November 1975 at the age of eighty.

APACHE and APACHE HILLS

These two streets, found in Apache Hills subdivision, were named for the nomadic Apache tribes.

APPALOOSA

Saddle Ridge, developed by Bellamah Homes in the 1970s, is a subdivision designed to provide horse boarding and horse trails around the area, leaving plenty of riding area between houses.

The streets were given equine names, including Equestrian, Appaloosa, Arabian, Morgan, Mustang, and Palomino.

This street name honors the Appaloosa breed.

ARAGON

In Four Hills subdivision, created by Hicks and Associates in the early 1970s, Ralph Hicks chose street names that develop a Western or Spanish theme.

Aragon is a province of Spain that is located in the northeast section of the country.

ARENAL

Many of Albuquerque's streets are named for Indian tribes or pueblos, and this one is no exception. Arenal was one of the Tiguex pueblos. After Coronado's arrival, the Tiguex rebelled overtly because of the actions of the Spaniards, who were disliked by the Indians because the Spaniards bothered their women and were gradually taking over more and more of their land.

ARENAL

In the winter of 1541, a war party from Arenal stole a herd of horses from the Spaniards and slaughtered them. As a result, Coronado's troops sacked and burned the Arenal Pueblo. Braves were lanced or taken captive and roasted alive while tied to stakes.

ARENAS PLACE

This Four Hills subdivision street takes its name from the Spanish word meaning "sands." The street is appropriately named because the homes located along it border the Manzano Open Space, which is a part of the desert.

ASTAIR

In Santa Fé Village, the streets were named for actors and actresses who were popular during the early twentieth century.

Though this street was named for Fred Astaire (born Frederick Austerlitz in Omaha, Nebraska, May 10, 1899), the street name omitted the *e* at the end of his name.

Educated at Alvienne School of Dance, Astaire and his partner Ginger Rogers helped to redefine musical comedy during the 1930s.

His first small film appearance was opposite Joan Crawford in *Dancing Lady* in 1933. Then he made ten films with Ginger Rogers. Other partners were Lucille Bremer, Rita Hayworth, Eleanor Powell, and Cyd Charisse.

With a long list of film credits, Fred Astaire died in Los Angeles on June 22, 1987.

ATLANTIC

The railroad came to Albuquerque in 1880, setting the course for Albuquerque to become the major city in the area. Albuquerque became the center for major railroad repair at the shops located in the area of Atlantic, Pacific, and Santa Fé Streets. These street names were given for the Atlantic and Pacific Railroad and the Atchison, Topeka, and Santa Fé Railroad.

This street is located in the Atlantic and Pacific Addition, which attracted many of the railway employees.

ATRISCO DRIVE

The street was named for the nearby village of the same name. Though written *Atlisco* by Fray Atanasio Dominguez in 1776, the name was probably Atlixco, the name of a valley and city southwest of Puebla, Mexico. Probably the valley of the Río Grande reminded the first settlers of their previous home in Mexico.

This settlement pre-dated the founding of Albuquerque. It was located on the west bank of the Río Grande, facing the site of what was later to become Albuquerque. Atrisco was a community of farms at least as early as 1703.

AVENIDA LA COSTA

Spanish for "riverside avenue," this name signifies the location of the street in Academy Acres near Pino Arroyo and Borealis Arroyo.

B

BACA

The Baca family is one of the oldest families in Albuquerque. The Bacas have been prominent and deeply involved in financing and promoting local enterprises. Bartolomé Baca served as governor of New Mexico from 1823 to 1825. He was a competent leader in warfare with the Indians and was commander of Albuquerque's Cavalry Company of Volunteer Militia in 1815.

Elfego Baca was a local lawyer and, from all reports, quite a town personality. (See Elfego Baca Street.)

BALLOON PARK ROAD

Albuquerque is a major center for hot-air ballooning because of the favorable air currents.

Balloon Park Road derived its name from the Balloon Park, from which the balloon fiesta is held. During

Though this photo was taken of balloons ascending from old Alameda Airport, Balloon Park Road derives its name from Balloon Park, where the annual Kodak Albuquerque Balloon Fiesta is held each October.

most of the remainder of the year, the balloons ascend from the abandoned Alameda Airport.

On the first and second weekends in October, the Kodak Albuquerque International Balloon Fiesta is held at Balloon Park. Kodak says that the balloon fiesta is the most photographed event in the United States. It holds the distinction of having had the most hot-air balloons participating in a mass ascension. In 1992 there were 650 balloons involved in the fiesta.

BARELAS

The street derives its name from the community or plaza that bore the same name. In 1809 Don Juan Barela purchased land in the area that is now south Broadway, at a ranch called El Torreon. By 1870 the settlement had grown to some four hundred farmers and ranchers.

The word *torreon* is Spanish for "tower." During the early European period in New Mexico, it was not uncommon for a family to build a *torreon* or tower in conjunction with their home. The *torreon* was usually made of brick and was located at the end of the home and used as a defense against intruders.

The street name apparently goes farther back into Albuquerque history, however. According to Marc Simmons (*Albuquerque: A Narrative History*), Pedro Varela (or Barela) de Losado owned an estancia or estate believed to have been located somewhere near present-day Albuquerque, possibly in the area of the South Valley known as Los Barelas. (In Spanish, the letter *v* is often pronounced as a *b*.) In 1662, Governor Diego de Peñalosa came down from Santa Fé and, at a meeting held at the Varela estancia, drew up an order for the creation of a town. Twelve to fifteen people agreed to participate in the founding of the town and signed their names to the document, but the venture did not develop.

BARNHART STREET and COURT

This street and this court in Academy Acres were named by Tom Burlison for Charles "Charlie" Barnhart, who was a member of the Albuquerque City Commission when the subdivision was developed in 1972.

BEAR CANYON

In the eastern portion of Academy Acres, developed in the 1970s, the streets were given New Mexico place names.

Bear Canyon is located not far from this street on the western slope of the nearby Sandia Mountains. Bear Canyon Arroyo flows—when there is water—quite near this street.

BEAR DANCER

In Kachina Hills, this street was named for one of the kachinas of the Hopi Pueblo. (See Kachina Place.)

BECK DRIVE

Ed Beck was a traffic engineer for the City of Albuquerque. His name was given to this street by Tom Burlison, formerly of Home Planning Corporation, the company

that platted Academy Acres in northeast Albuquerque in 1972.

BELCHER AVENUE and COURT

Tom Burlison of Home Planning Corporation named this street for "Stretch" Belcher, who was CEO of the mortgage company owned by Ed Leslie, one of the builders.

BELLAMAH

Dale Bellamah was born in San Juan (now Veguita) in northern Socorro County in 1914, the son of an immigrant Lebanese teacher who opened a grocery story in the Barelas area of Albuquerque in 1918. Though his real name was Abdul Hamid Bellamah, "slave of God," the boy became known as Dale.

In his youth, Bellamah worked at the Santa Fé Railroad for $3 a day. He went to the University of New Mexico, worked at the railroad, and slept in the fire house for the pay of a half-dollar a night.

He was married to Jeanne Lees, of Albuquerque, whom he called Princess Jeanne; and in every town in which he built homes, he named a street Princess Jeanne. In Santa Fé, the equivalent is Calle Princesa Juana. Jeanne died in 1970, two years before Dale's death.

Bellamah built Princess Jeanne Park subdivision in 1954. He was a famous builder, one of the top six builders in the United States.

In 1961 Bellamah was the recipient of the American Success Story Award. Beginning with $250, he had developed his business into twenty corporations that were building about one thousand houses a year and were grossing more than $50 million annually.

Bellamah died April 19, 1972. He was survived by a niece, Mrs. D. E. Boyle of Albuquerque, and a grandnephew, Daniel Boyle III. The Bellamahs had no children.

BELLEHAVEN AVENUE, LANE, PLACE

Bellehaven subdivision was created by Dale Bellamah. Though the spelling of the name suggests the French

"beautiful" plus *haven*, "a place of refuge," the name was actually derived from Dale Bellamah's last name.

BENAVIDES

Father Alonzo de Benavides, a Catholic missionary to the Española Valley in the 1630s, may be the person honored in this street name. Two of the churches were placed among the Tewa, at Sandia Pueblo and at Isleta Pueblo.

BENT

In Heritage East, developed in the early 1970s, the streets were named for governors or heroes of New Mexico.

A native of Virginia, Charles Bent was born in 1797 in Charlestown. He graduated from the United States Military Academy at West Point and served in the Army for a time. After he resigned from the Army, he operated a mercantile business in St. Louis.

In 1832 Bent went to Santa Fé and, with his brother William, opened a general merchandise store there. He also was a business partner with Céran St. Vrain. Bent was married to María Ignacio Jaramillo.

With the coming of the Americans, Indians and many Spanish alike were displeased, and plans were made for a revolt in December 1846. Tomás Ortiz, Colonel Diego Archuleta, members of the Piño family, some of the Armijos from Albuquerque, and several clergymen, including Fr. Antonio José Martínez, were involved. These people plotted to kill Bent, then acting governor, on December 19; then they postponed the assassination to Christmas Eve. The authorities discovered this plot, but nothing happened when the planned time came. Governor Bent journeyed from Santa Fé to Taos to spend Christmas at home, thinking that nothing would happen. However, on January 19, 1847, an uprising occurred in Taos, and Governor Bent and five other men of importance were slain.

Bent reportedly died attempting to crawl through a hole in the adobe wall of his home with arrows protruding from his body, having been scalped while he was still alive. His wife, María, and their daughters escaped through the hole in the wall into an adjoining building.

According to Teresina Scheurich, one of his daughters, the women had dug through the adobe wall of the house with a poker and a spoon.

Others slain with him were Louis Lee, acting sheriff of Taos, Cornelius Vigil, prefect, J.W. Leal, district attorney, Pablo Jaramillo, a brother of Mrs. Bent, and Narcisco Beaubien, a son of Don Carlos Beaubien, circuit judge. Bent was buried in the National Cemetery in Santa Fé.

Bent Street honors Governor Bent.

BENT TREE DRIVE

Located next to Ladera Golf Course, this street was fittingly named for the famous Bent Tree Golf Course in the Dallas-Fort Worth, Texas, area.

BERNALILLO PLACE

In Four Hills subdivision, developed by Hicks and Associates in the early 1970s, Ralph Hicks chose street names that develop a theme of the Old West or of New Mexico. Bernalillo is the name of the county in which Albuquerque is located and the name of a small town seventeen miles north of Albuquerque.

The name means "little Bernal" and apparently refers to someone in the Bernal family who settled in the area before the Pueblo Revolt of 1680.

BETTS

This street is located in Princess Jeanne Park, which was developed by Dale Bellamah in the early 1950s and named for Bellamah's wife, Jeanne Lees. Oscar Love first owned the land and subdivided a portion of it.

Betts Street, Betts Place, Betts Court, and Betts Drive were named by Love for E. O. Betts, who was a city engineer at the time. Betts died in 1964.

BIENVENIDA

In Quaker Heights, located on the west side of Albuquerque, the street names develop the theme of the peaceful-

ness and friendliness of the Quakers. *Bienvenida* is Spanish for "welcome."

BJORN BORG

In Wimbledon West, developed by Centex Homes in the 1980s, the street names develop the theme of tennis.

Bjorn Borg, a Swede, was a big name in tennis during the late 1970s and early 1980s. He first won the Wimbledon title in 1976 and won that title five consecutive times. He also won the French Open five times. In 1980 he won the Pepsi Grand Slam and the Colgate Grand Prix Masters as well.

Other streets in this subdivision include Wimbledon and Flushing Meadows.

BLUEWATER ROAD

Bluewater is a small settlement located 112 miles west of Albuquerque. A dam was completed for an irrigation project on Bluewater Creek in 1910.

BLUECORN MAIDEN

In Kachina Hills, this street was named for one of the kachinas, or deities. (See Kachina Place.)

BOATRIGHT DRIVE and STREET

The Boatright family have been in Albuquerque for many years. David Boatright owned a home at 220 Edith S.E., believed to have been built before 1888. He married Rose Casady in 1888.

Boatright was mayor of Albuquerque 1915–1916; while in office, he cleaned up the city's red-light district. Later, he became president of Co-Op Building and Loan Company.

Born in Otterville, Missouri, on March 25, 1859, Boatright was schooled in Otterville and in Sedalia, Missouri.

He began working with the Missouri Pacific Railroad Company as a painter. In March 1881, he moved to Albuquerque and took a position with Atlantic and Pacific Railroad Company in charge of the paint shops. He left Albuquerque for a time, then returned in 1889 and opened a shop called The Racket.

BOGART

In Santa Fé Village, the streets were named for actors and actresses who were popular during the early to mid-twentieth century.

Humphrey DeForest Bogart was born January 23, 1899, in New York, New York, to a prominent family. He had a minor career in the theater in the 1920s and became one of Hollywood's most distinctive leading men of the 1940s and 1950s. Most of his fame was achieved through three major movies—*The Maltese Falcon* (1941), *Casablanca* (1942), and the Oscar-winning *The African Queen* (1951). His list of credits is long.

"Bogey" died in 1957.

BOLACK DRIVE

This street in Heritage East subdivision was named for Tom Bolack, who served as governor of New Mexico for only thirty-two days when Governor Edwin L. Mechem was appointed to the United States Senate. John N. Campbell had already been elected governor for the next term, so rather than moving into the governor's mansion, the Bolacks just maintained their home in Farmington. Bolack had served as lieutenant-governor since 1961.

Originally from Kansas, Bolack worked in oil fields, evenutally becoming very wealthy through oil and gas explorations.

He married Alice Schwerdtfeger on March 14, 1946, in Council Grove, Kansas. Reportedly, he had seen her photograph in a newspaper and carried it until he finally met her. They had two children: Duane Thomas, born in 1951, and Terry Ellen, born in 1954.

The family owned and lived at the B-Square Ranch near Farmington. Bolack served as mayor of Farmington and as state representative.

Bolack was seriously injured in an automobile accident in 1973 and spent many months in an Albuquerque hospital. His wife died of cancer on October 6, 1978.

BOSQUE ROAD and CIRCLE

These two streets located near the Río Grande were named for nearby *bosques* (Spanish for "grove of trees"). Along the river, there are many bosques, constituted primarily of cottonwood trees and Russian olive trees.

BRANDING IRON

In Four Hills subdivision, developed by Hicks and Associates in the 1970s, Ralph Hicks chose names that illustrate a Western theme.

BRAZOS COURT and PLACE

For these Four Hills subdivison streets, Hicks chose a name that developed the theme of the West or of New Mexico. *Brazos,* Spanish for "arms of a human" or "branches of a stream," is the name of a town in northern New Mexico and also a reference to the branches of the North Chama River.

BROADWAY

When the railroad came in 1880, the New Mexico Town Company developed the townsite of New Albuquerque. The company appointed Colonel Walter G. Marmon, a civil engineer, to lay out the town. According to Eldred Harrington (*An Engineer Writes*), Marmon thought that every city should have a Broadway, so he surveyed a wide street and gave it that name.

BURKE

William Smith Burke was a newspaper editor of Albuquerque and the father of the public school system in Bernalillo County.

He was born in Brownsville, Pennsylvania, on November 2, 1835. Though he never went to school, he learned the printer's trade in the Intelligence office in Wheeling, West Virginia, and served in the Seventeenth Iowa Infantry during the Civil War. He owned newspapers in Leavenworth, Kansas.

Burke came to Albuquerque in 1880 and bought an interest in the Albuquerque *Journal* in 1881. He was editor most of the time from 1881 until his death in 1910.

Burke was the first Superintendent of Public Instruction of Bernalillo County because of his interest in education.

BUENA VISTA

Situated on the edge of the East Mesa, the street does allow for a "good view" of the Río Grande Valley and downtown Albuquerque.

BUFFALO DANCER

In Kachina Hills, this street was named for one of the kachinas of the Hopi Pueblo. (See Kachina Place.)

BURGAN AVENUE

When Academy Place was platted in the early 1970s by Home Planning Corporation, Tom Burlison honored Bob Burgan, who was director of Albuquerque City Parks and Recreation Department at the time, in the naming of this street.

BURLISON DRIVE

Thomas Burlison, former employee of Bellamah Homes and, later, of Home Planning Corporation, is honored in this street name in Academy Acres, developed in the early 1970s.

In 1972, Ralph Hicks, his boss, went to the Planning and Zoning Commission to record the names of the new streets of the subdivision. One of the names was a duplicate of an existing street name. So, on the spot, Hicks changed the name to Burlison in honor of his employee. When he returned to the office, he said, "Well, Tom, you now have a street named for you."

BURTON

Solomon L. Burton was a physician in Albuquerque during the early 1900s. He maintained a residence at 610 S. Walter and an office at #9 Barnett Building. He was a strong advocate of the water supply company for the city.

BUSH COURT

Located next to Sagebrush Trail, this Four Hills street was called simply Bush Court.

BUTTERFLY MAIDEN

This Kachina Hills street was named for one of the Hopi deities. (See Kachina Place.)

CABALLERO

In Four Hills subdivision, Ralph Hicks chose street names that create a Western or New Mexican theme. *Caballero* is Spanish for "gentleman" or "horseman."

CABEZON ROAD

The road was named for nearby Cabezon Channel, which connects to the Río Grande. The channel was probably named for Cabezon Peak in nearby Sandoval County. According to T.M. Pearce (*New Mexico Place Names*), Cabezon Peak is a great volcanic hill that rises about 2,200 feet above the plain forty miles northeast of Albuquerque. The Navajos call it *tse najin*, "black rock," and they identify it as the head of a giant killed by the Twin War Gods. On the Miera y Pacheco map of 1775, it was called *El Cabezón de Los Montoyas*. *Cabezón* is Spanish for "neck" or "yoke."

CALHOUN DRIVE

In Heritage East subdivision, developed in the early 1970s, the streets were named for governors or heroes of New Mexico.

James S. Calhoun went to New Mexico as an Indian agent in 1849. He served as the first territorial governor, from March 3, 1851.

In May 1852 he left New Mexico to return to the United States and died in June while en route.

CALLE DE ALAMO

In a small addition near the Río Grande, at the west end of Campbell Road, the streets were given names that are descriptive of their surroundings. Along the Río Grande, numerous *bosques* (groves of trees, especially cottonwood) prevail. *Alamo* is Spanish for "poplar" or "cottonwood." The cottonwood tree is a variety of poplar.

CALLE DEL BOSQUE

Lying near Calle de Alamo, Calle del Bosque derived its name from the same *bosques* discussed above.

CALLE DE ENTRADA

In Las Lomitas ("little hills"), developed in the early 1990s by Presley Homes, James Hicks said that the planners chose Spanish names for the streets, names that develop the theme of the countryside.

Calle de Entrada, Spanish for "entrance street," is the entrance street for the subdivision.

CALLE DEL PALOMA

Like the other streets in this small addition at the west end of Campbell Road, Calle del Paloma was given a name descriptive of its surroundings.

Calle del Paloma is Spanish for "street of the dove," though whoever named the street made a bit of an error. *Paloma* is a feminine noun, so the name should be *Calle de*

la Paloma. Nevertheless, doves are plentiful in the Albuquerque area, especially around the *bosques* along the Río Grande.

CALLE DEL RIO

In this same subdivision, *Calle del Río,* "street of the river," lies parallel to the Río Grande and adjacent to the river.

CALLE GRANDE

In this same subdivision, this street is the main or "big" street of the addition.

CALLE OCHO

In Thomas Village, developed around 1980 by Ed Leslie, the streets were named primarily for Miguel de Cervantes Saavedra's picaresque romance, *Don Quixote de la Mancha,* though some other names were added. There are eight side streets radiating from La Mancha Drive and Toboso Drive. Apparently the street platters ran out of names and named the eighth street simply *Calle Ocho,* "street eight."

CALLE DE PANZA

In *Don Quixote de la Mancha,* Sancho Panza was the uncouth rustic who fell in with the dreamer Don Quixote and became his squire. (See Don Quixote Drive.)

CALLE DE SANCHO

Near Calle de Panza lies Calle de Sancho, also named for Sancho Panza from *Don Quixote de la Mancha.*

CALLE DE REAL

In Thomas Village also, this little side street was named "royal street," tying in with the Don Quixote theme, as Quixote was trying to be a chivalrous knight.

CALLE NUESTRA

In College Heights, developed by Bellamah, this is an attractive street name, Spanish for "our street."

CAMINO CERRITOS

Literally meaning "hills road," this Spanish name was chosen by Ralph Hicks of Hicks and Associates, the company that developed the Four Hills subdivision in the late 1970s.

CAMINO DE AGUILA

In Las Lomitas ("little hills"), developed by Presley Homes, the company chose Spanish names for the streets.

Camino de Aguila means "road of eagle" or "eagle road."

CAMINO DON DIEGO

Near Eldorado High School, this street was named in honor of Don Diego de Vargas Ponce de Léon y Contreras, who was appointed governor and sent to New Mexico to reconquer the land in 1692 after the Pueblo Revolt of 1680 had ridded the land of the European settlers. (See De Vargas for complete story.)

CAMINO PAISANO

The name of this Las Lomitas street translates as "road of the same country" or perhaps "country road."

CAMINO PLACIDO

In the eastern portion of Academy Acres, developed in the 1970s, the streets were given names descriptive of their location.

Camino Placido, Spanish for "placid road," supposedly is a description of the quiet little side street that it is.

CAMINO REAL COURT

This short street was named in memory of *El Camino Real,* "the royal road," which once was the principal artery of travel and trade in the area. It connected New Mexico with the southern provinces of Spain. This trade route was one of the leading assets of Albuquerque, as Albuquerque was on the Camino Real, which stretched between Santa Fé and Mexico.

CAMINO SANDIA

Spanish for "watermelon road," the name was derived from the nearby Sandia Mountains, east and northeast of Albuquerque.

The name apparently was given by the Spanish because, particularly when the evening sun is splashing on the reddish granite on the western face, the mountain resembles a slice of watermelon. The thin layers of pale limestone near the summit and a cover of dark timber even suggest a banded green rind, according to Marc Simmons (*Albuquerque: A Narrative History*).

CAMPUS BOULEVARD and ROAD

Campus Boulevard traverses the University of New Mexico north campus, and Campus Road makes a circle of sorts through the Albuquerque Academy grounds.

CANDELARIA

The street was named in honor of the prominent Candelaria family of the city. Juan Candelaria was one of the first settlers in Albuquerque.

CAPULIN

In a portion of Loma Del Norte, the streets were named for towns or counties in New Mexico.

According to *New Mexico Place Names,* Capulin is a village in Río Arriba County and a town in Union County. The name is Spanish for "wild cherry," and the

name was given to the town because of its proximity to Mount Capulin, so named because of the wild cherries or chokeberries that grew inside the cone of the extinct volcano.

CARDENAS

Though probably named for a local Cárdenas family, the street may be a remembrance of García López de Cárdenas, who was on Coronado's great expedition to New Mexico. Cárdenas led an advance guard to Cíbola, which was actually Zuni Pueblo.

CARGO

In Heritage East subdivision, this street was named for David F. Cargo, born in Dowagiac, Michigan, in 1929. He earned the B.A. and M.S. degrees from the University of Michigan.

He moved to New Mexico after a tour of duty in the United States Army.

A Republican, he served two terms as governor, 1967–1970, and was the youngest person to serve as governor of New Mexico up to that time. He was nicknamed Lonesome Dave.

CARNEY

In Santa Fé Village, the streets were named for actors or actresses of the early twentieth century.

Art Carney (Arthur William Matthew Carney) was born November 4, 1918, in Mount Vernon, New York.

As Jackie Gleason's goofy sidekick, Ed Norton, on "The Jackie Gleason Show/The Honeymooners," he showed his brilliance as a comic performer. He originated the role of Felix Unger in the Broadway production of *The Odd Couple* in 1965 opposite Walter Matthau.

Carney has a long list of credits.

CARRUTHERS

George C. Carruthers was employed in the City Planning Department when Academy Place was platted by Home Planning Corporation in the early 1970s.

CASA LOMA

In the eastern portion of Academy Acres, developed in the 1970s, the streets were given names descriptive of their locations.

Casa Loma is a somewhat strange Spanish structure, translating as "little hill house."

CARLISLE

The United States Indian Training School, commonly known as the Albuquerque Indian School, which opened in 1881, was modeled after the Indian Industrial School at Carlisle, Pennsylvania. Possibly this street was named in honor of that city, or perhaps it was named for a Carlisle family.

CARLOS REY

This street in southwestern Albuquerque honors King Charles II, who was king of Spain during De Vargas' Reconquest of New Mexico in 1692. De Vargas reclaimed New Mexico in the name of Carlos Rey.

CARSON

This street in Old Town was probably named for Cale Wellman Carson, president of First National Bank in the 1930s and 1940s.

Carson was born November 19, 1891, in Ashland, Kansas. He earned the B.A. degree from the University of Kansas in 1915.

Carson came to Albuquerque in 1933 from Washington, D.C.

He was married to Alice Coors of Las Vegas, New Mexico; the couple had two children.

CASTELLANO COURT and ROAD

In Four Hills subdivision, created by Hicks and Associates during the early 1970s, Ralph Hicks chose street

names that develop a Western or New Mexican/Spanish theme. This street name is a Spanish word that means "Castillian," as an adjective or noun. Castillian is the Spanish dialect that most Spanish speakers consider the "correct" one.

CATRON

In Four Hills subdivision, this street name contributes to the New Mexico theme.

Thomas B. Catron came to Santa Fé from Missouri in 1866. He served in the Constitutional Convention of 1910 and was chosen United States Senator at the first State Legislature in 1912. (See more of the Catron story under his name in Santa Fé.)

Catron County was created in 1921 and was named for Thomas B. Catron.

CENTRAL

Originally Railroad Avenue, this street was given its new name because it was the central street through Albuquerque before the city began its big sprawl. Central is a portion of the old U.S. Route 66, which began at Grant Park in Chicago and dead-ended in Santa Monica, Cali-

Vestiges of old U. S. Route 66 are still evident along Central Avenue in Albuquerque. At Route 66 Diner, one can get a good meal at a fair price.

fornia, at Santa Monica Boulevard and Ocean Avenue. The highway was over 2,400 miles long and traversed Illinois, Missouri, Kansas, Oklahoma, Texas, New Mexico, Arizona, and California.

Route 66 first opened in 1926 and began to be supplanted by the interstate highway system in 1956.

CERROS DE MORADO

This Four Hills street name translates from Spanish as "hills of home."

CHACO

In the eastern portion of Academy Acres, developed in the 1970s, the streets were named for New Mexico place names.

Chaco is a regional Spanish word for "desert." The street name probably was selected in honor of Chaco Canyon National Monument, which contains some of the greatest surface ruins in the United States. Archeologists have identified home sites of the Basketmakers dating back approximately 1,500 years.

CHACON

Don Joseph Chacón, the Marqués de la Peñuela, became governor of the Spanish territory of New Mexico in 1706 shortly after Francisco Cuervo y Valdés, who had been appointed provisional governor by the viceroy, founded the city of Albuquerque. Chacón purchased the position from the Spanish king Felipe IV.

CHAMBERS PLACE

This street in Academy Place, platted by Home Planning Corporation in the early 1970s, was named for Dr. Frank Chambers, head of the history department at Valley High School. Tom Burlison, an employee of Home Planning Corporation at the time, named the street to honor his best friend from high school.

CHAMISA

The *chamisa* is a grayish-colored, narrow-leaved plant that grows along stretches of northern New Mexico, especially around Santa Fé and Taos. It is also called the rabbitbrush.

Another bush that is similar to the *chamisa* is the *chamiso,* commonly called the saltbush. *Chamisal* is Spanish for "place overgrown with chamiso."

In addition to Corte de Chamisa in Las Lomitas, there are six other streets in the area with names that derive from the word, including Chamisa Court in Taylor Ranch, Chamisal Drive in Paradise Hills, Chamisal Place in Paradise Hills, Chamisal Road in the North Valley, Chamisal Road in Los Ranchos de Albuquerque, Chamiso Lane in the North Valley, and Corte de Chamisa in Las Lomitas subdivision.

CHAPLIN

In Santa Fé Village, the streets were named for movie actors of the early twentieth century.

Sir Charles Chaplin (Charlie Chaplin) was born in London in April 1889, the son of music hall entertainers. He became involved in the theater and was playing a feature role by the age of sixteen.

Chaplin was noted for his pantomime. According to the *Encyclopedia of Film,* Chaplin "revolutionized film comedy, transforming it from the rag-tag knockabout farces of Sennett into an art form by introducing characterization, mime and slapstick pathos."

Chaplin was an actor, director, screenwriter, producer, and composer. His greatest popularity was achieved between 1915 and 1925.

Chaplin died December 25, 1977.

CHARLEVOIX

Presumably this short street in Old Town was named for Pierre François Xavier de Charlevoix (1682–1761). Charlevoix was a French Jesuit traveler and historian. He was born in St. Quentin, France, on October 24, 1682, and died at La Flèche, France, February 1, 1761.

Charlevoix taught at the Jesuit college in Québec from 1705 to 1709, went to France, then returned to Québec in 1720 with a commission from the French government to report on the best route to the so-called western sea. In 1721 he set out for the west and worked his way slowly down the Mississippi River, visiting all the military outposts of the French frontier in North America. He arrived in New Orleans in January 1722 and returned to France the next year.

The Louisiana Territory was ceded to Spain by France in 1763. Perhaps there is some connection between Spain and Charlevoix that would explain a street by that name in Old Town Albuquerque.

Charlevoix wrote *Histoire et description générale de la Nouvelle France, avec le Journal historique,* a three-volume history published in Paris in 1744.

CHAVEZ ROAD and AVENUE

According to E.E. "Babe" Osuna, a long-time resident of the North Valley, Chavez Avenue and Chavez Road were named for "a whole row of Chavez families" in that area.

Also, Don Nicolás de Chavez was head of one of the oldest families in the Middle Valley. This family owned land south of Albuquerque and in the Isleta area as well.

CHILDERS

The street was probably named for William B. Childers, a prominent attorney in Albuquerque. Childers was elected representative to the city council in 1882 and to the position of mayor in 1887.

However, it may have been named for K. Clark Childers, who was manager of Breece Lumber and Supply Company during the 1930s and 1940s.

CHOLLA PLACE

In Four Hills subdivision, created by Hicks and Associates in the early 1970s, Ralph Hicks chose names which develop a western or Spanish theme. *Cholla* is a Spanish name which means "nut, head, or brains."

CHRISTY AVENUE

Bill Christy was an employee of Home Planning Corporation, the company that platted Academy Acres in northeast Albuquerque in 1972.

CHURCH

San Felipe de Neri Catholic Church is located between this street and North Plaza, across from the Plaza of Old Town Albuquerque.

Founded in 1706 by the Franciscan friars, this church has been in continuous service since that time. The original building, however, was located on the west side of the Old Town Plaza. The church on the present site northwest of the Plaza was built about 1793.

CIELO GRANDE

in the eastern portion of Academy Acres, developed in the 1970s, the streets were given Spanish names descriptive of their locations or of views from the streets.

Cielo Grande, Spanish for "big sky," is a fitting name for a street in almost any place in New Mexico where the views are usually unobstructed.

CLANCY

Possibly this street was named for Frank W. Clancy or his descendants. Clancy was an attorney who served as district attorney for the Second Judicial District. He was born in Dover, New Hampshire, in 1852, and he settled in New Mexico in 1879.

CLEOPATRA

Near Don Juan Onate Park lies a subdivision of streets named for Shakespearean characters. Cleopatra, from *Antony and Cleopatra,* is the Queen of the Nile, the woman of "infinite variety," who, in her tragedy, places the asp upon her breast and dies. (See also Macbeth, Hamlet, Othello, Adonis, and Venus.)

COAL

When the railroad came in 1880, New Albuquerque was created by sales of lots through New Mexico Town Company, developed by the Santa Fé Railroad and Franz Huning, William Hazeldine, and Elias Stover.

The company appointed Colonel Walter Marmon, a civil engineer, to lay out the townsite and to plat the streets and lots. Marmon chose the names. He named the cross streets after minerals, apparently an indication of the hope at the time that Albuquerque would develop into a major shipping point for the mining of the area. He chose Coal, Copper, Gold, Lead, and Silver. Apparently someone else later added Marble, Slate, and Granite as the streets near Old Town developed.

COCHITI

This street name honors the Cochiti Pueblo, possibly a Spanish derivation of Tewa *Kao Tay-ay*, "stone kiva." A Keresan-speaking pueblo, Cochiti is about halfway between Albuquerque and Santa Fé. Its population was about nine hundred in 1986, and its land area is 28,779 acres.

Cochiti is noted for its jewelry and its drums, particularly double-headed ones made from aspen or cottonwood.

The Spanish mission, San Buenaventura de Cochiti, was built in the early seventeenth century and is still in use today.

CODA

Coda Roberson, of Roberson Homes, built homes during the mid-1900s and following. One of the subdivisions in which he used creative street names was Westwind subdivision, in which two streets were named Landry and Staubach for the Dallas Cowboys and in which other streets were named for other NFL players.

COLFAX

In a portion of Loma Del Norte, the streets were named for towns or counties of New Mexico.

COLFAX

Colfax, the town, and Colfax County, which was created on January 25, 1869, were named for Schuyler Colfax, who was vice-president of the United States, 1869–1873, during the first term of President Ulysses S. Grant.

COLLEGE and COLLEGE HEIGHTS

These streets were named for their proximity to the University of Albuquerque on the west side of the Río Grande. Unfortunately, the University of Albuquerque has closed.

COLLEGES AND UNIVERSITIES

Near the University of New Mexico, many streets are appropriately named after colleges and universities throughout the United States and England. These include the following: Harvard, Cornell, Stanford, Eton, Oxford, Columbia, Princeton, Vassar, Girard, Dartmouth, Richmond, Bryn Mawr, Wellesley, Lafayette, Tulane, Purdue, Berkeley, Marquette, and Amherst.

COMANCHE ROAD

The Comanche tribe of Indians were fierce and often wreaked havoc on European civilization in New Mexico; however, Governor Anza struck a peace with the Comanche in 1786. This peace almost came to an end, however, when the so-called alliance fund was cut in 1821, eliminating the money for purchasing gifts for the Comanches, Jicarilla Apaches, and Utes in order to maintain the peace.

COMPADRE

In a portion of Academy Estates, four streets were named with Spanish words denoting or connoting friendship. *El compadre* means "a friend, pal, or buddy."

CONCHAS COURT and CONCHAS STREET

The street was probably named for the Concha family, known as *Los Conchas*. The name has long been associated with New Mexico, as Fernando de la Concha was governor of New Mexico in 1793.

CONESTOGA DRIVE

In Four Hills subdivision, developed by Hicks and Associates in the 1970s, Ralph Hicks chose street names that generally create a Western theme. Crossing Wagon Train, Conestoga Drive was named for the covered wagons which constituted the wagon trains of the old West.

CONRAD

In Santa Fé Village, the streets were generally named for actors/actresses who were popular during the early to mid twentieth century. Apparently this street name commemorates William Conrad, who has been popular on television in recent years but who has been in films for many years.

COORS, COORS BYPASS, and COORS TRAIL

These three streets on the west side of Albuquerque were named for Henry G. Coors and his family.

Coors was born February 20, 1885, in Las Vegas, New Mexico. He attended New Mexico Normal School (now New Mexico Highlands University), Kentucky Military Institute, and the University of Michigan, from which he was granted a law degree in 1907.

He practiced law in Las Vegas for about two years, then moved to Clovis. He moved to Albuquerque in 1913.

Coors served as president of the Clovis National Bank, as member and president of the University of New Mexico Board of Regents for many years, and as chairman of the board of First National Bank of Albuquerque.

He served as assistant district attorney, 1913–1920.

In 1942 Governor John E. Miles appointed him to the district court bench, and he was elected to that same post in November 1942 and re-elected in 1948.

In 1950 he was elected to the New Mexico Supreme Court, but he resigned in 1953 because the high elevation of Santa Fé caused him to tire easily.

Coors died January 1, 1961.

COPPER

The street was named by Colonel Walter G. Marmon after a mineral that is present in New Mexico, apparently an indication of the hope that Albuquerque would become a major shipping point for the mining industry after the railroad came in 1880.

CORONADO FREEWAY, CORONADO AVENUE, and CORONADO ROAD

An early Spanish explorer, Francisco Vásquez de Coronado (1510–1554) led an expedition into the American southwest in search of the Seven Cities of Cíbola and Gran Quivira. Indians and other explorers had reported that these cities were rich in gold. With a force of three hundred Spaniards and several hundred Indians, Coronado began his search early in 1540, visiting the area that now includes Arizona and New Mexico. He and his group found Indian pueblos, but no golden cities.

In the spring of 1541, he led his army across *El Llano Estacado* ("The Staked Plains"), in the Texas Pandhandle, discovering Palo Duro Canyon near present-day Amarillo. Pushing on to central Kansas, the group discovered the Quivira Indians, but no golden cities.

Born in Salamanca, Spain, Coronado went to Mexico in 1535 and became governor of New Galicia, northwest of Mexico City, in 1538.

CORRALES ROAD

The street known as Corrales Road was so named because it leads to the town of Corrales, which was named, according to local tradition, *Los Corrales* for the corrals

that were built by the founder of Alameda, rancher Juan González.

CORTE DEL VIENTO

In Las Lomitas ("little hills"), developed in the early 1990s by Presley Homes, James Hicks said they chose Spanish names for the streets, names that develop the theme of the countryside.

This street name is Spanish for "court of the wind"; in the Albuquerque area, wind is a common occurrence.

CORTE DE LOMA

In Las Lomitas, this street name is Spanish for "court of the hill" or "hill court."

COULSON DRIVE

Situated in Loma Del Norte in northeast Albuquerque, this street was named by Tom Burlison, formerly of M. and Q. Southwest Company, for Diane Coulson, a high school friend. Diane married Burlison's best friend, Dr. Frank Chambers, who currently is head of the history department at Valley High. There is a street just off Spain Road named for him.

COUNTRYWOOD

In a small addition to Loma Del Norte, the *wood* theme was used, with Countrywood being the east-west street and those radiating from it beginning with *Wood*—Woodridge, Woodleaf, and Woodhaven.

CROMWELL

Oliver E. Cromwell, a New Yorker who came to Albuquerque in 1879, invested heavily in real estate after his arrival. One of the founders of the Street Railway Company, which was incorporated in 1880, Cromwell was president and the chief driving force of the company. The Plaza was connected with New Town and Barelas by three miles of track and the use of eight mule-drawn cars.

CUATRO CERROS

In Four Hills subdivision, developed by Hicks and Associates in the 1970s, Ralph Hicks chose the name *Cuatro Cerros,* Spanish for "four hills," as a fitting name. On the other side of the subdivision lie two streets called Four Hills Court and Four Hills Road.

CUBERO

In the eastern portion of Academy Acres, developed in the 1970s, the streets were named for New Mexico place names.

Cubero is the name of a small town northwest of Laguna. It was probably named for Governor Don Pedro Rodríguez Cubero, who succeeded Don Diego de Vargas. He served as governor of New Mexico from 1697 to 1703.

Cubero was a native of Calatayud, Spain; before coming to North America, he had been in the royal service for twenty-six years. He had served in the royal armada of the ocean and in the Spanish army of Sicily.

CUERVO

Francisco Cuervo y Valdés was provisional governor of New Mexico, and it was he who founded the city of

At the north entrance to Old Town stands this equestrian statue of Francisco Cuervo y Valdés, who founded the city of Albuquerque on April 23, 1706. The sculpture was created by Buck McCain, artist, and cast by the foundry of Santa Fé Bronze, Inc.

Albuquerque in 1706. He had been appointed as provisional governor of the Spanish territory of New Mexico by the viceroy, with the appointment to be approved by the king. However, in 1706, after the founding of the city, Felipe IV, Spanish king, sold the position of governor to Don Joseph Chacón, the Marqués de la Peñuela.

CURRY AVENUE

In a portion of Loma Del Norte, streets were named for towns or counties of New Mexico. This street was named for Curry County, which was named for George Curry. Curry was one of Teddy Roosevelt's Rough Riders and was appointed governor of the Territory of New Mexico in 1907.

CURT WALTERS

In Nor Este Manor, developed by Presley Homes, the streets were named for New Mexico artists, and the names were recommended by the Nor Este Art Association. Many of the artists came out for the dedication ceremony, and their hand prints are in the fountain in the park near La Cueva High School.

CUTLER

Abraham Cutler, a native of New York, was appointed by President Lincoln as marshal during the Civil War. He took office August 16, 1862. It was his duty to attach and dispose of the property belonging to those who were accused of collaboration and treason. (See Marc Simmons' *Albuquerque: A Narrative History* for this story.)

The street was probably named for some of Abraham Cutler's descendants.

CUTTER and CUTTER ROAD

The street and road were named for the Cutter family. William P. Cutter was a vital part of aviation in Albuquerque from 1929 to his death in 1963 at the age of seventy-four. He was one of the first pilots for Wyoming Airways, which established a sales agency, aerial taxi,

and flight-training business at the airport in 1929. Cutter and William Carr, another of the early pilots, created the Cutter-Carr Flying Service, which operated from 1939 to 1947. Cutter later managed Cutter Flying Service.

D

D. REED COURT

In Nor Este Manor, Presley Homes named the streets for New Mexico artists who were recommended by the Nor Este Art Association. Many of the artists attended the dedication ceremony and left their hand prints in the concrete of the park fountain near La Cueva High School.

Born in 1895 in Indiana, Doel Reed began his career as an architect, but painting and etching were his real loves. He studied art at the Art Academy in Cincinnati.

He served in France during World War I and taught art at Oklahoma State University for thirty-five years. He retired as Professor Emeritus in 1959, then moved to Taos in 1960.

Internationally known as a master of the aquatint, Reed emphasized drawing for artists.

DANIEL

Daniel Sedillo bought ten acres of land, piece by piece. Intersecting Los Ranchos Road, Daniel Road or Daniel Circle was named for Daniel Sedillo, as he built his house there.

Sedillo was born in Martíneztown in 1895 and settled in the North Valley in 1942.

Juan Bautista de Anza served as second governor of New Mexico, 1778 to 1788. (Photo courtesy New Mexico State Records Center and Archives, SRC Misc. Collection, #9447)

DE ANZA DRIVE

The name of this street in Atrisco Village honors Juan Bautista de Anza, who served as governor of New Mexico from 1778 to 1788.

De Anza received his formal education in Mexico City, but he had been born in Primería Alta, where his father and grandfather had been distinguished in their service to the crown. He saw an opportunity to open an overland route to the missions in California through Arizona. In 1772 he wrote the viceroy a recommendation that De Anza be permitted to explore the route to Cali-

fornia. The viceroy was very much in favor of the exploration. On January 8, 1774, De Anza and his party departed from Tubac, in present-day Arizona. Afterward, he went to New Mexico.

DE VARGAS LOOP, COURT, and ROAD

In Heritage East subdivision, developed in the early 1970s, the streets were named for governors or heroes of New Mexico. De Vargas Court and De Vargas Loop are located there. De Vargas Road is located in southwestern Atrisco.

After the Pueblo Revolt of 1680, Don Diego de Vargas Zapata y Lujan Ponce de Léon y Contreras was appointed governor and sent to New Mexico to reconquer the land. During the revolt, the Europeans were wiped out of New Mexico.

De Vargas went to New Mexico in 1691. In August 1692, he took about two hundred men and marched up the Río Grande valley. He met no resistance and found most of the villages deserted. When he arrived in Santa Fé on September 13, however, he found the village surrounded by walled entrenchments filled with numerous Indians. When his negotiations with the Indians failed, he laid siege, cut off the water supply in the aqueduct, and issued an ultimatum for peaceful surrender. The strategy a success, he and his men entered Santa Fé; and he proclaimed the city repossessed for King Charles II of Spain.

He served as governor from 1693 to 1697 and from 1703 to 1704.

DEE DRIVE

In Academy Place, platted by Home Planning Corporation in the early 1970s, this street was named for Dee Hines, wife of Frank Hines, who was an employee of the company.

DEER DANCER

In Kachina Hills, this street was named for one of the kachinas of the Hopi Pueblo. (See Kachina Place.)

DELGADO DRIVE

This street located in southwest Albuquerque was obviously named for the Delgado family. Records show that Fr. Carlos Delgado, a missionary to the Indians, along with Fr. Pedro Ignacios Pino, went to a Hopi village in 1742 to convert the people of that village. They were successful in converting some of them.

DEMICA

In Loma Del Norte, Kent Henderson named one street Demica for Demica Vigil, daughter of Ann Vigil, who worked for Henderson.

DEMING

In a portion of Loma Del Norte, the streets were named for towns or counties in New Mexico.

According to *New Mexico Place Names,* Deming, county seat of Luna County, was settled *circa* 1880 and was named for Ann Deming, daughter of John Jay Deming, a sawmill owner in Indiana. Ann married Charles Crocker, one of the men who built the early railroad lines in the territory.

DEMPSEY

In Heritage East, developed in the early 1970s, the streets were named for governors or heroes of New Mexico.

John J. Dempsey was born on June 22, 1879, in Whitehaven, Pennsylvania. He married, and the couple lived in Santa Fé and had three children.

Dempsey worked as a water boy with a railroad crew at age thirteen. He worked in various positions with Brooklyn Union Elevator Company, served as vice-president of Brooklyn Rapid Transit Company, then as vice-president of Continental Oil and Asphalt Company, 1919–1920. He was an oil operator, 1920–1928, and president of United States Asphalt Corporation from 1928.

He was a member of the 74th Congress, elected at large in New Mexico, and he was re-elected in 1936.

He was a Democrat, and he served as governor of New Mexico, 1943–1947.

DIETZ FARM CIRCLE, ROAD, PLACE, COURT, and LOOP

These streets are located in an addition built on the farm owned by the Dietz family, an old established family who lived in Los Ranchos de Albuquerque and in the edge of Albuquerque.

DONA ANA PLACE

This is a popular place name and street name in New Mexico. Apparently the name memorializes Doña Ana Robledo, who, according to *New Mexico Place Names,* was a legendary woman who was reputed to have lived in this place a few miles north of Las Cruces during the seventeenth century. She was outstanding for her charity and good deeds and for opening her home to soldiers.

Also, the governor of Chihuahua issued a land grant that was known as *El Anco de Doña Ana.*

DONAHOO CIRCLE

Bert Donahoo was a realtor and a partner who helped develop a small section of Academy Place. His name was given to this street by Tom Burlison, employee of Home Planning Corporation, when Academy Place was developed during the early 1970s.

DON DIEGO STREET

In Heritage East subdivision, developed in the early 1970s, the streets were named for governors or heroes of New Mexico.

This street was named in honor of Don Diego de Vargas Ponce de Léon y Contreras, who was appointed governor and sent to New Mexico to reconquer the land in 1692 after the Pueblo Revolt of 1680 had ridded the land of the European settlers.

See De Vargas for complete story.

DON PEDRO

In Thomas Village, developed around 1980 by Ed Leslie, the streets were named primarily for Miguel de Cervantes Saavedra's Picaresque romance, *Don Quixote de la Mancha.*

On Don Quixote's first outing, he was beaten by a group of traveling merchants who thought the old man mad when he challenged them to a passage at arms. Back in his village, he was watched over by Pedro Perez, the village priest, while his bruises and cuts healed. This street, then, honors the village priest.

DON QUIXOTE DRIVE and PLACE

In the subdivision mentioned above, this street was named for the title character in *Don Quixote de la Mancha.*

Don Quixote, a retired and impoverished gentleman, loved reading romances of chivalry. He was dubbed knight by a rascally publican at an inn that Quixote had mistaken for a turreted castle.

After his first beating by some traveling merchants, he returned home and was watched over by Pedro Perez, the village priest. He fell in with Sancho Panza, an uncouth rustic who became his squire. And as the mistress to whom he would dedicate his deeds of valor, he chose Dulcinea del Toboso, a buxom peasant wench who was famous only for her skill in salting pork.

La Mancha Drive and Toboso Drive each make a semi-circle around Don Quixote. Calle Real ("royal street"), Calle Panza, and Calle de Sancho are short side streets radiating from the semi-circle. Calle Ocho, "street eight," is one of eight side streets. Apparently the people who platted the streets ran out of names.

DON TOMAS

Don Tomás C. de Baca held the extensive Las Vegas Land Grant given by the Viceroy of Mexico. One of his descendants, Ezequiel C. de Baca, was governor of the State of New Mexico for forty-nine days in January-February 1917 before dying of pernicious anemia.

DORIS STEIDER

In Nor Este Manor, Presley Homes named the streets for New Mexico artists who were recommended by the Nor Este Art Association. Many of the artists attended the dedication ceremony and left their hand prints in the concrete of the park fountain near La Cueva High School.

Doris Steider was born April 10, 1924, in Decatur, Illinois. She was granted a Bachelor of Science degree from Purdue University in 1945 and became a certified laboratory technician at Kirksville College of Osteopathy in 1949.

She is married to C. B. McCampbell.

Steider works in oils and egg tempera and bronze. She resides in Albuquerque and maintains a gallery on Silver Hills Lane.

Steider has won numerous awards for her paintings and has had many shows. She is one of twelve artists featured in *Masters of Western Art* and is listed in *Who's Who in American Art*. She has participated in over two hundred major exhibitions, including one at the Smithsonian.

DOUGLAS MACARTHUR

General Douglas MacArthur, one of the leading United States generals in World War II, is honored in this street name. MacArthur was chief of staff of the famous Forty-second Division in World War I, served as superintendent of the United States Military Academy for a time, and served in Australia as commander of the Allied forces in the Southwest Pacific during World War II. It was on his way to take command of troops in Australia that he made his famous promise, "I shall return."

DUKE

Albuquerque was named for Viceroy Francisco Fernández de la Cueva, Duke of Alburquerque (note two *r*s). Albuquerque is called the Duke City in the Duke's honor, and the professional baseball team is called the Albuquerque Dukes. Definitely the city needed a Duke street.

DUMAS DRIVE

Will Dumas was chief draftsman for M. and Q. Southwest when the company platted Loma Del Norte in the early 1970s. Tom Burlison was in charge of naming the street, and he chose this name to honor the chief draftsman.

DURANES

The Durán family was one of the original old families of Albuquerque. In fact, the first *alcalde mayor* of Albuquerque was Fernando Durán y Chávez. (In Spanish the first surname is the father's surname.) He was one of the leading men of the valley.

A number of Durán families settled in an area north of the *Plaza Vieja*, and the area was known as *Los Duranes*.

E

EAGLE DANCER

In Kachina Hills, this street was named for one of the kachinas at the Hopi Pueblo. (See Kachina Place.)

EAGLE RANCH ROAD

Connecting Coors Road to Paseo del Norte, Eagle Ranch Road is located on the old Eagle Ranch. The Taylors, of Taylor Ranch, think that either the Bullington family or Jack and Van "Dude" Turner and their brother owned Eagle Ranch. They all lived up in that area.

EASTERDAY DRIVE

The Easterday family came to Albuquerque during the frontier days, and this street honors their name.

George S. Easterday, M.D., was born in Jefferson County, Ohio, September 12, 1849. He received his schooling in Ohio and earned the M.D. degree in 1878 at Eclectic Medical College in Cincinnati, Ohio. He practiced medicine in Nebraska for a time, then moved to Albuquerque in 1881.

His brother, J. S. Easterday, M.D., became associated with him in 1894.

George Easterday lived at 410 Gold. He invested heavily in real estate and building projects.

He was married to Catherine Haller of California in 1881.

In 1887 Easterday was chosen as one of the aldermen of Albuquerque. In 1891 he was elected as one of the school trustees, and in 1892 he was elected mayor of Albuquerque.

EDDY

In a portion of Loma Del Norte, the streets were named for towns or counties in New Mexico.

Eddy County, organized from Lincoln County on February 25, 1889, was named for Charles B. Eddy, who was a promoter of Carlsbad Irrigation Project. Eddy owned ranches in New Mexico and played a major role in building the railroad from Pecos, Texas, to Carlsbad and on to Roswell.

EDITH

Colonel Walter G. Marmon was the civil engineer employed to lay out the townsite of New Albuquerque when the railroad came in 1880. Marmon had worked for the Santa Fé Railroad occasionally. He named two of the streets for his children, Edith and Walter. Colonel Marmon settled and married at Laguna, where he taught school.

Lee Marmon, his great nephew, lives in Laguna today and operates the Blue-Eyed Indian Bookshop in New Laguna.

EL ENSUENO ROAD

Near Vineyard Addition, perhaps a part of it (see Vineyard Road), lies a street with the Spanish name *El Ensueño,* "dream or fantasy." Perhaps this name was given because someone had finally built a dream home or because some other dream had been realized.

EL MORRO

In the eastern portion of Academy Acres, the streets were named for New Mexico place names.

Spanish for "headland, bluff, fortress," El Morro was the name given to the great rock in El Morro National Monument. According to *New Mexico Place Names,* the huge triangular rock known as Inscription Rock is made of light-colored sandstone that is soft enough to be cut with a knife or sword. Spaniards, over the centuries, have carved names and dates and short messages on the rock. More than five hundred inscriptions are there. Juan Oñate, who became the colonizer of New Mexico and its first governor in 1598, inscribed the earliest message. In translation, it reads, "Passed by here the *Adelantado* Don Juan de Oñate from the discovery of the Sea of the South, the 16th of April of 1605." Oñate was returning from the Pacific Coast, and the Gulf of California was the "Sea of the South."

El Morro is the name given to what is often called Inscription Rock. Among others, Don Juan de Oñate carved his name on the rock with the earliest message. (Photo courtesy New Mexico State Records Center and Archives, McNitt Collection #6390)

EL PUEBLO

According to Miguel Sena, in an interview for *Shining River Precious Land,* the road was so named because it led to a *placita* or *pueblo.* It was called Camino al Pueblo.

ELFEGO BACA

In Atrisco Village, this street was named for Elfego Baca, a colorful personage from New Mexico.

Baca served as sheriff of Reserve, in Catron County. He is famous for a fight in 1882 when he was attempting to arrest a drunken cowboy. McCarthy, the cowboy, rode up and down the street looking for trouble and found it. Baca disarmed the cowboy and placed him under arrest, but McCarthy's friends gathered into a mob and rode into town to free McCarthy. Baca killed one of the mob and injured another. Hanging on to his prisoner, he chased the mob down the street by putting bullets into the dust behind them.

After a justice-of-the-peace verdict, Baca went to a cabin to rest but was attacked again. Another mob member was killed, and several more were injured as they tried to break the door down. Some stories credit Baca with holding off eighty or more members of the mob for more than thirty-three hours before surrendering for trial in the local court and being acquitted.

In early years, Baca once shot up Albuquerque with William Bonney (Billy the Kid). Later he was on the other side of the law in Reserve (as described above). He was acquitted in two trials.

He once went to Chihuahua, Mexico, where he negotiated with Pancho Villa for a notorious cattle rustler wanted in the United States. Villa and Baca became friends, but Baca betrayed Villa and stole his rifle. Villa placed a $30,000 bounty on Baca, but Baca escaped to the United States.

In later years he settled down to a life as an attorney and became involved in politics in Socorro, his home. He served as county clerk, district attorney, school superintendent, and mayor. He ran for governor of New Mexico on the Republican ticket but was defeated.

Baca died in 1945 at the age of eighty.

In 1958 Disney filmed the story of Elfego Baca, with Robert Loggia playing the role of Baca.

ELIZABETH

In Princess Jeanne Park, developed by Dale Bellamah in the early 1950s and named for his wife, Jeanne Lees, the streets were generally named for friends or relatives of the Bellamahs.

Oscar Mahlon Love owned some of the property and had named some of the streets before selling the property to Bellamah. Elizabeth street was named for Love's wife, Elizabeth.

EMBUDITO

A Spanish word meaning "little funnel," the name derives from nearby Embudo Arroyo.

EMBUDO

A Spanish word meaning "a funnel," the name derives from nearby Embudo Arroyo, which apparently was so named because it funnels the rain water from the Sandia Mountains. Embudo Dam is located on the arroyo in Embudo Park.

ERBBE

The Erbbe family operated a drug store in Albuquerque in the early twentieth century.

ESCALANTE

This street in an area of streets named for historical figures may have been named for Sylvestre Vélez de Escalante, one of the friars who, accompanied by Francisco Domínguez and eight others, explored the Chama Valley and up to Utah Lake in 1776. Their explorations opened the way for later development of a commercial route to the west, known then as the Old Spanish Trail.

ESPEJO STREET and ESPEJO ROAD

Though these streets may have been named for an Espejo family of the area, they are also reminiscent of Antonio de Espejo, who, in 1582, led an expedition to New Mexico, apparently to learn what had happened to three priests who had journeyed there in 1581 to convert the pueblos. All three of the priests had been killed, he discovered. Espejo remained there for several months prospecting for silver and gold.

EUBANK

When the Albuquerque Army Air Base (later renamed Kirtland Air Force Base) was completed on August 8, 1941, the 19th Bombardment Group was transferred to Albuquerque to train its air crews before being sent to the Philippines. Lt. Colonel Eugene L. Eubank was commander of the 19th Bombardment Group, and this major artery of the city was later named for him.

FARRAGUT

In Academy Estates, Gary Swearingen with Academy Developing Company chose admirals' names for the names of the streets.

Admiral David Glasgow Farragut (1801–1870) lived in New Orleans as a boy and was befriended and later adopted by Captain (later Commodore) David Dixon Porter. As a youngster, Farragut served in the War of 1812. In 1861 he was assigned to command the blockading squadron in the west Gulf of Mexico and to enter the Mississippi River and capture New Orleans. Ironically, a man who, as a boy, lived in New Orleans was responsible for the fall of the city during the Civil War.

FATHER SKY

In Kachina Hills, this street was named for one of the Indian dieties. (See Kachina Hills.)

FLUSHING MEADOWS

In Wimbledon West subdivision, developed by Centex Homes in the 1980s, the street names develop a theme of tennis.

FLUSHING MEADOWS

The U.S. Open tennis tournament, sponsored by the United States Tennis Association, is held each year in Flushing Meadow, New York. The street name is in the plural form, *Meadows,* though the correct name of the city is *Meadow.* It is a fairly common practice to add the *s.* Even some of the U.S. Open announcers add the *s.*

The United States National Lawn Tennis Association was established in 1881. Later it became the United States Tennis Association. In 1968 the U. S. Open was moved to hard court.

Other streets in the subdivision include Wimbledon and Bjorn Borg.

FLYNN

In Santa Fé Village, the streets were named for actors and actresses of the early twentieth century.

Errol Leslie Thomson Flynn was born June 20, 1909, in Hobart, Tasmania. He was educated at the University of Tasmania and was a swash-buckling adventure hero of the 1930s and 1940s. He came to Hollywood in 1935 and became a sex symbol and leading adventure star in films such as *Robin Hood* and *Captain Blood.*

His list of movie credits is long, though he was known for his dissipated life style as well as for his movies.

Flynn died October 14, 1959.

FOREST HILLS DRIVE and COURT

Tom Burlison, former employee of Home Planning Corporation, said that he chose this name because it sounded good. In Academy Acres, there are hills, but there are no forests. He chuckled when he said that he had originally misspelled *forest* by including a double *r.*

FORRESTER

Reverend Henry Forrester, first rector of St. John's Episcopal Church, developed a housing project called Coronado Place Addition, located to the east of Park Addition and north of New York Avenue (now Lomas).

FORTY-NINERS STREET

In Prospectors Ridge, developed by Presley Homes, the street names develop a theme of mining or prospecting.

Forty-Niners Street recalls the Gold Rush days of California, which began when James W. Marshall, who had been hired by John A. Sutter to help build a sawmill, discovered the first gleaming nuggets of gold at Sutter's mill. And thus began the massive gold rush to California, with hordes of people streaming there in 1849.

FOUR HILLS COURT and ROAD

Four Hills subdivision surrounds Four Hills Country Club, whence the subdivision and these two streets derive their names. Four Hills was developed by Hicks and Associates in the 1970s.

FRANCES

Edward H. Snow, owner of Snow Construction, Inc., developed Snow Heights subdivision, naming some of the streets Snow Street, Snow Heights Boulevard, and Snow Heights Circle.

Frances street was named for Snow's wife, Frances.

FRANTZ DRIVE

Mary Frantz was secretary for Wood Brothers, a home building company, during the 1970s when Academy Acres in northeast Albuquerque was developed.

FRANZ HUNING AVENUE

Born in Hanover, Germany, on October 28, 1827, Franz Huning was educated in Germany and gained experience in general merchandising.

He came to the United States in 1848, eventually arriving in New Mexico in 1849. He was on his way to California during the Gold Rush. Bad weather caused him to stay in Santa Fé for awhile; then he went to Albuquerque. During that time he went on a military expe-

dition to Gran Quivira in search of $40 million in gold, but was, of course, unsuccessful.

In 1855 Huning opened a general merchandising store in Albuquerque and continued that enterprise for thirty-four years, until 1889.

Along with Elias Stover and William Hazeldine, Huning purchased the land for New Albuquerque in conjunction with the New Mexico Town Company. The three men gave the land for the depot to the railroad and land for school house sites. In 1864 Huning opened a flour mill.

Huning married Ernestine Franke, from Germany, in 1863.

He developed Huning Highland Addition and was active in real estate development and the development of Albuquerque in general. In 1883, he erected the famous Huning Castle, his home.

FREMONT ELLIS COURT

In Nor Este Manor, Presley Homes named the streets for New Mexico artists who were recommended by the Nor Este Art Association. Many of the artists attended the dedication ceremony and left their hand prints in the concrete of the park fountain near La Cueva High School.

Fremont Ellis was born in Virgina City, Montana, in 1897. He spent a short time studying at the Art Students League of New York but decided that an eastern art school was not much help in teaching him to paint the southwestern landscapes that he loved. He came back to the west and taught himself.

Ellis trained to be an optometrist and practiced in El Paso for a time, but he settled in Santa Fé in 1919. In Santa Fé, Ellis and four other young men formed the *Cinco Pintores*, the Five Painters, who settled on and made known the Camino del Monte Sol, where he owned an attractive studio home, most of which he built himself.

He married Laurenta Gonzales, from an old Spanish family. They had two children—a daughter, Bambi, and a son, Frederick.

Ellis was awarded the Huntington Prize for landscape at the Los Angeles Museum exhibition of California and southwestern painters in 1924 for his *When Evening Comes*. He also won the Springville, Utah, Mu-

seum Purchase Award in 1958, the Governor of New Mexico's Award for Excellence in the Arts in 1981, and the Rody International Award in 1981. The National Academy of Western Arts dedicated its 8th annual exhibition to him in 1981 and made him an honorary member.

FRIENDLY PLACE and FRIENDLY COURT

In Quaker Heights, located on the west side of Albuquerque, the street names develop the theme of the peacefulness and friendliness of the Quakers.

The names Friendly Place and Friendly Court contribute to the friendly ambiance of the subdivision.

FRUIT

According to E. E. "Babe" Osuna, former Albuquerque postman and life-long resident of the area, the street was named for the fruit produced by the orchards of the area, in keeping with Walter Marmon's practice of naming streets for New Mexico products, such as gold, silver, lead, coal, and copper.

G

GABALDON

This street in Los Ranchos de Albuquerque was named for Raphael Gabaldón in the early 1900s. Gabaldón died in 1917.

GABLE

In Santa Fé Village, the streets were named for actors/ actresses who were popular during the early to mid twentieth century.

William Clark Gable was born in Cadiz, Ohio, February 1, 1901. A former blue-collar worker in Ohio, Cable became the leading male box office attraction throughout the 1930s.

He played bit parts in several silent Hollywood films but became a leading man on Broadway in the late 1920s.

In films, he played the macho man in many movies, being shown bare-chested in *It Happened One Night* and *Mutiny on the Bounty*. And, of course, his "I don't give a damn" in *Gone With the Wind* in 1939 made audiences gasp.

Many of Gable's films won Oscars, and he played opposite many of Hollywood's leading ladies.

He died November 16, 1960, shortly before his fifth wife gave birth to John Clark Gable, the son that he had always wanted.

GALACIA

In Four Hills subdivision, created by Hicks and Associates in the early 1970s, Ralph Hicks chose street names that develop a Western or Spanish theme.

Galicia is a province of Spain, located in the northwest corner of the country. The street name is misspelled. The second *a* should be *i*.

GALLEGOS ROAD

The Gallegos name has long been present in the Albuquerque area. The lands on which Los Ranchos de Albuquerque was founded during the 1700s once were part of the Elena Gallegos lands. Originally, what became known as the Elena Gallegos grant had been granted to Captain Diego Montoya by Governor Peñuela in 1712. Shortly after that time, however, these lands were conveyed to Elena Gallegos, widow of Santiago Gurulé. Elena Gallegos died in 1731.

This property consisted of approximately seventy thousand acres, much of which was on the East Mesa and in the Sandia Mountains. Later, much of this property was purchased by Albert Simms, and he donated much of the property to Albuquerque Academy. (See Simms Avenue, Montoya Road, and Academy Parkway.)

GANADO COURT

In Four Hills subdivision, this street contributes to the Spanish theme of the street names. *Ganado* is Spanish for "cattle" or "a herd."

Nearby are Oveja ("ewe") Court and Toro ("bull") Street.

GARCIA STREET

Though Garcia is now a common surname in Albuquerque, the name goes back to the 1600s. Alonzo Garciá de Noriega owned a hacienda near, or possibly within, modern-day Albuquerque. He established a place called *Estancia de San Antonio* on the west bank of the Río Grande during the 1600s. In 1670 he was *alcalde mayor,* and in 1680 he was lieutenant-governor.

Possibly this street is a remembrance of him or of some of his descendants.

GENERAL ARNOLD

In Park Addition, this street was named for Major General Henry H. "Hap" Arnold, who was chief of the Army Air Corps. Arnold was a friend of Major Albert D. Smith, who was regional manager of TWA assigned to Albuquerque. Arnold was helpful in arranging for Governor Tingley and other officials to see the right people in Washington in an effort to get an air base at Albuquerque. Arnold visited Albuquerque in 1939 while the municipal air base was under construction.

GENERAL BRADLEY

In Park Addition, names of United States generals were chosen for street names.

Omar Nelson Bradley (1893–1981) was born in Clark, Missouri, on February 12, 1893. He moved to Moberly, Missouri, with his family when he was fifteen. There he met Mary Quayle, whom he later married. He was graduated from the United States Military Academy at West Point in 1915.

During World War I he served with the 14th Infantry Regiment. During World War II he served as commandant of the Infantry School, commanded an infantry division in training, and, in 1943, commanded the 2nd Corps in North Africa and in Sicily.

He was chosen by General Dwight D. Eisenhower to command the 1st United States Army, which was the American contingent in the invasion of Normandy in June 1944. The troops that he led broke out of the Normandy beachhead, liberated the city of Paris, defeated a counter offensive by the Germans in 1944–1945, seized the first bridgehead over the Rhine, and drove through Germany to establish the first contact by Allies with troops of the Soviet Union.

Bradley died in New York City on April 8, 1981.

GENERAL CHENNAULT

Also in Park Addition, this street was named for General Claire Lee Chennault (1890–1958), who was born in Commerce, Texas, but was brought up in Louisiana. He was a principal in a high school in Texas until World War I, when he joined the Army Air Service. He became an expert pilot, flying in a precision flying exhibition team. In 1937 he became air adviser to Generalissimo Chiang Kai-shek of China.

Before the United States entered World War II in 1941, he led the Flying Tigers, a small group of American pilots who supported China in its war against Japan.

In 1943 Chennault became commander of the United States 14th Air Force in China. He retired in 1945 as a major general and became head of a Chinese airline.

An air base in Lake Charles, Louisiana, was also named after General Chennault.

GENERAL HODGES

Also in Park Addition, this street was named for General Courtney Hicks Hodges (1887–1966), who was born at Perry, Georgia. He attended the United States Military Academy, but failed geometry. So he enlisted as a private and received a commission only a year behind his former classmates.

He fought Pancho Villa in Mexico, then commanded a machine-gun company in the Meuse-Argonne campaign during World War I and received the Distinguished Service Cross.

Hodges became chief of infantry in World War II and went to France to command the 1st Army after the invasion of Normandy. He led the 1st Army in liberating Paris and made the first penetration of Germany's frontier. He established the first crossing of the Rhine at the Remagen Bridge and made the first Allied contact with Russian armies at the Elbe River.

When he retired in 1949, he moved to Texas. He died in San Antonio on January 16, 1966.

GENERAL KEARNEY COURT

In 1846, during the Mexican War, Brigadier General Stephen Watts Kearny led United States Army forces to claim New Mexico for the United States. He set up a quartermaster supply depot on the Plaza and marched to Santa Fé, where Governor Armijo capitulated without a fight.

The street name is misspelled with an extra *e* at the end.

GENERAL MARSHALL

In Park Addition, the streets were named for United States generals.

George Catlett Marshall (1880–1959) was born December 31, 1880, in Uniontown, Pennsylvania. He graduated from Virginia Military Institute in 1901 and received a commission as second lieutenant of infantry in 1902.

He began his army career with duty in the Philippines in 1902. When the United States entered World War I, he went to France with the first field units, serving as training officer and then as chief of operations of the 1st Division. He transferred to the 1st Army in 1918 and served as chief of operations in the latter part of the war.

He was promoted to brigadier general in 1938 and became chief of staff of the U.S. Army. He did a great deal of reorganizing and building in the Army. In 1944 he became a general. After the war was over, President Truman appointed him special representative to China.

In 1947 he returned to the United States and became secretary of state under Truman. He urged Congress to pass the European Recovery Program, the Marshall Plan,

which rebuilt the European countries and helped stave off Communism. His role in the reconstruction of Europe earned him the Nobel peace prize in 1953.

Marshall died in 1959 and was buried in Arlington National Cemetery.

GENERAL PATCH

Also in Park Addition, this street was named for Alexander McCarrell Patch, Jr., who was born in Fort Huachuca, Arizona. He graduated from the United States Military Academy in West Point in 1913.

Patch led United States armies in the Pacific and European theaters during World War II. He commanded United States forces at Guadalcanal in the south Pacific in 1942. In 1944 Patch commanded the 7th Army in the Allied invasion of southern France. He died in 1945.

GENERAL SOMERVELL

This street in Park Addition was named for General Brehon Burke Somervell (1892–1955), who was born in Little Rock, Arkansas, on May 9, 1892. He was graduated from the United States Military Academy at West Point, New York, in 1914.

Somervell served in France in the Corps of Engineers branch during World War I, building installations and briefly working in an office in the Meuse-Argonne offensive.

In World War II he was appointed commander of the newly formed Service of Supply, with the rank of lieutenant-general. His job was to ascertain the needs of United States Army troops in all areas of the world and to spur the industries of the nation to produce the necessary goods and the transportation services to deliver them. He was a presidential adviser.

Somervell retired in 1946 and went into private industry. He died on February 13, 1955, at Ocala, Florida.

GENERAL STILLWELL

Also in Park Addition, this street was named for General Joseph Warren Stilwell (1883–1946). Though the street

name has a double *l* in the first syllable, the name really has only one *l* in the first syllable. Stilwell was born in Palatka, Florida, in 1904. During World War I he served with the American Expeditionary Forces in France. Having studied Chinese, he served as military attaché in China from 1935 to 1937.

During World War II, General Stilwell commanded all the United States forces in the China-Burma-India theater of war. He served as chief of staff to Generalissimo Chiang Kai-shek, who was supreme commander of the Chinese theater, and he was the first American general to command a Chinese army.

Because of Stilwell's forthright manner, he was nicknamed Vinegar Joe.

In 1944 General Stilwell and Chiang Kai-shek disagreed on military policy, and Stilwell was re-assigned to Washington, D. C. In June 1945 he took command of the United States 10th Army on Okinawa. After the war was over, he continued to hold an Army command in the United States.

GEORGIA O'KEEFFE DRIVE

In Nor Este Manor, Presley Homes named the streets for New Mexico artists who were recommended by the Nor Este Art Association. Many of the artists attended the dedication ceremony and left their hand prints in the concrete of the park fountain near La Cueva High School.

Georgia O'Keeffe was born in Sun Prairie, Wisconsin, in 1887. Deciding at an early age that she wanted to become an artist, she took private lessons and then studied at the Art Institute of Chicago and at the Art Students League in New York.

She began teaching in Amarillo, Texas, in 1912, and was apparently influenced greatly by the barren landscape of the Texas Panhandle.

Several years later, she returned to New York and met and married Alfred Stieglitz, a photographer and proponent of modern art.

She made her first extended visit to New Mexico in the summer of 1929. After that time, she continued to spend most of her summers in the state, finally moving to Abiquiú in 1949.

She died in 1986 in Santa Fé.

GIBSON

Edward J. Gibson was division superintendent for the Santa Fé Railroad during the early twentieth century. In 1907 he lived at 611 W. Coal Avenue, according to the city directory for that year.

GIDDINGS

In Heritage East subdivision, developed in the early 1970s, the streets were named for governors or heroes of New Mexico.

Marsh Giddings was appointed governor by President Ulysses S. Grant in 1871. He served for about four years, dying in office on June 3, 1875.

GILA

In the eastern portion of Academy Acres, developed in the 1970s, the streets were named for New Mexico place names.

A mining community north of Silver City, Gila was named for a New Mexico Indian tribe. In *New Mexico Place Names,* Pearce says that the word is possibly the Spanish spelling of the Apache word for "mountain," *tsihl* or *dzihl.* Gila Cliff Dwellings National Monument in Catron County consists of three groups of small prehistoric dwellings north of Silver City.

GILL

Possibly the street was named for D. F. Gill, an employee of the Albuquerque *Morning Journal* during the early 1900s, or for his descendants. Gill lived at 715 Gold S.E. through 1913.

GISELE DRIVE

Tom Burlison, former employee of Home Planning Corporation, the company that platted Academy Acres in northeast Albuquerque, named this street for Gisele Gatenole, who was City Clerk in the early 1970s.

GOFF

The Goff family have lived in Albuquerque for many years.

Lloyd Lozes Goff, Ph. D., was born in 1929 in Dallas, Texas. He studied art at the University of New Mexico and was an assistant professor at the University of New Mexico in 1943–45 before going to New York. While living in Albuquerque, he owned a home on Edith that was built *circa* 1755 by early settlers in the Río Grande.

He became internationally known as an artist and illustrator of books and magazine articles.

GOLD

The street was named by Colonel Walter G. Marmon after a mineral, apparently an indication of the hope that Albuquerque would become a major shipping point for the mining industry after the railroad arrived in 1880.

GRANITE

When the railroad came in 1880, Colonel Walter G. Marmon named five of the cross streets after minerals (See Coal). He chose Coal, Copper, Gold, Lead, and Silver. Apparently, as the section around Old Town developed, someone decided to continue the naming trend by adding Granite, Marble, and Slate.

GRIEGOS ROAD

This road was named for the Griegos community, which was located off the present-day road and which began as an extended family settlement, with six of the twenty-five families living there in 1795 being named Griego.

The name is Spanish, meaning "the Greek." According to Pearce in *New Mexico Place Names,* the original ancestor of the Griego family was Juan Griego, "John the Greek," a native of Greece who came to New Mexico with Oñate in 1598.

GROGAN STREET

In Westwind Subdivision, created in 1979 by Coda Roberson, of Roberson Homes, this street was named in honor of Steve Grogan, quarterback for the New England Patriots football team. Grogan was the quarterback at Kansas State University, leaving there in 1975. He played with the New England Patriots from 1975 to 1990.

Roberson was a Dallas Cowboys fan, and he named two of the streets in this subdivision for Tom Landry, coach, and for Roger Staubach, quarterback, of the Dallas Cowboys when he built the subdivision.

Though Roberson was a Cowboy fan and could have named more streets for Cowboys, instead he chose other professional football players as well, including Steve Grogan, Joe Namath, and Billy Kilmer.

GUADALUPE TRAIL (LANE and COURT)

In the North Valley, this road was named for Guadalupe Gutiérrez, who was one of the prominent citizens of the North Valley who profited by the presence of a permanent garrison of soldiers near the plaza in Albuquerque after General Stephen Kearney claimed New Mexico as a United States territory.

Gutiérrez owned a great deal of land in the valley during the last half of the nineteenth century. Supposedly, Gutiérrez drove his cattle and sheep along this trail.

GUTIERREZ

The Gutiérrez name has long been prominent in Albuquerque. Juan Gutiérrez was an owner of the 45,000-acre Pajarito land grant in the South Valley. When he died, his daughter, Julianita, inherited the massive land grant. She married James Lawrence Hubbell. (See Hubbell.)

HAGEN ROAD

Vern Hagen was employed by the Albuquerque City Planning Commission in the 1970s when Academy Place was platted by Home Planning Corporation and developed by Wood Brothers, Inc.

HAGERMAN AVENUE

In Heritage East subdivision, developed in the early 1970s, the streets were named for governors or heroes of New Mexico.

Herbert J. Hagerman was appointed territorial governor in early 1906 and served until 1907, when he resigned.

Hagerman was born in Milwaukee, Wisconsin, on December 15, 1871. He received his early schooling in public schools and graduated from Cornell University. After graduation, he entered the diplomatic service of the United States and was assistant secretary under two American ambassadors to Russia.

After his term as governor, he lived in Roswell.

HAMLET

Near Don Juan Onate Park lies a subdivsion of streets named for Shakespearean tragic characters.

Hamlet, of course, is the indecisive Danish prince who cannot act to revenge his father's death at the hands of Hamlet's uncle.

See Othello, Macbeth, Cleopatra, Adonis, Venus, and Saturn.

HANNETT

Arthur Thomas Hannet lived in Albuquerque after serving as governor of the State of New Mexico, 1925–1927.

Hannett was born in Lyons, New York. He married Louise Westfall, of Clyde, New York. The couple had one son, William.

The family moved to Gallup, New Mexico, in 1911. Hannett served as city attorney for Gallup, 1914–1916, mayor of Gallup, 1918–1922, and chairman of the New Mexico Highway Commission, 1923–1925. Then he was elected governor, taking office in 1925.

HARPER

This street located in northeast Albuquerque near the Albuquerque Academy was named for Ashby T. Harper, the third headmaster of Albuquerque Academy. Harper served as headmaster from 1964 to 1984.

HAZELDINE

William C. Hazeldine was an attorney who came from Arkansas in his late twenties. He had served as a state legislator and as a district judge. He went to Santa Fé and, in 1875, formed a partnership with William Breeden. In 1877 he moved to Albuquerque and opened a branch office of the firm.

Hazeldine was frequently involved in speculative ventures, particularly in land deals. He was an investor in the New Mexico Town Company, which sold the real estate when New Albuquerque was first developing. The New Mexico Town Company was composed of the Santa Fé Railroad and Franz Huning, Elias Stover, and William Hazeldine, three local investors. They had purchased land for the railroad, then transferred title to the New Mexico Town Company for a share of the profits. Merchants who wanted to establish businesses near the railroad had to buy their lots from the railroad. The three streets south of Coal were named for the three men.

Hazeldine served as judge, served on the first town government known as the Board of Trade, and served as secretary for the Albuquerque Publishing Company, which published the Albuquerque *Daily Journal*. He was one of the founders of the Street Railway Company, which connected New Albuquerque with Old Town and Barelas. Hazeldine was a real pillar of early Albuquerque.

HELEN HARDIN STREET

In Nor Este Manor, Presley Homes named the streets for New Mexico artists who were recommended by the Nor Este Art Association. Many of the artists attended the dedication ceremony and left their hand prints in the concrete of the park fountain near La Cueva High School.

Helen Hardin was born in Albuquerque on May 28, 1943. She studied at the University of New Mexico and at the Special School of Indian Arts at the University of Arizona in Tucson. She lives in Santa Fé.

She has exhibited in many shows and has done numerous commissions.

Hardin won the Grand Award in the Best Art Work in Painting and Sculpture Category and Best in Acrylic

Division at the 11th National Indian Arts Exhibit in Scottsdale, Arizona; First and Second Awards, Santa Fé Indian Market; and the Patrick Swazo Hinds Award for Excellence in Painting.

HENRIETTE WYETH

Also in Nor Este Manor (See Helen Hardin Street above), this street was named for Henriette Wyeth, the older sister of Andrew Wyeth. She was born in Wilmington, Delaware, in 1907. She studied art under her famous father, N. C. Wyeth, and at the Normal Art School in Boston and at the Philadelphia Academy of Fine Arts.

Wyeth married Peter Hurd while he was studying at Chadds Ford in 1929. She specializes in painting portraits and murals.

HENSCH AVENUE

Irv Hensch was director of the City of Albuquerque Public Works when Academy Acres in northeast Albuquerque was platted in the early 1970s. The street was named for Hensch by Tom Burlison.

HIDEAWAY LANE

In Four Hills subdivision, developed by Hicks and Associates in the early 1970s, Ralph Hicks chose names that generally developed a Western or New Mexico theme. This name is a departure from that pattern, however. Stemming from Stage Coach Road, Hideaway Lane provides a hideaway for those living along it, as it is a dead-end street.

HIGH

When the railroad came in 1880, the New Mexico Town Company (See Hazeldine) appointed Colonel Walter Marmon, a civil engineer, to lay out the streets for New Albuquerque. The last street on the east was called High street, because it ran through the gravely hills on the edge of the valley.

HIGHLAND

This street lies near Highland High School, named for Huning's Highland Addition, a subdivision that was developed during the 1880s. The addition was founded east of the railroad tracks, convenient to the railroad and on elevated ground that sloped up toward the sandhills. It quickly became a prestige suburb. This street, however, is far from the old Huning Highland Addition, but obviously a borrowing from it.

Franz Huning was the main backer of the development, and another street was named for him.

HILDEGARDE DRIVE

Tom Burlison, former employee of M. and Q. Southwest Company, said that thinking up names for new streets was often a problem. And in their search for names, they selected for this street in Academy Acres the name of the pet dachshund owned by Jim Berg, a draftsman for the company.

Berg's wife, Luella Anne, also has a street named for her.

HILTON

Conrad Hilton was born in New Mexico. He built a ten-story Hilton Hotel in Albuquerque in 1939.

August Holver Hilton and his brother emigrated from near Oslo, Norway, in 1854, arriving in New Mexico in 1881. A. H. Hilton erected a hotel in San Antonio, New Mexico; his son, Conrad Nicholas Hilton, who was born in San Antonio, New Mexico, on December 25, 1887, became the creator of the great Hilton Hotel empire.

HINES DRIVE

In Academy Place, platted by Home Planning Corporation in the early 1970s, this street was named for Frank Hines, an employee of Home Planning Corporation.

Dee, a nearby street, was named for his wife.

HINKLE

James F. Hinkle was manager of the large C. A. Bar Cattle Company and was involved in politics and government.

In 1892 he was elected to the territorial legislature and married Lillie Roberts on December 14 of that same year.

In 1901 the couple moved to Roswell, where Hinkle was involved in real estate and banking. He served in the New Mexico House of Representatives and in the Senate. He was elected governor in 1922, taking office January 1, 1923. He served a two-year term as governor (1923–1925) and was known as the Cowboy Governor.

Hinkle died in 1951.

HOKONA PLACE

In Taylor Ranch subdivision, in which many of the streets have names derived from Indian languages, this street bears a pueblo-language name that means "virgin butterfly." This was also the name given to the first women's dormitory at the University of New Mexico. The dormitory was built around 1910.

HOPI ROAD

The Hopi Indians live about one hundred miles west of Gallup in the northern part of Arizona, in the land called Tusayan. The Hopi villages were built on three mesas, including the villages of Hano, Sichomovi, Walpi (the oldest of the Hopi towns), Mishongnovi, Shipaulovi, Shimopovi, Hotevila, and Bacabi.

The word *Hopi* is derived from the word *Hopitu*, which means "peaceful people." These people are home-loving, agricultural, and peaceful. Their silver jewelry work is distinctively different from the work of other tribes and is particularly attractive.

The Hopi believe in a number of kachinas or spirits, and they make replicas of these spirits, which they call kachina dolls.

HOTEL CIRCLE and HOTEL AVENUE

Near Lomas, Eubank, and I-40, Hotel Circle is a relatively new street. It is fittingly named, as Ramada Inn, Freeway Inn, Howard Johnson Lodge, Econo Lodge, and Days Inn are all located on it. Hotel Avenue crosses the area in the middle of the "circle," forming a diameter, so to speak.

HUBBELL CIRCLE

Located in the South Valley, this street was named for the Hubbell family, probably descendants of James Lawence Hubbell, who was a wealthy rancher in the South Valley during the 1800s. He served in the territorial militia and fought against the Confederates at the Battle of Valverde.

Hubbell was born in Connecticut. He was in the United States military in 1846; when he left military service, he stayed in New Mexico and settled downstream from Albuquerque. He married Julianita Gutiérrez, daughter of Juan Gutiérrez, who was heiress to the 45,000-acre Pajarito land grant.

Hubbell was known as Santiago to his Hispanic neighbors.

HUGH GRAHAM

Hugh Graham was the chief executive officer of Albuquerque Federal Savings and Loan.

It was reported that Hugh Graham was involved in the development of South Glenwood Hills II subdivision and that the street was named for him for that reason.

I

ILFIELD

Though listed on the map as Ilfield, this was probably named for descendants of the Ilfeld family who arrived in Albuquerque during the frontier days.

Noa, Bernard, and Louis Ilfeld were merchants during the middle and late nineteenth century. Louis Ilfeld became an automobile dealer in 1906, ordering three Maxwells. Their business occupied the first floor of the Grant Building, built by Agnus A. Grant in 1883 and located at the northwest corner of Railroad Avenue (now Central) and Third Street. The building was destroyed by fire in June 1898 but was later rebuilt.

The family came from Las Vegas, New Mexico, and their father was Charles Ilfeld, a pioneer merchant there.

Louis C. Ilfeld was a member of the first New Mexico Senate.

Though the street name is mistakenly spelled Ilfield, the street name remembers the Ilfeld family. Pictured at age 60 is Charles Ilfeld, father of Noa, Bernard, and Louis. (Photo courtesy New Mexico State Records Center and Archives, Ilfeld Collection #129)

INDIAN SCHOOL ROAD

The road runs in front of the Albuquerque Indian School, which was constructed on its permanent site beginning in 1882 and being completed in 1884.

The school first opened in rented quarters in Los Duránes on January 1, 1881. The first class had forty students, composed mainly of Pueblos, Apaches, and Utes. The school was a boarding school operated originally by the Presbyterian Church. In 1886 the United States government took over management of the school.

Commonly known as Albuquerque Indian School, the school was officially the United States Indian Training School. The permanent site of the school was on a sixty-six acre farm, which was donated by Albuquerque businessmen to the Department of the Interior.

The school was modeled after the Indian Industrial School at Carlisle, Pennsylvania.

No longer in use, the buildings stand idle, and periodically fires occur in the buildings.

ISLETA

The street was named in honor of Isleta Pueblo. The name is Spanish, "little island." Located thirteen miles south of Albuquerque, Isleta is the largest of the Tiwa-speaking pueblos. It has about three thousand residents and 210,948 acres of land.

Hornas (ovens) are still used for baking bread at Isleta Pueblo south of Albuquerque and at other pueblos.

The street was named for Isleta Pueblo. St. Augustine church is one of the oldest mission churches in the United States, having been established in 1613. Originally called St. Anthony, the church was destroyed during the Pueblo Revolt of 1680, though the walls remained. It was rebuilt in 1716 on the original walls and renamed St. Augustine.

Isleta has occupied the same site since before Coronado explored the area in 1540. It was the only pueblo that did not join in the Pueblo Revolt of 1680.

J

JAFFA

Henry Jaffa, a local merchant, was Albuquerque's first mayor. Albuquerque was incorporated as a town in 1885 and as a city in 1891. Jaffa served one one-year term, as was the rule at first before the mayoral term was extended to two, then to four, years.

JEAN PARISH COURT

In Nor Este Manor, Presley Homes named the streets for New Mexico artists who were recommended by the Nor Este Art Association. Many of the artists attended the dedication ceremony and left their hand prints in the concrete of the park fountain near La Cueva High School.

JEMEZ

This street was named in honor of the Jemez Pueblo, located about twenty miles northwest of Bernalillo. A rather large pueblo, Jemez has about 1,900 residents and 88,867 acres of land. According to Edelman (*Summer People Winter People*), the present site has been occupied since the sixteenth century, but the actual pueblo was not constructed until after the Pueblo Revolt of 1680.

Jemez women make pottery, some in the beautiful traditional style. The women still weave yucca baskets. Also, some fine stone sculpture is being produced there, especially by Victor Vigil.

Joseph Montoya spent most of his life in public service, serving in the New Mexico state legislature, as lieutenant governor, and in the United States House of Representatives and Senate. (Photo courtesy of New Mexico State Records Center and Archives, R.H. Martin Collection #10200)

JOE MONTOYA

Joseph M. Montoya was born September 24, 1915, in Peña Blanca, in northwest New Mexico, of parents descended from Spanish immigrants.

He graduated from Bernalillo High School, then attended Regis College in Denver in 1931. Three years later he transferred to Georgetown University Law School in Washington, D. C. He earned a law degree in 1938 and was admitted to the New Mexico Bar in 1939.

He served twelve years in the New Mexico state legislature (in both houses) and four terms as lieutenant governor. He was elected to Congress in 1959 and then to the Senate in 1964.

Montoya died in 1978 of complications from surgery for cancer.

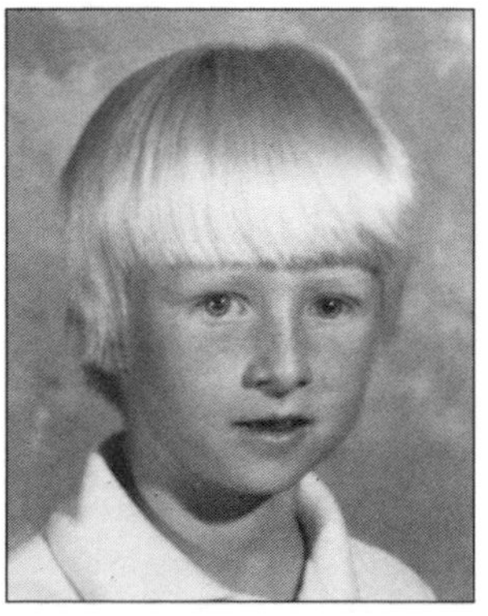

Born in 1969, John Thomas Pexa is now a commercial pilot. John Thomas Street bears his name. (Photo, 1977, courtesy Mr. and Mrs. Revi Pexa)

JOHN THOMAS DRIVE

This street was named for John Thomas Pexa, son of Revi and Dana Pexa. The Pexa family are close friends with Tom Burlison, who worked for Home Planning Corporation in the early 1970s when Academy Place was platted. A part of Burlison's job was to name streets in the new subdivisions.

Names of nearby streets honor the other two Pexa sons, Revi Don and Van Christopher.

JOSEPH SHARP STREET

In Nor Este Manor, Presley Homes named the streets for New Mexico artists who were recommended by the Nor

Este Art Association. Many of the artists attended the dedication ceremony and left their hand prints in the concrete of the park fountain near La Cueva High School.

Born in 1859, Sharp enrolled at the McMicken School of Design in Cincinnati at the age of fourteen. In 1881 he took his first study trip abroad. After each of his three trips abroad, he visited New Mexico and the Columbia River basin. He spent a part of the summer of 1893 in Taos and touted its artistic resources to Ernest Blumenschein and Bert Phillips, artists whom he had met in Paris in 1895.

For about twenty years, he taught at the Cincinnati Art Academy, sketched in the Columbia River basin, and summered in Taos. He finally established a permanent residence in Taos in 1912. His enthusiastic support of Taos caused several artists to visit Taos and some to stay there.

The subjects of his work were mostly Pueblo Indians.

Sharp died in 1953.

JUAN TABO

According to Marc Simmons (*Albuquerque: A Narrative History*), the identity of Juan Tabo has not been satisfactorily determined. One legend says that he was a priest who lived nearby, but no such name occurs in early church records. Another story says that he was a sheep herder who grazed his flocks in Tijeras Canyon, a portion of which is designated the Juan Tabó Recreation Area.

T. M. Pearce (*New Mexico Place Names*) says that on April 5, 1748, a petition designated *La Cañada de Juan Taboso* as west of the Sandia Mountains. The Taboso Indians were akin to the Texas Apaches. Pearce also suggests that *tabo* is a Spanish word in the Philippines meaning "cup made from coconut shell."

The name is also listed by Elsie Clews Parsons as one used by members of a ceremonial society at Jemez Pueblo, northwest of the Juan Tabó Canyon, according to Pearce.

JULIAN ROBLES STREET

In Nor Este Manor, Presley Homes named the streets for New Mexico artists who were recommended by the Nor

Este Art Association. Many of the artists attended the dedication ceremony and left their hand prints in the concrete of the park fountain near La Cueva High School.

Julian Robles, painter and sculptor, was born in the Bronx, New York, on June 24, 1933. He studied at the National Academy of Art and Design with Robert Phillip and at the Art Students League of New York with Sidney Dickinson. He lives in Taos.

In addition to private collections, Robles' work hangs in the New Mexico State Permanent Collection in Albuquerque, the Diamond M Museum in Snyder, Texas, the 3M Collection in Houston, and the Cowboy Hall of Fame.

He won the Rosenthal Award for the Pastel Society of America in 1983, the Silver Medal for Oils and Third Place for Pastels at the National Western Art Show in 1983, and many other national and regional awards.

KACHINA PLACE

This street in Kachina Hills subdivision bears the name of the subdivision. Kachina Hills, in East Heights, was developed during the late 1970s.

Kachinas are benevolent beings who live in nature—in lakes, mountains, springs. When treated properly, they bring blessings of rain, sunshine, crops, and healing. The Hopi Pueblo particularly believed in the kachina. Often, members of the pueblo will don masks and costumes and perform the dance of the kachina.

In this subdivision, the streets are names of kachinas—Bear Dancer, Bluecorn Maiden, Buffalo Dancer, Butterfly Maiden, Deer Dancer, Eagle Dancer, Father Sky, and White Cloud.

KAP STREET

Tom Burlison, former employee of Home Planning Corporation, the company which platted Academy Acres in northeast Albuquerque, named this street for Dennis Kapperman, an outside consultant and computer programer. Kapperman did a great deal of work for Home Planning Corporation.

George A. Kaseman's wealth made possible, through his wife, the Anna Kaseman Hospital. (Photo from *History of New Mexico*, Los Angeles: Pacific States Publishing Company, 1907)

KASEMAN

George A. Kaseman was born in Shamokin, Pennsylvania, in 1868. He was educated at Bucknell University in Pennsylvania. He married Anna Traxler of Pennsylvania, and they moved to New Mexico in 1887.

For many years Kaseman was director and for two years was president of Albuquerque Chamber of Commerce. He was in the telephone business, 1902–1907, coal mining, from 1906, and banking, from 1924. He was affiliated with Albuquerque National Trust and Savings Bank. He was also involved in merchandising from 1897.

Kaseman was a member of the New Mexico Senate, 1917 and 1919.

During the early 1900s, Kaseman was active in a number of business ventures and made a fortune. It was through his financial help that the city took options on over two thousand acres of land southeast of the city in 1935 to create a new airport to replace the privately-owned airport developed by Speakman and Franklin.

It was Kaseman's wealth that made possible, through his wife, the Anna Kaseman Hospital.

KEARNY

In 1846, during the Mexican War, Brigadier General Stephen Watts Kearny led United States Army forces to claim New Mexico for the United States. He set up a quartermaster supply depot on the *Plaza Vieja* in Albuquerque; then he and his men marched to Santa Fé, where Mexican Governor Manuel Armijo capitulated without a fight.

KELEHER

Will Keleher was an attorney and historian who wrote several books. In 1908, before gaining his law degree, he was city editor of the Albuquerque *Journal*, after having previously worked as a reporter. He served on the board of regents for New Mexico A & M (now New Mexico State University), and a building on that campus was named for him.

Keleher came to Albuquerque in 1888 when his parents moved there, when he was two years old.

He died December 18, 1972, at the age of eighty-six.

KELICH

When Academy Place was platted in the 1970s by Home Planning Corporation and was developed by Wood Brothers, Inc., Tom Burlison named this street for Bob Kelich, who was assistant city engineer for the City of Albuquerque.

KELLY

In Loma Del Norte, Ken Henderson named this street for his son, Kelly Henderson.

KENT

In February 1881, the United States Post Office issued a charter to the new town of Albuquerque establishing a post office there and naming Frederick H. Kent the postmaster. The post office was housed in a small building owned by Kent on Third Street. According to Marc Simmons (*Albuquerque: A Narrative History*), it contained only twelve boxes, and customers had to line up outside to get to the delivery window.

There was a problem, however, with incoming mail, since there was also a post office in Old Albuquerque at the *Plaza Vieja*. In 1882 a postal inspector decided to close down the post office at the *Plaza Vieja*, thereby making the residents of that area extremely angry. They petitioned the Postal Department to have their post office re-opened. With enough pressure exerted, they were successful; however, the Plaza-area post office was called Armijo, and the new town had the sole right to be called Albuquerque.

Local controversy over the ownership of the name Albuquerque continued to rage. Finally, in 1886, the Postal Department compromised by designating the plaza post office Old Albuquerque and the new one New Albuquerque. Therefore, people referred to Old Town and

New Town. Now, however, with the addition of Uptown, Albuquerque residents refer to Old Town, Downtown, and Uptown.

KILMER

Located in Westwind Sudivision, developed by Coda Roberson, of Roberson Homes, in 1979, this street was named for Billy Kilmer, who played quarterback for the Washington Redskins when the Redskins were the nemesis of the Dallas Cowboys.

Roberson was a Dallas Cowboys fan, and he and engineer John Leverton named two of the streets in this subdivision for Tom Landry, coach, and for Roger Staubach, quarterback, of the Cowboys when this subdivision was created. However, instead of naming all the streets for Dallas Cowboys, they named some of the streets for other professional football players, including Joe Namath, Steve Grogan, and Billy Kilmer.

Billy Kilmer played single-wing tailback for UCLA, leaving there in 1960. He played quarterback for the San Francisco Forty-Niners from 1961 to 1966. Coach Red Hickey devised the shotgun formation to amplify his talents. But Kilmer broke his ankle and was considered washed up. The New Orleans Saints, however, hired him from 1967 to 1970; then he was a star for the Washington Redskins from 1971 to 1978.

KINLEY

Named for President McKinley, the street was always called McKinley until sometime in recent years when the *Mc* was dropped. Evangeline Hernandez, wife of Judge B. C. Hernandez and descendant of the Armijo family, says that her girlhood friend lived on McKinley Street and that she used to visit her friend there when they were youngsters.

KIRTLAND DRIVE and ROAD

The Albuquerque Army Air Base was completed on August 8, 1941. On February 25, 1942, the base became

Kirtland Field and was named for Colonel Roy C. Kirtland, one of the pioneer aviators in the United States.

In 1912 Kirtland was the pilot of the first plane from which a machine gun was fired. He commanded the 3rd Regiment in France during World War I. He retired from the military in 1938, but three years later, he returned to active duty at the West Coast Air Corps Training Center in California. Kirtland died of a heart attack in California on May 2, 1941.

KIT CARSON

Running alongside Kit Carson Park, this street was named for Kit Carson, Indian scout and most famous of the mountain men who came to Taos, arriving there in 1826.

Carson was first married to an Arapaho woman named Waa-nike but later married a Taoseña named Josefa Jaramillo. They had eight children.

He served as John Fremont's guide to California, was an Indian fighter and spoke several Indian languages, and also served as Jicarilla Apache Indian Agent on three appointments in 1854, 1857, and 1858.

Carson died of an aneurism in 1868, just a month after Josefa had died of complications in childbirth. They died near Fort Lyons, in Colorado, and were buried there. But their remains were returned, within the year, to Taos, where they were buried in Kit Carson Memorial Cemetery.

Kit Carson Street and Park were named for Kit Carson, Indian scout and most famous of the mountain men who settled in Taos in the early 1800s. (Photo courtesy Kit Carson Memorial Museum, Taos, New Mexico)

KIVA

In Four Hills subdivision, created by Hicks and Associates in the early 1970s, Ralph Hicks chose street names that develop a Western or Spanish theme. The kiva, of course, is the ceremonial structure found in pueblos, partially above and partially below ground.

KLONDIKE

In Prospector's Ridge, developed by Presley Homes, the street names develop the theme of prospecting or mining.

KLONDIKE

Klondike is a region in the Yukon Territory of northwestern Canada. In August 1896, George W. Carmack and his wife found gold in the gravel of a creek, which he called the Bonanza. When news of the gold discovery reached the outer world, a horde of gold prospectors stampeded the Klondike in 1897 and 1898.

KRIM DRIVE

When Loma Del Norte was platted in the early 1970s by M. and Q. Southwest, Tom Burlison named the street for Frank Krim, who was a draftsman for the company.

L

LA CABRA

In Four Hills subdivsion, developed by Hicks and Associates in the early 1970s, Ralph Hicks chose the name *La Cabra,* Spanish for "she-goat" or "nanny goat," to tie in with an intersecting street called Pedrogoso Place, which was named for a pet goat belonging to one of the city draftsmen.

LA CIENEGA STREET

Just off Montaño Road, La Cienega Street apparently is derived from the small community located fifteen miles southwest of Santa Fe.

The name is Spanish for "swamp." In Santa Fé, there is also a street by this name, and that name was given because the area around the street once was a swamp.

LA JARA

In the eastern portion of Academy Acres, developed in the 1970s, the streets were named for New Mexico place names.

According to *New Mexico Place Names,* this name in Spain refers to the European labdanum tree, but in New Mexico the name refers to the scrub willow. La Jara is a place name in wide use in New Mexico. There are two communities named La Jara, two La Jara Canyons, five La Jara Creeks, and one La Jara Park.

LA MADERA

Also in the eastern portion of Academy Acres, this street was named after a place name. *La Madera,* Spanish for "wood or lumber," is the name of a winter sports area in the Sandia Mountains near Albuquerque.

LA MANCHA

In Thomas Village, developed around 1980 by Ed Leslie, the streets were named primarily after Miguel de Cervantes Saavedra's picaresque romance, *Don Quixote de la Mancha.* (See Don Quixote Drive.)

La Mancha, of course, is the home of Don Quixote.

LA ORILLA

Spanish for "the border," this street serves as the border between Albuquerque and Los Ranchos de Albuquerque.

LA TUNA

In Four Hills subdivision, created by Hicks and Associates in the 1970s, Ralph Hicks chose street names that develop a Western or New Mexican/Spanish theme. This name is Spanish for "prickly pear," a common species of flora of the area.

LADERA

Ladera Street derived its name from a section in the North Valley known as *La Ladera,* "hillside or slope," on north Edith. The general area was known as La Ladera, so named for its location on the West Mesa. Today, Ladera Golf Course and Ladera Heights Addition bear the same name.

LADRONES

The name of this street in Atrisco Village commemorates the Ladron Mountains, or *Los Ladrones,* which lie southwest of Albuquerque. *Ladrón* is a Spanish word that means "thief," and the word was applied to these moun-

tains because they provided cover originally for Navajo and Apache horse thieves and later for American rustlers. The mountains are quite rocky, and the trails are passable only on foot or on horseback. One of the American rustlers had a ranch in the area, which provided cover for his thieving activities. Some say that he had a spy in Socorro who was thought to be a simpleton but who reported information which helped his master in the robberies.

LAGUNA

After the Pueblo Revolt of 1680 and the Reconquest of 1692, Keresan-speaking refugees from Santo Domingo, Ácoma, Cochiti, and other pueblos founded the Pueblo of Laguna. The Spaniards named the pueblo for a marshy lake located to the west, *laguna,* meaning "a pool or lagoon." The pueblo still occupies its original hilltop site. Laguna is the only pueblo which was created after the Spanish came to New Mexico.

LAMAR

In Santa Fé Village, the streets were named for actors and actresses who were popular during the early part of the twentieth century.

Laguna street was named for the Laguna Pueblo located on a hill west of Albuquerque.

Hedy Lamarr (usually spelled with a double *r*, though the street name has only one) was born Hedwig Eva Maria Kiesler on November 9, 1913. She was a beautiful bit player in Austrian-German films. She caused a furor when she appeared nude in the 1932 Czech film *Ecstasy*. She came to the United States in 1938, where, according to *Encyclopedia of Film*, "she contributed little but her exotic beauty to a host of productions, mostly at MGM."

LAMP POST CIRCLE and COURT

In Four Hills subdivision, developed by Hicks and Associates in the early 1970s, Ralph Hicks chose street names that generally create a Western or New Mexico theme. This name suggests the method of lighting in the Old West towns.

LAMY

Rt. Rev. Jean Baptiste Lamy was assigned to Santa Fé and went there in 1850. Accompanied by Father Joseph Projectus Macheboeuf, his friend and fellow priest who had accompanied him from France in 1839, Lamy made the trip to Santa Fé from Ohio, where the two had been previously assigned, on horseback. However, although he was well received by the people of Santa Fé, the clergy resented him and refused to accept his authority. As a result, he journeyed into Mexico in order to gain assistance from his former bishop. He became Bishop of Santa Fé when the Diocese of Santa Fé was officially established in 1853.

He brought the Sisters of Loretto from Kentucky to Santa Fé, and they opened an academy. He also brought European priests and various teaching orders to serve in Santa Fé.

A French priest who expected the utmost in rectitude, apparently, he disciplined those who needed disciplining. It is said that he excommunicated Padre Martínez in Taos, and he once sent Father Macheboeuf to Albuquerque to correct the wandering ways of Father José Manuel Gallegos.

Archbishop Jean Baptiste Lamy was first bishop, then archbishop, in Santa Fé, having jurisdiction over Albuquerque. (See Bishops Lodge Road in Santa Fé for more story and photographs.) (Photo courtesy New Mexico State Records Center and Archives, McNitt Collection #6522)

Bishop Lamy built his own personal chapel at Bishop's Lodge, the bishop's retreat located north of Santa Fé.

Lamy was born on October 11, 1814, at Lempdes, France. He was educated and ordained in the Diocese of Clermont. In 1839 he came to Ohio with Bishop of Cincinnati J. B. Purcell, who had been to France to recruit missionary priests to come to the United States.

It was Lamy who brought about the construction of the beautiful Cathedral of St. Francis in Santa Fé.

LANDRY AVENUE

When Coda Roberson, of Roberson Homes, developed Westwind Subdivision on the West Mesa in 1979, he and engineer John Leverton named two of the streets for the Dallas Cowboys because Roberson was such a Cowboys fan. Tom Landry was coach and Roger Staubach was quarterback of the Cowboys team when this subdivision was created.

Landry had played a back position at the University of Texas, leaving there in 1949. He played defensive back for the New York Giants, 1950 to 1955, and was assistant coach for the Giants from 1956 to 1959. In 1960, when the Dallas Cowboys came into being, Landry became the first coach for the Cowboys, staying with them until 1988, when he was released by Jerry Jones.

LAS LOMAS

Spanish for "the hills," *Las Lomas* is the name of a street that is situated in the hills of the East Mesa, around the campus of the University of New Mexico.

LEAD

The street was named by Colonel Walter Marmon after a mineral, apparently an indication of the hope that Albuquerque would become a major shipping point for the mining industry. This street and other streets named after minerals were given their names by Marmon when he laid out New Albuquerque when the railroad came in 1880.

LESLIE PLACE

Ed Leslie built a large number of homes in Albuquerque, including many in Academy Acres in northeast Albuquerque. Tom Burlison of Home Planning Corporation, the company that platted this subdivision, named the street for Leslie.

LEW WALLACE

In Heritage East subdivision, the streets were named for New Mexico governors, mostly those who served prior to statehood.

Lew Wallace was born in Brookville, Indiana, in 1827.

He worked as a court and legislative reporter and studied law. During the Mexican War, he served as a vol-

unteer in the Army. After the war, he practiced law and participated in politics.

When the Civil War began, he became adjutant general of Indiana, and he quickly won promotion to the rank of major general of volunteers. At that time, he was the youngest Union general in the Civil War. In 1864 he temporarily stopped a Confederate offensive at the Battle of Monocacy, probably saving Washington, D.C., from capture.

After the Civil War, President Rutherford B. Hayes appointed Wallace territorial governor of New Mexico and sent him to restore order from the havoc that was being created by Billy the Kid (William H. Bonney) and the Tunstall-McSween faction. They were rustling and causing many problems in Lincoln County. (Sheriff Pat Garrett was finally successful in shooting Billy the Kid on July 14, 1881.)

Wallace arrived in New Mexico during the turbulent years of mining, land speculation, and railroad building. He served as territorial governor from 1878 to 1881.

He is best remembered as the author of *Ben Hur: A Tale of the Christ,* which was written while he resided in Santa Fé as governor of the territory.

After his tenure as governor, he served as minister to Turkey, 1881–1885. He died in 1905.

LINN AVENUE

John Floyd Linn was a masonic official in Albuquerque. He was born October 12, 1884, in Agricola, Kansas. He married Mazie E. Woodworth, and they had no children. He arrived in New Mexico in 1914 from Topeka, Kansas.

Linn served in many positions with the Masons. He was employed as an official in the Masonic Temple in Albuquerque and lived on Fruit Street.

LLANO COURT

Spanish for "level, flat, smooth," *llano* is a fitting name for a street in this area of north Albuquerque. The East Mesa has traditionally been called *El Llano,* though this street is not so far east as the East Mesa.

LOBO PLACE and LOBO COURT

Located near the University of New Mexico, these two streets were named for the mascot of the athletic teams of the University of New Mexico. *El lobo* is the Spanish word for "wolf."

LOMA DEL NORTE ROAD

Spanish for "hill of the north" (or "north hill"), Loma Del Norte is also the name of a subdivision in northeast Albuquerque. The name seems a bit strange, suggesting that there is only one hill; however, Tom Burlison, formerly of M. and Q. Southwest, said that they chose names that sounded good and that they may have taken liberties with Spanish occasionally.

LOMAS

Originally New York Avenue, this street name was later changed to *Lomas,* Spanish for "hills." The name is reminiscent of the hills that it traverses as it links Old Town to New Town to the University of New Mexico and all the way east to Tramway.

LONA LANE

In the northeast part of Albuquerque, just off Spain and Eubank, lies Lona Lane. This street was platted and named in the early 1970s by Hicks and Associates. Though Lona, in the interest of discretion, cannot be identified here, she was a brief romantic interest of Tom Burlison, who was an employee of the company. According to Burlison, he and a group of young adults had gone to Conchas Lake for the weekend, and the group of them were camping, so to speak, in a mobile home. He said that he made a proposition to Lona that if she would spend the night with him on the beach of the lake, he would name a street in Albuquerque for her. She did, and he did.

LOS LUNAS

In a portion of Loma Del Norte, the streets were named for towns or counties in New Mexico.

According to *New Mexico Place Names,* the town of Los Lunas, Spanish for "the Luna folks or people," was named for the Luna family, descendants of Diego de Luna, who was born in 1635.

Though the word *Luna* means "moon," the presence of the masculine article *los* indicates a family name. If the word referred to "moon," the feminine article *las* would be used.

LOS POBLANOS LANE and PLACE

Located in Los Ranchos de Albuquerque, an enclave within the city of Albuquerque, the streets were given the name Los Poblanos, a name that referred to the Armijo family, who had come from Puebla, Mexico. The name also referred to their hacienda.

Albert Simms ultimately bought the land in this area.

LOS VOLCANES

The street name is a remembrance of the fury that was once visited upon many parts of New Mexico in the form of volcanic eruptions. Much of the land, especially that west of Albuquerque and in parts of the south and southwest of New Mexico, is covered by lava flow, as much as twenty feet thick in some areas. On the escarpment just west of the Río Grande, the cones of three extinct volcanoes are visible, and much of the land in the vicinity is lava-covered. The lands covered by lava flow are called *Malpais,* Spanish for "badlands." (See Malpais Road and Volcano Road.)

LOST DUTCHMAN

In Prospector's Ridge, developed by Presley Homes, the names of the streets develop the theme of prospecting or mining. This street commemorates the famous Lost Dutchman mine.

LOVE

Oscar Mahlon Love was a native of Hamilton, Virginia. He moved to Albuquerque in 1921 and was assistant secretary of the Albuquerque YMCA.

In 1925 he began a career with Albuquerque National Bank. Beginning as assistant cashier, he became cashier and a bank director in 1930, vice-president in 1941, senior vice-president in 1957, and president in 1963.

He served as president of Albuquerque Chamber of Commerce, 1935–1941. He was on the executive board of Bataan Methodist Hospital and a trustee of the Lovelace Foundation for Medical Research.

Love died in January 1977 at the age of eighty-five.

This street was named for Love, as he had owned the property on which Dale Bellamah built Princess Jeanne Park, which was named for Bellamah's wife, Jeanne Lees. Love had named some of the streets before he sold the property to Bellamah, apparently, including Elizabeth, for his wife, and Mahlon, for his son, Oscar Mahlon Love, Jr.

LOVELACE ROAD

Dr. William Randolph Lovelace was born at Rolla, Missouri, on July 27, 1883. He attended private schools, then medical school at Saint Louis University.

Dr. Lovelace was a pioneer in aerospace medicine. Aside from private practice, he was consulting surgeon for the Atchison, Topeka, and Santa Fé Hospital and for a number of other hospitals.

He served on the Board of Regents for the University of New Mexico and on the State Board of Medical Examiners.

Lovelace died on December 4, 1968.

LOWE STREET

Bob Lowe was employed by the City of Albuquerque Public Works Department in the 1970s when Academy

Place was platted by Home Planning Corporation and developed by Wood Brothers, Inc.

LUELLA ANNE DRIVE and COURT

This street name honors Luella Anne Berg, wife of Jim Berg, a draftsman for Home Planning Corporation, the company that platted Academy Acres in northeast Albuquerque in the early 1970s.

Nearby lies a street named for the family's pet dachshund, Hildegarde.

LUNA

Solomon Luna was president of the Albuquerque Bank of Commerce and the largest individual raiser of sheep in New Mexico in the early 1900s when Luna Place, a subdivision east of the old Perea Addition, was named for him.

He was once vice-president of First National Bank and was a member of the Republican National Committee. He was actually a resident of Los Lunas, but was active in Albuquerque's business life and real estate.

LUTHY CIRCLE, COURT, and DRIVE

Fred Luthy was born in 1895. He served as president of Albuquerque National Bank. He lost his sight in an explosion of a nitroglycerin bomb near Hobbs, New Mexico, in 1938, but trained himself to keep figures in his head.

His daughter, Cyrene Jane Luthy, married John W. Inman, a home builder; because of this connection, three streets were named for him. Luthy died in January 1963.

MABRY AVENUE

In Heritage East subdivision, developed in the early 1970s, the streets were named for governors or heroes of New Mexico.

Thomas J. Mabry, a Democrat, served as governor of New Mexico, 1947–1951.

Born October 17, 1885, in Carlisle County, Kentucky, he came to New Mexico in 1907 from Weatherford, Oklahoma. He was educated at the University of New Mexico and at the University of Oklahoma.

Mabry married Katherine Burns of Clovis, New Mexico, and they had three children.

Mabry was the youngest member of the New Mexico Constitutional Convention in 1910. He was admitted to the New Mexico Bar in 1915. He was a member of the first New Mexico Senate, 1912–1917, and served as district attorney of the Second Judicial District, 1933–1936. In 1936 he was elected district judge of the Second Judicial District of New Mexico.

Thomas J. Mabry served as governor of New Mexico from 1947 to 1951. This photograph was taken in 1948. (Photo courtesy New Mexico State Records Center and Archives, D.O.D. #1637)

MAHLON

In Princess Jeanne Park, developed by Dale Bellamah in the early 1950s and named for his wife, Jeanne Lees, the streets were generally named for people.

Oscar Mahlon Love owned some of the property on which Princess Jeanne Park was developed, and he named some of the streets before selling the property to Bellamah. Mahlon Street was named for Love's son, Oscar Mahlon Love, Jr.

MALAGA

In a portion of Loma Del Norte, the streets were named for towns or counties in New Mexico.

Malaga, according to *New Mexico Place Names,* was founded in 1892 and was named for a sweet Spanish wine made from a variety of grape that grew there. Malaga, in Eddy County, is located fifteen miles southeast of Carlsbad.

MALPAIS COURT and ROAD

Spanish for "badlands," this name refers especially to the area west of Albuquerque, which is largely covered by lava flow from volcanoes that erupted in the area hundreds of years ago. West of Albuquerque, over one hundred extinct volcanic cones stand in mute affirmation of the volcanic fury that has been visited upon parts of New Mexico in the past. The escarpment just west of the Río Grande is covered by lava, and three major cones are easily visible from Albuquerque.

MANKIN

Ed Mankin was a builder in Albuquerque during the early 1900s, and his name is remembered on a street in the Park Addition, developed by Martin P. Stamm. Located near Los Altos Park, this subdivision contains several streets named for generals.

MANZANO

El manzano is Spanish for a variety of apple tree that produces a small, sweet Mexican apple. According to Marc Simmons (*Albuquerque: A Narrative History*), a stray band of colonists created a small settlement on the lower edge of the wooded eastern slope of the mountains now called the Manzanos. Along with fields of grain, they put in a couple of orchards of *manzanos*. The new community and the entire chain of mountains south of Tijeras Canyon took their names from the orchards.

Pearce, in *New Mexico Place Names,* gives a similar story. He says that there are two old apple orchards there, reputedly planted during the mission period before 1676. But Dr. Florence H. Ellis dated the trees, from the ring growth, as no earlier than 1800. Tradition says that they were planted when Manzano was still one of the pueblos in the Salinas region, but the Spanish village dates only from 1829.

The street, however, takes its name from the mountains and the village.

MANUEL CIA PLACE

In Nor Este Manor, Presley Homes named the streets for New Mexico artists who were recommended by the Nor Este Art Association. Many of the artists attended the

dedication ceremony, and their hand prints are in the fountain in the park near La Cueva High School.

Manuel Cia is of both Spanish and Navajo heritage. Cia was born in Las Cruces, New Mexico. He studied at the American Academy of Art in Chicago, the San Francisco Art Institute, and the Los Angeles Trade Technical School.

His work is a blend of strong composition and design with impressionist technique.

MARBLE

When the railroad came in 1880, Colonel Walter G. Marmon named five of the cross streets after minerals (See Coal). He chose Coal, Copper, Gold, Lead, and Silver. As the section around Old Town developed, apparently someone decided to continue the naming trend by adding Granite, Marble, and Slate.

MARTINEZ

Martinez Road lies on the west side of the Río Grande, and Martinez Avenue lies on the east.

During the early settlement of the area, there was the large central plaza, or *Plaza Vieja,* near which other families would settle and create their own small plazas.

Such was the case when around 1850 Don Manuel Martínez moved his family onto the land northeast of Old Town Plaza, between what later were Broadway and the sandhills. His plaza and surrounding homes were called Martíneztown, which was a suburb of Old Town. Eventually, Martíneztown was engulfed by Albuquerque.

MARTINGALE LANE

In Four Hills subdivision, developed by Hicks and Associates in the early 1970s, Ralph Hicks chose street names that would create a Western or New Mexico theme.

A martingale is a part of a horse's harness that steadies a horse's head or checks its upward movement. It is usually a strap that is fastened to the girth and, after passing between the forelegs, divides and ends in two rings through which the reins pass.

MATADOR

In Four Hills subdivision, this street name celebrates the bullfighter or the one who kills the bull. Nearby is Toro Street, in honor of the bull.

MAVERICK COURT and TRAIL

In Four Hills, this name refers to an unbranded range animal or an independent person who refuses to conform with his group.

The word is an eponym, deriving from the name of Samuel Maverick, an American pioneer of the late nineteenth century who refused to brand his calves.

McDONALD ROAD

W. W. McDonald was a resident of Albuquerque when Will Keleher was growing up. McDonald was a Civil War veteran. The street was probably named for some of his descendants.

MECHEM

Merritt C. Mechem was governor of New Mexico in 1921–1922.

Mechem migrated to New Mexico for his health, seeking relief from the asthma that troubled him in Arkansas. He was a lawyer and was well known in political circles.

He moved to Tucumcari and married Eleanor O'Heir in 1910; they moved to Socorro in 1912.

A Republican, Mechem was elected governor in the fall of 1920 and took office in January 1921.

The Mechems lived in Albuquerque after his term of office was completed. He died in 1946, and Mrs. Mechem lived until 1973.

MEDICAL ARTS AVENUE

The huge medical arts building lies between Medical Arts Avenue and Lomas Boulevard.

MENAUL BOULEVARD

The boulevard was named for Menaul School, which was named for Reverend James Menaul, synod executive of the Presbyterian Church for New Mexico. The beginnings of the Menaul School are quite complicated, as a number of different schools for girls and boys ultimately were combined to create the Menaul School. According to "100 Years From Founding of Menaul School 1881–1981," a "contract school" arranged between the United States government and the Presbyterian Church was opened in Albuquerque on January 1, 1881, in an adobe house located about a mile north of Old Town in Duranes Plaza. Most of the first students were Pueblos, Navajos, and Utes. Benjamin M. Thomas, a Pueblo Indian agent in Santa Fé, had been corresponding with Dr. Henry Kendall, secretary of the Presbyterian Board of Home Missions, and with Sheldon Jackson, superintendent of Presbyterian Missions in the Territories, and he apparently was partially responsible for the bringing about of this school. Records are not clear as to whether Miss Lora B. Shields or Professor J. S. Shearer actually opened the school, but Shearer was soon recognized as superintendent and served in that position until July 1882.

In 1887 the principal building of the school burned. Most of the students transferred to the nearby government school, but the church rebuilt the school and continued it as an Indian school for boys until 1892.

The buildings were then vacant until 1896, when Rev. James Menaul arranged for the boarding department of the Presbyterian school in Las Vegas to be transferred to Albuquerque. The next year, the school was named for Rev. Menaul.

MENDIUS AVENUE

John Mendius was a surveyor for Home Planning Corporation, the company that platted Academy Acres in northeast Albuquerque in 1972.

MERIWETHER

In Heritage East, developed in the early 1970s, the streets were named for governors or heroes of New Mexico.

David Meriwether served as territorial governor of New Mexico, 1853 to 1857. (Photo courtesy New Mexico State Records Center and Archives, McNitt Collection #6526)

David Meriwether served as territorial governor of New Mexico, 1853 to 1857. His previous experience with New Mexico was none too pleasant, however, While he and his Negro servant were crossing the plains with a group of Pawnee Indians in 1819, they were arrested by a group of cavalry men and accused of being spies. Melgares, governor at the time, released them.

He left New Mexico in May 1857, though his term did not end until November. He returned to his farm near Louisville and became active in politics there.

During Meriwether's term as territorial governor, the Gadsden Purchase was completed.

Meriwether was born October 30, 1800, and died in 1893.

MERRITT

Ross Merritt was a banker in Albuquerque in the early twentieth century.

MESQUITE

In the eastern portion of Academy Acres, developed in the 1970s, the streets were named for New Mexico place names.

Mesquite is the name of a community south of Las Cruces, so named because of the many mesquite bushes.

The word derives from Mexico-Spanish *mezquite,* "desert shrub."

MESSERVY

In Heritage East subdivision, developed in the early 1970s, the streets were named for governors or heroes of New Mexico.

William S. Messervy served as acting territorial governor of New Mexico when Governor William Carr Lane left the state after he lost the election for delegate to Congress to José Manuel Gallegos. Messervy served as governor until the arrival of Governor David Meriwether in 1853.

A native of Massachusetts, Messervy came to New Mexico long before the Mexican War. He was engaged in business in Santa Fé for several years and amassed a fortune.

MIDGE STREET

Midge Sprenger, wife of Robert Sprenger, is honored in this street name. Robert Sprenger was a draftsman for M. and Q. Southwest when Loma Del Norte was platted in the early 1970s.

Sprenger Street, located nearby, was named for Bob Sprenger.

MILL POND ROAD

This street was named for the pond at the sawmill owned by Albuquerque Lumber Company. The lumber company opened a sawmill at this site in the early 1880s, and the mill continued production into the twentieth century.

Mill Pond Road intersects Sawmill Road.

MILNE

In 1908, John Milne was teaching mathematics in the high school. Later he became superintendent of schools for the Albuquerque public schools and remained in that position for nearly fifty years. He worked as a plumber part time to supplement his salary.

Milne refused to segregate the schools, and he believed that the ability to speak Spanish was an asset rather than a liability. He enlarged the Albuquerque school system from five to sixty-three schools during his superintendency.

MIMBRES

Mimbres is a Spanish word meaning "willow trees." The Spaniards gave the name *mimbreños* to an early Indian tribe who built pit houses and lived near the river which is called the Mimbres River. Willows, of course, are common along waterways in New Mexico.

MISSION

In the Vineyard Addition, platted by Henry G. Coors in 1923, the streets were named for varieties of grapes or vineyard-associated words. (See Vineyard Road.)

MOLLY BROWN AVENUE

In Prospector's Ridge, developed by Presley Homes, the names of the streets develop a theme of prospecting or mining.

Molly Brown was the wife of "Leadville" Johnny Brown, owner of the richest silver mine in the world, which was located near Leadville, Colorado. Molly was an under-educated mountain girl who married Johnny Brown. They moved to Denver but were not accepted by the "genteel" people there because of their boorish ways. So they went to Europe, where Molly in particular, was a favorite with royalty and the élite. She was on the *Titanic* when it sank, and she emerged from the tragedy a heroine for her rescue efforts on the ship.

MONTANO (MONTANO PLAZA)

In Los Ranchos de Albuquerque, the Montaño family owned land in the area of the present-day Montaño Road. The small plaza of Los Montaños or Los Ranchitos is shown on an 1882 map of the Elena Gallegos Grant.

Montaño Place, at Montaño Road and Coors Boulevard, was built on land owned by Joel P. Taylor. (See Taylor Ranch Road.)

MONTGOMERY BOULEVARD

Montgomery Boulevard was named for the Montgomery family. According to Mrs. Grant Montgomery, wife of the eldest son of Earl Montgomery, the name was brought to Albuquerque when Elizabeth Montgomery and her three sons—Earl Cyrus, Eugene Christopher, and Paul Loren—homesteaded land that is now in the vicinity of Carlisle

Boulevard and Montgomery Boulevard. They homesteaded in the early 1900s, around 1910 to 1912.

When the boys grew old enough to qualify for homesteading, Earl and Eugene also homesteaded in the area. Earl had almost a section of land that is now bounded by San Mateo Boulevard on the west, Montgomery Boulevard on the north, Louisiana Boulevard on the east, and Candelaria Boulevard on the south.

Eugene's land was a strip along the north section line, which is now Montgomery Boulevard, and then west to the gravel pit. San Mateo and Montgomery are intersecting section lines.

The boulevard was given its name in honor of the Montgomery family in the late 1940s.

MONTOYA STREET and MONTOYA ROAD

The Montoya name has been in the Albuquerque area for almost three hundred years. In 1712 Governor Peñuela granted the lands on which Los Ranchos de Albuquerque was founded to Captain Diego Montoya. Shortly after that time, however, the lands were conveyed to Elena Gallegos, widow of Santiago Gurulé. Known as the Elena Gallegos grant, this land consisted of some seventy thousand acres of land on the north of Albuquerque, much of which was on the East Mesa and in the Sandia Mountains. Later much of this property came under the ownership of Albert Simms, and he later donated much of the property to the Albuquerque Academy. (See also Gallegos Road, Simms Avenue, and Academy Parkway.)

MOON

The Moon family have lived in Albuquerque for some time. Z.B. Moon was a state senator during the 1930s.

MORNINGSIDE DRIVE

When Morningside addition was created, it was on the east—or morning side—of the city. In the Ridgecrest addition, through which Morningside Drive runs, Sun-

rise Place lies on the east side of the addition, and Sundown Place lies on the west.

MORRIS RIPPEL PLACE

In Nor Este Manor, Presley Homes named the streets for New Mexico artists who were recommended by the Nor Este Art Association. Many of the artists attended the dedication ceremony and left their hand prints in the concrete of the park fountain near La Cueva High School.

A native of New Mexico, Morris Rippel was born in Albuquerque in 1932. He attended Albuquerque High School and entered the University of New Mexico College of Engineering in 1947. He was granted a degree in architectural engineering in 1958 and practiced architecture for nine years before devoting himself to painting full time.

Rippel won four consecutive gold medals for watercolor and the 1979 Prix de West in the National Academy of Western Art competition.

MORROW

John Morrow was a businessman in Albuquerque. After the City Electric Company, which operated the street cars, went out of business in 1928, Morrow and several associates brought a bus company franchise to Albuquerque. The Albuquerque Bus Company was a private business until it became the Albuquerque Transit System in 1965, owned by the city.

MOSQUERO

In a portion of Loma Del Norte, the streets were named for towns or counties in New Mexico.

According to *New Mexico Place Names,* the name is a Spanish word which, in New Mexico, means "a swarm of flies, fleas, or mosquitoes." Mosquero is the county seat of Harding County.

MOUNTAIN ROAD

Mountain Road extends to the north of Old Town and New Town, along a high area. According to E. E. "Babe"

Osuna, Mountain Road was the north boundary of the city back in "the old days" when he was a postman in the city. Back then, he said, Mountain Road never went more than a few blocks.

MUSCATEL

In the Vineyard Addition, platted by Henry G. Coors in 1923, the streets were named for varieties of grapes or for vineyard-associated words. (See Vineyard Road.)

NAMASTE ROAD

N

In Quaker Heights, located on the west side of Albuquerque, the street names develop the theme of the peacefulness and friendliness of the Quakers.

Namaste means "hello," "welcome," "good day," etc., in Nepali and some dialects of India.

NAMATH AVENUE

Located in Westwind Subdivision, which was developed in 1979 by Coda Roberson, of Roberson Homes, this street name honors Joe Namath of the National Football League.

Roberson was a fan of the Dallas Cowboys; when he built this subdivision, he and engineer John Leverton named two streets for Roger Staubach, quarterback, and Tom Landry, coach, of the Dallas Cowboys when the subdivision was developed.

Rather than naming all the streets for Dallas Cowboys, however, he spread the honors around the NFL, naming streets also for Steve Grogan, Billy Kilmer, and Joe Namath.

NAMBE

The Nambe Pueblo, its name deriving from Tewa *nambyongwee* "people of the roundish earth," is located about sixteen miles north of Santa Fé. The population is about 420, and the pueblo has 19,076 acres of land.

Nambe has been continuously occupied since about A.D. 1300. It was active during the Pueblo Revolt of 1680,

and the people there murdered their priest and destroyed their church.

Nambe is making a comeback in weaving and pottery making. Their pottery is black-on-black or white-on-red in style.

In 1951 the Nambe Pueblo created and began producing Nambe ware, beautiful and rather expensive, designer-like serving pieces made of a pewter-like metal. This is the kind of serving ware that my wife's aunt says you accidentally leave the price tag on when you give it as a gift.

NAVARRA WAY

In Four Hills subdivision, created by Hicks and Associates in the early 1970s, Ralph Hicks chose street names that develop a Western or Spanish theme.

This street is a remembrance of Navarre (Spanish *Navarra*), a province located in north-central Spain.

NEWCOMB AVENUE

Linda Newcomb was secretary for Wood Brothers, Inc., the company that built many of the homes in Academy Place. Her name was selected by Tom Burlison, an employee of Home Planning Corporation, the company that platted the subdivision in the early 1970s.

NIAGRA

In the Vineyard Addition, platted by Henry G. Coors in 1923, the streets were named for varieties of grapes or vineyard-associated words. (See Vineyard Road.)

NORMENT ROAD

In South Valley, this street was named for James Norment, who was president of the Mutual Investment Agency and of the Security Investment Agency. In the early 1900s, he came into ownership of a great deal of land, some by simply paying back taxes. He acquired the vast Pajarito Grant in the South Valley, once owned by the Hubbell family and originally owned by Juan Gutiérrez.

NORTH VIEW

This street lies on the north end of Quaker Heights, a subdivision located on the west side of Albuquerque with streets whose names develop the theme of the peacefulness and friendliness of the Quakers.

NORTHERN TRAIL

Also in Quaker Heights, this street, unlike the other streets in this subdivision, seems to have no particular meaning in that scheme of names that develop the theme of peacefulness and friendliness. This name was probably suggested by the presence of nearby Western Trail.

NUGGET COURT and NUGGET STREET

The names of the streets in Prospector's Ridge develop a theme of prospecting or mining. These two street names celebrate the nugget, the most exciting form in which to find gold.

ONATE COURT and ONATE STREET

Don Juan de Oñate, after much preparation and waiting, led a group of settlers and priests to New Mexico in 1598. When he arrived at the Río Grande, he took possession of New Mexico in an elaborate ceremony, claiming it for the Spanish king.

The people settled at the Pueblo of Ohke in July, at the confluence of the Río Grande and the Río Chama, and they re-named the site Don Juan Bautista. They erected a church building and dedicated it on September 8, 1598.

Oñate's expedition was a private one, one which he had proposed, and he was governor.

Later, however, having fallen into disfavor with the Spanish government and facing the prospect of removal from his position as governor, he resigned his post on August 24, 1607. Investigation into his conduct was begun in 1612, and in 1614 he was convicted of a number of charges. But later he filed appeals, and in 1622 his petition for leniency and restoration of his titles apparently was granted by the king.

ORR AVENUE

Rip Orr was assistant director of the City of Albuquerque Public Works in the early 1970s when Academy Place was platted by Home Planning Corporation.

Osuna street was named for Dr. Elijio Osuna, physician, surgeon, and professor of medicine. (Photo courtesy of Katharine Osuna, wife of the late Ben Osuna, son of Dr. Elijio Osuna)

OSUNA

This street was named for the Osuna family.

Dr. Elijio Osuna and his wife came to Albuquerque in the 1890s. Dr. Osuna came from Monterrey, Mexico; his wife, Aurelia Martínez y Montemaior, familiarly known as Mamacita, came from Sca Sca, Mexico, near Monterrey. Osuna was a professor of medicine, and he maintained a practice in Albuquerque. According to Katharine Osuna, his daughter-in-law, Dr. Osuna "delivered lots of babies." He was also coroner.

Dr. Osuna had an office in downtown Albuquerque and used a buggy drawn by Old Bones, his horse, to make his rounds.

The Osunas had nine children, eight of whom survived. There were five sons (one died at the age of two) and three daughters. The oldest daughter, Anita Osuna y Martínez de Carr, was the first Hispanic woman on the faculty of the University of New Mexico.

Ben Osuna, Katharine's husband, was an attorney in Albuquerque. Elijio Edward "Babe" Osuna still lives in Albuquerque; Tomás lives in Mexico.

Mrs. Katharine Osuna related an interesting story about her brother-in-law Tomás: When he was younger, Tomás was selling Fuller brushes door-to-door in Santa Fé. At one home, the woman said that she had guests and could not talk to him at the moment. But on reflection, she asked, "Do you play bridge?" Upon receiving a positive answer, she said, "We need a fourth. If you will come in and play bridge with us, I promise that everyone here will buy something from you when we finish." He did, and they did.

Dr. Osuna died in 1916 after many years of practicing medicine in Albuquerque.

The original Osunas came from Spain; the title for the Duke of Osuna still exists today. The name itself comes from *Osa*, "bear."

When Dr. Osuna was practicing medicine in Albuquerque, he bought land here and there. He came into a long, narrow strip of land running along Guadalupe Trail over to Island (now Edith). As "Babe" Osuna explained it, this was called a "shoe-string" addition because it was long and narrow. The land was not very valuable. But they were able to develop an addition in it, and in 1945 this street was created and was named Osuna Road.

OTERO

The Otero family are one of the oldest families in Albuquerque. They have long been extremely active in financing and promoting local enterprises.

Mariana Otero, who died in 1904, was one of the most influential Albuquerqueans of the late 1800s. He owned Jemez Hot Springs and Sulphur Springs and was a banker and financier.

However, the street is located in Loma Del Norte, a subdivision in which the streets were named for towns or counties in New Mexico. This street, then, was probably named for Otero County, which was named for Miguel Otero, territorial governor when the county was created in 1899. Appointed by President William McKinley in 1897, Otero served as territorial governor until 1906.

OTHELLO

Near Don Juan Onate Park lies a subdivision of streets named for Shakespearean tragic characters.

Othello, of course, is the title character in *Othello.* He is the jealous Moor who smothers his wife, Desdemona.

See Hamlet, Macbeth, Cleopatra, Adonis, and Venus.

OVEJA COURT

In Four Hills subdivision, created by Hicks and Associates in the early 1970s, Ralph Hicks chose street names

that develop a Western or New Mexican/Spanish theme. *Oveja* is Spanish for "ewe," a female sheep.

Nearby are Ganado ("cattle" or "herd") Court and Toro ("bull") Street.

P

PACIFIC

When the railroad came to Albuquerque in 1880, it set the course for Albuquerque to become the major city in the area. The town became the center for major railroad repair at the shops located in the area of the streets named Atlantic, Pacific, and Santa Fé. The names were given for the Atlantic and Pacific Railroad and the Atchison, Topeka, and Santa Fé railroad.

This street is located in the Atlantic and Pacific Addition, which attracted many of the railway employees.

PADILLAS

The street runs near Los Padillas school, which is located in the South Valley. It was begun in the 1880s by Fr. Padilla, a Catholic priest, in order to care for children whose parents had been killed by Indians. It later became a public school, and rooms were added to it in 1912.

The structure of the name of the school indicates that it was named for the Padilla family, as the article *los* indicates the plural of the family name.

PARK AVENUE

Park Avenue runs beside Forest Park between Central and the Albuquerque Country Club. It was given its name for its proximity to the park.

PASEO DE LADERA

According to James Hicks, the streets in Las Lomitas ("little hills"), a subdivision that was developed in the early 1990s by Presley Homes, were given Spanish names that develop a theme of the countryside.

Paseo de Ladera means "hillside walk or stroll."

PATRICIA DRIVE

The street was named for Patricia Lantz, wife of Raymond Lantz, who was a party chief of surveyors for M. and Q. Southwest Company, the company that platted Loma Del Norte subdivision in northeast Albuquerque.

Raymond, a nearby street, was named for Lantz himself.

PEDROGOSO COURT and PLACE

In Four Hills subdivision, created by Hicks and Associates in the early 1970s, Pedrogoso Court and Place reportedly were named after a pet goat that belonged to one of the city draftsmen.

Pedrogoso is a Spanish adjective which means "stony or rocky," a fitting name for a goat.

Intersecting Pedrogoso Place is La Cabra street, from a Spanish noun meaning "she-goat" or "nanny goat."

PERALTA ROAD

In Heritage East subdivision, developed in the early 1970s, the streets were named for governors or heroes of New Mexico.

Pedro de Peralta was appointed governor of New Mexico in 1609, succeeding Governor Oñate. He founded *La Villa Real de Santa Fé* ("Royal Town of the Holy Faith") in 1610, ten years before the Pilgrims landed at Plymouth Rock. He and a few settlers from San Gabriel selected a site on the north bank of the Río Santa Fé, at the southern end of the Sangre de Cristo ("blood of Christ") range of mountains. They laid out the town in the spring of 1610.

Peralta set up a government of four *regidores* (councilmen), two of whom served as *alcaldes ordinarios* (judges) to hear criminal and civil cases within the boundary of the villa. These officers were selected annually.

Each resident of the town was given two lots for a house and garden, two fields for vegetable gardens, two others for vineyards and olive groves, and about 133 acres of land.

Thus, Santa Fé was founded by Pedro de Peralta and is one of the oldest settlements in the United States.

PEREA

The Perea family were some of the early settlers in The Narrows of Bernalillo in the mid-1600s. This street in Bernalillo was obviously named for the descendants of that family.

PETER HURD STREET

In Nor Este Manor, Presley Homes named the streets for New Mexico artists who had been recommended by the Nor Este Art Association. Many of the artists attended the dedication ceremony and left their hand prints in the concrete of the park fountain near La Cueva High School.

A native of Roswell, Peter Hurd was born in 1904. He attended New Mexico Military Institute in Roswell and was appointed to attend the United States Military Academy in West Point, New York. His artistic talent was discovered while he was at West Point, and his art work was encouraged.

After leaving college, he studied at the Pennsylvania Academy of Fine Arts, where he became a private student of the famous N. C. Wyeth, whose oldest daughter, Henriette, Hurd ultimately married.

In the 1930s the Hurds moved back to New Mexico and settled in San Patricio. He died in 1984.

Hurd is the only native New Mexican artist who has earned membership in the elite National Academy of Design.

Pexa street was named by Tom Burlison for the Pexa family, his friends. The street name honors Revi and Dana. (Photos courtesy Mr. and Mrs. Revi Pexa)

PEXA

Tom Burlison, employee of Home Planning Corporation in the early 1970s when the company platted Academy Place, named this street for his friends Revi and Dana Pexa. Names of nearby streets honor their three sons—Revi Don, John Thomas, and Van Christopher.

PLAZA (NORTH and SOUTH)

The streets on either side of the Plaza in Old Town are called North Plaza and South Plaza. *La Plaza Vieja* was

The Armijo House, one of the oldest in *Plaza Vieja*, is now a restaurant, located on San Felipe street at South Plaza.

North Plaza and South Plaza lie on either side of the Plaza in Old Town. Even today, the Plaza is a popular place for weddings, events, and just relaxing in the shade on a sweltering day.

the nucleus of old Albuquerque, which was founded in 1706 and named for Don Francisco Fernández de la Cueva Enríquez, Duke of Alburquerque (note two *r*s in the name), Viceroy of New Spain, 1702–1711.

South Plaza was once called James Street.

POCO CERRO

In Four Hills subdivision, Ralph Hicks of Hicks and Associates chose a humorous name for this very short street. *Poco Cerro* is Spanish for "little hill."

POJOAQUE

This is the smallest of the Tewa Pueblos, with 130 residents and 11,601 acres of land. Its name is a Spanish derivative of a Tewa word meaning "place where the flowers grow along the stream" or "drink water place."

Pojoaque was extinct for several decades because its small population was totally eliminated in 1918 by the influenza epidemic. The survivors, unable to sustain themselves, moved to other pueblos. In 1932 the reestablishment of the pueblo began. Some of the buidings date back to the time of Coronado. The church was built in 1706, the year of the founding of Albuquerque.

Interestingly, in 1973 Pojoaque became the first pueblo to elect a woman governor.

POOL ROAD

William Pool was a resident of Albuquerque during the late 1800s and was elected alderman in 1863. He later was a housing developer, and this street was probably named for him or for one of his descendants.

PORTALES

In a portion of Loma Del Norte, the streets were named for towns or counties of New Mexico.

Portales, which was given a Spanish name meaning "porches or gates," is a town located in eastern New Mexico. The town was named for the nearby Portales Springs, which, according to *New Mexico Place Names*, flow from caves that resemble the porches of Mexican adobe houses.

PRESIDENTS OF THE UNITED STATES

Naming streets for presidents of the United States is a popular custom throughout the United States, and Albuquerque is no exception. However, oddly enough, not all the presidents are represented. A few blocks east of the University of New Mexico, several streets are named for United States presidents. There are nine streets named for presidents, including Washington, Adams, Jefferson, Madison, Monroe, Quincy, Jackson, Van Buren, and Truman. These appear in order of their elections, but a skip of many years occurs between Van Buren and Truman. A few others are scattered throughout the city.

PRICE

In Santa Fé Village, the streets were named for actors and actresses who were popular during the early twentieth century.

Vincent Price, born in St. Louis, Missouri, May 27, 1911, was educated at Yale, the University of London, and Nuremberg University.

Price gained initial attention in England as a cultured stage star. He made his Hollywood debut in 1938. He soon became associated almost exclusively with horror films, through *House of Wax, The Fly, House on Haunted Hill,* and others, as well as through a series of Edgar Allen Poe adaptations.

Price died of lung cancer on October 26, 1993, at the age of eighty-two. He had a list of 110 films to his credit.

PRINCESS JEANNE

Jeanne Lees Bellamah was the wife of builder Dale Bellamah. Princess Jeanne Park subdivision was built in 1954 and named for Bellamah's wife. Princess Jeanne street lies in this subdivision and commemorates Jeanne Lees Bellamah as well.

In each town in which Bellamah built homes, he named a street for his wife. In Santa Fé, in order to conform to the Spanish naming practice in the city, the street is called Calle Princesa Juana.

See Bellamah.

PURCELL DRIVE

When Academy Place was platted in the early 1970s by Home Planning Corporation and was developed by Wood Brothers, Inc., Tom Burlison named this street for Don Purcell, his colleague at Home Planning Corporation.

QUAKER HEIGHTS

Q

Quaker is the popular name for a member of the Religious Society of Friends. Though a majority of the followers of Quakerism live in the United States, the religion developed in England during the 1600s. Quakers have been known for their humanitarian activities. Among other attributes, they stress peace.

Quaker Heights, located on the west side of Albuquerque, consists of streets with names suggesting friendship, peacefulness, and quietude. Street names include Friendly Place and Friendly Court, Namaste Road, Bienvenida, Trail's End, Westward, Northern Trail, Western Trail, and North View.

QUARAI

Sometimes referred to as Coara, Quarai was a pueblo established on the eastern slope of the Manzano Mountains near what is modern-day Mountainair, New Mexico. It was established in 1629 but was abandoned sometime before the Pueblo Revolt of 1680, possibly between 1671 and 1680, because of its exposed position to the Apaches.

QUEMADO

In the eastern portion of Academy Acres, developed in the 1970s, the streets were named for New Mexico place names.

The word *quemado* is Spanish for "burned" and is the name of a town in north-central Catron County. According to T. M. Pearce's *New Mexico Place Names,* José Antonio Padilla and his family moved from Belen in 1880 to a place they called Rito Quemado because the *chamiso* or rabbitbrush had been burned on both sides of the creek. Later the name was shortened to Quemado. Another explanation is that the town is situated in the area of an extinct volcano and that the area around it appears to be scorched.

Rito is Spanish for "ceremony."

QUIMERA

In Four Hills subdivision, developed by Hicks and Associates in the early 1970s, Ralph Hicks chose names generally that developed a Western or New Mexican theme. The name of this short street is Spanish for "pipe dream" or "a fantasy," roughly synonymous with *el ensueño.*

QUINTANA

In Heritage East, developed in the early 1970s, the streets were named for governors or heroes of New Mexico.

Captain Luis Quintana led the settlers at La Cañada (now Santa Cruz) to protect their settlement during the Pueblo Revolt of 1680.

QUIVERA CIRCLE and QUIVERA COURT

In April 1541 Coronado led his Spanish soldiers east to *El Llano Estacado* ("the Staked Plains") in the Texas Panhandle in search of the golden cities that had been rumored to exist. Disappointed at finding no golden cities, he sent the main expedition back to New Mexico under the command of Captain Alvarado. He and thirty of his soldiers went on to Quivira, which was the home of the Wichita Indians in central Kansas. Greeted by the poverty of this group, he and his men realized that the cities of gold apparently did not exist.

Though the street names are spelled *Quivera,* the generally accepted spelling is *Quivira.*

RANCH TRAIL

In Four Hills subdivision, this name contributes to the Western theme that Ralph Hicks chose to develop.

RATON PLACE

In Four Hills subdivision, the names develop a Western or Spanish theme. *Raton* is a Spanish word for "mouse," but it is also the name of a town in northern New Mexico, named for the nearby Raton Mountains. The mountains were so named because of the numerous mice and rats that feed on the piñon nuts in the mountains.

RAYMOND DRIVE

Raymond Lantz was a party chief of surveyors for M. and Q. Southwest Company, the company that platted Loma Del Norte in northeast Albuquerque. Tom Burlison named this street for him.

Patricia Street, nearby, honors Lantz's wife.

RAYNOLDS

The Raynolds brothers owned Central Bank, the first bank in Albuquerque, which was founded *circa* 1880. Jefferson Raynolds was president, and Frederick and Joshua Raynolds were involved in the bank. It was located in Old Town at James and Santiago streets (now South Plaza and Romero) across from the southwest corner of the Plaza. With the coming of the railroad in 1880, the bank moved to New Albuquerque in 1881 to a two-story brick building on the corner of Second and Gold.

R. C. GORMAN AVENUE

In Nor Este Manor, Presley Homes named the streets for New Mexico artists who were recommended by the Nor Este Art Association. Many of the artists attended the dedication ceremony and left their hand prints in the fountain in the park near La Cueva High School.

Born in 1932, R. C. Gorman is a Navajo who was brought up in a hogan on an Arizona reservation. He now lives in a three-hundred-year-old adobe home in Taos.

As an artist, he deals in oils, bronzes, ceramics, pastels, tapestries, and paper castings. His trademark is serene Indian women, easily recognizable as R. C. Gorman in style.

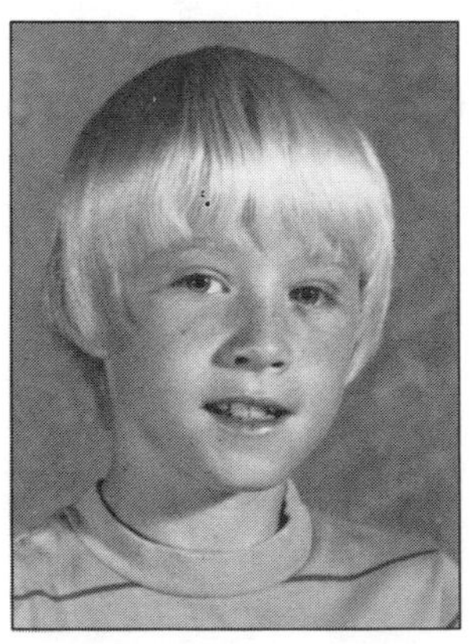

Born in 1966, Revi Don Pexa is now a surgical first assistant in Albuquerque. Revi Don street bears his name. (Photo courtesy Mr. and Mrs. Revi Pexa)

REVI DON DRIVE

Tom Burlison, employee of Home Planning Corporation in the early 1970s when the company platted Academy Place, named this street for Revi Don Pexa, oldest son of his friends Revi and Dana Pexa.

Names of nearby streets honor their other two sons, John Thomas and Van Christopher.

RIO

This is a very short street that runs alongside Río Grande Park near the Río Grande. The name is Spanish for "river."

RIO ABAJA ROAD

This street was named for one of the administrative units of the region of the Río Grande. Río Arriba (upper sec-

tion) and Río Abaja (lower section) were the two divisions of the province. The dividing line was the high east-west escarpment known as *La Bajada,* located about nineteen miles south of Santa Fé.

RIO ARRIBA

In Four Hills subdivision, the street names generally illustrated a Western theme. *Río Arriba,* Spanish for "upper river," refers to the upper section of the Río Grande. La Bajada Mesa, situated nineteen miles south of Santa Fé, is the dividing line between Río Arriba ("upper river") and Río Abaja ("lower river").

RIO GRANDE BOULEVARD

Originally Main Street, this principal street on the west side of *Plaza Vieja* ("Old Town") is now called Río Grande in honor of the river that gives life to Albuquerque.

Stretching some 1,885 miles from its source to its mouth, the Río Grande brings life to arid New Mexico.

The Río Grande stretches some 1,885 miles from its source to its mouth at the Gulf of Mexico. Though it is dry during most summers, partially because most of its water is diverted into irrigation canals and partially because rain in New Mexico is rather sparse, it can become a raging torrent in the spring when snow melts in the high mountain ranges.

RIO HONDO

In the eastern portion of Academy Acres, developed in the 1970s, the streets were named for New Mexico place names.

Río Hondo, Spanish for "deep river," is formed west of Roswell by the confluence of Bonito River and Ruidoso River. The word *hondo* also appears in several other New Mexico place names.

ROBERTS STREET

Platted in the early 1970s by M. and Q. Southwest, this street was named for Tom Burlison's brother-in-law, now his ex-brother-in-law. Burlison was in charge of naming all the streets in the subdivision.

ROMERO

Originally Santiago Street, probably named for Santiago Baca, this street in Old Town, located on the west side of the *Plaza Vieja,* became Romero in the early twentieth century.

Originally, the land on which the Romero house is located was owned by Nestor Montoya, who purchased additional adjoining acreage from Ambrosia Baca and his sister, Juana Baca, in 1854, and from Manuel Armijo in 1855.

Ultimately the land was owned by James Murphy, whose heirs sold the property to Jesus Romero (born 1859) and his wife, Mary Springer de Romero. They built the Romero house in 1915. Jesus Romero died in 1935 and left the house to his wife. She later sold it to his sister Luciana in 1937. The Romero house now contains several shops.

Romero street was named for Jesus Romero, who built the Romero House (pictured), now containing several shops. Romero operated a grocery store near the plaza and was sheriff of Old Albuquerque.

Jesus Romero also owned a grocery store on the southwest corner of the plaza and served as sheriff of Old Albuquerque.

RUIDOSO

In a portion of Loma Del Norte, the streets were named for towns or counties in New Mexico.

Ruidoso is a Spanish word meaning "noisy," and the name was given because of a fast-flowing noisy creek which flows through the town. Ruidoso is a beautiful tourist and ranching town located in the mountains southeast of Carrizozo. Ruidoso Downs draws many horse-racing fans.

RUNNING WATER CIRCLE

In Four Hills subdivision, developed by Hicks and Associates in the 1970s, Ralph Hicks chose names that generally illustrate a Western theme. This street name calls to mind the flowing of the nearby Río Grande and of numerous arroyos in the area, dry except after rains.

S

SAAVEDRA

Louis E. Saavedra was born in Tokay but went to school in Socorro. He served in the Army and earned a degree from Eastern New Mexico University in Portales. He became an employee of the Albuquerque school system in 1960.

He was appointed to the City Commission in December 1967 and was elected to a four-year term in 1970. In 1973 he became chairman of the City Commission.

He served as principal of the Albuquerque Technical-Vocational Institute.

Saavedra served as mayor of Albuquerque, 1983 to 1993.

SAGEBRUSH

In Four Hills subdivision, this is one of the names that contribute to the development of the Western theme. Sagebrush, of course, is common on the desert.

S. SANDOVAL

In Nor Este Manor, Presley Homes named the streets for New Mexico artists who were recommended by the Nor Este Art Association. Many of the artists attended the dedication ceremony and left their hand prints in the concrete of the park fountain near La Cueva High School.

Secundio "Sec" Sandoval is a native of New Mexico, from Buena Vista, but he has lived in Los Alamos since 1943. He graduated from Los Alamos High School in 1952. He attended the University of New Mexico for a time, then went to Adams State College in Alamosa, Colorado, receiving the Bachelor of Arts degree in 1958.

He served as a technical illustrator for the United States Army Aggressor Center for two years, helping simulate the enemy for war games. From 1952 he worked, as a summer student employee or as a full-time employee, for the Los Alamos Scientific Laboratory as a draftsman and designer.

Sandoval paints in oils, acrylics, and water colors. He has exhibited in many shows and has won numerous awards.

SAN ANTONIO

San Antonio street commemorates Saint Anthony of Padua (1195–1231), a noted Franciscan scholar and teacher of theology.

Born in Lisbon, Portugal, of noble parents, Anthony was a great orator and reformer. He is reputed to have performed miracles.

The priests who came to christianize New Mexico were Franciscan; thus, San Antonio is a popular name in areas settled by Spain.

SAN FELIPE

This street which lies east of San Felipe de Neri Church, founded in 1706, was named for its proximity to the church. This church was the first church in Albuquerque and has been in continuous service since 1706.

St. Philip Neri was a sixteenth-century priest of the city of Rome, and he is the patron saint of the first church in Albuquerque.

San Felipe street was named for San Felipe de Neri Church, which was founded in 1706. Church street was also named for the church, which is located on both streets.

SAN ILDEFONSO

This street was named for the pueblo by the same name. Though the Tewa name is *pok-wo ghay ongwee,* the Spanish named the pueblo for St. Ildephonse, a seventh-century archbishop of Toledo. The pueblo is located twenty miles southwest of Santa Fé. A small pueblo, it has a population of about 450 and consists of about 28,000 acres of land.

Noted for its pottery and the friendliness of its people, San Ildefonso is primarily an agricultural community, but many of the people drive to Los Alamos for work.

SAN PASQUALE

Located in Old Town, this street commemorates Saint Pascal, pope of the Roman Catholic Church (817–824). He and Emperor Louis the Pious agreed to have free papal elections.

San Pasquale is the patron saint of kitchens.

The name *Paschal* comes from the Greek name for the Jewish passover, the season of the first Easter.

Originally this street was called Algiers Street.

SAN JUAN

San Juan, the largest of the Tewa Pueblos, provided the name for this street. The name is Spanish for "Saint John the Baptist." The pueblo had a population of 1,700 in 1986, and consisted of 12,238 acres.

The Spanish established the first capital of New Mexico in San Juan in 1598, across the river from the present site. It was called San Gabriel at first, but later the name was changed to San Juan de los Caballeros.

SAN MIGUEL

In a portion of Loma Del Norte, the streets were named for towns or counties in New Mexico.

San Miguel, Spanish for "Saint Michael," is the name of at least four towns in the state and of a county as well. San Miguel County was named for San Miguel del Bado.

SANDIA, SANDIA COURT, SANDIA LANE, SANDIA ROAD, SANDIA HEIGHTS, SANDIA HEIGHTS ROAD, SANDIA VIEW ROAD, SANDIA VISTA COURT

All of the Sandia streets derive their names from their proximity to the Sandia Mountains, east and northeast of Albuquerque.

Sandia is Spanish, meaning "watermelon." It is said that the name was given because the mountain resembles a slice of watermelon, particularly when the evening sun shines on the reddish granite on its western face. Near the ridge or crest line at the summit, the thin layers of pale limestone and a cover of dark-looking timber suggest a green rind, according to Marc Simmons.

The Pueblo Indians, however, perceived something different. They called the mountain *Oku Piñ,* "turtle mountain," as they saw the outline of the mountain as a

The Sandia mountains, Spanish for "watermelon," stand sentinel over Albuquerque.

turtle's shell. They believed the mountain holy and the home of many dieties.

According to Erna Fergusson, granddaughter of Franz Huning, developer of Huning's Highland Addition, the mountains were referred to as *la Sierra de la Santilla*, "the mountain of the little saint." Other records give *Santo Dia*, "holy day"; and in the Spanish language, it is possible that *Sandia* could have derived from that phrase.

But regardless of the origin of the term, the mountain is beautiful, always there but always changing. In *Albuquerque*, Erna Fergusson said it well:

> From Albuquerque the Sandia shows a true mountain blue by day with silvery rock slides and purplish patches where evergreens grow. Evening light brings on the show that a native daughter backs against the world. Then daytime blue shading in and out of all the purples is swallowed by rose and gold from the sunset sky. Leaping the valley in long shafts of light they inundate the mountains with color, rising from mesa to peak, and go off before the brain can quite register what it saw. The mountains are blue again, but an azure deepening into midnight blue and leaving the sky to stage the real show. Stars and stardust are near, planets close, and when the moon sails out above the city fathers cannily douse the electric street lights as mere impertinence.

SANTA ANA

This Keresan pueblo, located eight miles northwest of Bernalillo, on the banks of the Jemez River, bears the Spanish name for Saint Anne. It has about five hundred residents and 44,489 acres of land. However, many residents have moved away and return for religious ceremonies only.

SANTA ANNA

In Four Hills subdivision, created by Hicks and Associates during the early 1970s, Ralph Hicks chose street names that develop a Western or New Mexico/Spanish theme.

Saint Anne is the traditional name of the mother of the Virgin Mary. Usually spelled *Santa Ana* in Spanish, this name was probably misspelled with the extra *n* by Hicks. According to Tom Burlison, former employee of

Ralph Hicks, it is not uncommon for street namers to misspell a name, which is then recorded and made official.

SANTA FE

The railroad came to Albuquerque in 1880, setting the course for Albuquerque to become the major city in the area. The town became the center for major railroad repair at the shops located in the area of the streets named Atlantic, Pacific, and Santa Fé. The names were given for the Atlantic and Pacific Railroad and the Atchison, Topeka, and Santa Fé Railroad.

A locomotive on display in Coronado Park memorializes the railroad, which gave birth to New Albuquerque and the Albuquerque that we know today.

SAWMILL ROAD

Albuquerque Lumber Company opened a sawmill in the early 1880s near what is now Sawmill Road in Old Town. It continued production into the twentieth century.

Mill Pond Road, named for the pond at the sawmill, intersects Sawmill Road.

Arthur Seligman served as governor of New Mexico, 1931 to 1933. He is remembered in the name of a street in Heritage East. (Photo courtesy New Mexico State Records Center and Archives, Clara Olsen #22580)

SELIGMAN

In Heritage East subdivision, developed in the early 1970s, the streets were named for governors and heroes of New Mexico.

Arthur Seligman served as governor of New Mexico from 1931 to 1933. He served one term and was inaugurated for a second term in 1933. On September 24, 1933, he left for Albuquerque to address a banking association convention and by noon had died of a sudden heart attack.

Originally from Germany, Seligman came to Santa Fé in 1856 from Pennsylvania. He and his brother owned a wholesale and retail dry goods firm called Seligman Brothers.

He was actively involved in politics and community activities. A merchant, banker, politician, and property owner, he also served as mayor of Santa Fé.

Ironically, he had been commissioned through his store to buy the furnishings for the governor's mansion.

He married Franc Lacker in 1896 in Buffalo, New York. Seligman had met her when she and her fist husband, George Harris, lived in Santa Fé before they returned to New York when her husband fell ill.

SELLERS

Colonel D. K. B. Sellers came to Albuquerque during the early 1900s. In 1905 he platted and sold seven hundred lots in Perea Addition, then subdivided the Grant tract on North 5th Street. He also developed University Heights. Sellers owned a real estate office located at 204 S. Second Street.

Though this street lies farther east than the land that Sellers developed, the street probably was named for him or for his descendants.

Sellers became mayor of the city of Albuquerque later and was in charge of the opening festivities of the new city hall in 1914.

SHORT

In Heritage Hills, developed by Bellamah Homes during the 1970s, this street may have been named for R. Y. Short

or his descendants. Short was an employee of the Atchison, Topeka, and Santa Fé Railroad during the early twentieth century. He lived at 601 Coal S. W. from 1901 to 1909.

Since this is a very short street that connects Buckboard to Yeager, the name may be a description.

On the other hand, since the names of the streets in Heritage Hills develop a patriotic theme, this street may have been named for Lieutenant General Walter C. Short (1880–1949), one of the senior commanders at Pearl Harbor when it was attacked on December 7, 1941, by the Japanese.

SIGMA CHI

Sigma Chi fraternity is the only fraternity at the University of New Mexico to have a street named for it. According to a current member, Sigma Chi was the only fraternity on campus that owned land. They reportedly made a deal with the president of the university that Sigma Chi would donate to the university the land for what is now the University of New Mexico Golf Course North in exchange for having the street named after the fraternity and being granted the use of the number *1855* as their address. The year 1855 was the date of the founding of Sigma Chi, and the fraternity house bears that number, though that number is not in proper sequence among other addresses on the street. The fraternity house actually fronts on Yale, but Sigma Chi street runs beside it.

The interviewee chuckled as he said, "All the other fraternities have to have *Sigma Chi* as a part of their address."

SIGUARD COURT

Siguard Sabo was an automobile salesman from whom Tom Burlison, who named many of the streets in Loma Del Norte in the early 1970s, had purchased a used automobile or two. According to Burlison, Siguard Sabo asked him to name a street for him, so Burlison did just that.

SILVER

The street was named by Colonel Walter G. Marmon after a mineral, apparently an indication of the hope that Albuquerque would become a major shipping point for the mining in the area after the railroad came in 1880.

SIMMS

The Simms family have been prominent in Albuquerque history. Albert G. Simms was born October 8, 1882, in Washington, Arkansas. He attended the University of Arkansas and worked as an accountant in Monterrey, Mexico.

In 1912 he went to Silver City, New Mexico, and entered a tuberculosis sanitarium, and his brother John joined him soon thereafter.

Simms studied law and met and married Katherine Atherton Mather of Niagara, New York, who was also in New Mexico for her health. (She died in 1921.)

He moved to Albuquerque, was admitted to the bar in 1914, and opened Simms and Simms. He owned a ranch at Los Poblanos and was one of the richest men in New Mexico. At one time he owned the entire eastern section of the Elena Gallegos Grant, some 35,000 acres of it. Simms donated much of that land to Albuquerque Academy.

At Albert Simms' death in December 1964, former governor John F. Simms, Jr., and Dr. Albert G. Simms III his nephews, inherited Simms' Creamland Diaries, Inc., and his other properties. Simms and his wife had no children.

Simms Park in Paradise Hills was named for him also.

SLATE

When the railroad came to Albuquerque in 1880, Colonel Walter G. Marmon named five of the cross streets for minerals (See Coal). He chose Coal, Copper, Gold, Lead, and Silver. As the section around Old Town developed, apparently someone decided to continue the naming trend by adding Granite, Marble, and Slate.

SNOW STREET and SNOW HEIGHTS

Edward H. Snow, owner of Snow Construction, Inc., developed Snow Heights subdivision, naming some of the streets Snow Heights Boulevard, Snow Heights Circle, and Snow Street for his family name and Frances Street for his wife.

SNOWVISTA BOULEVARD

Located on the west side of the Río Grande, this street provides a magnificent view of the breath-taking Sandia Mountains, especially beautiful during the winter months when they are covered with snow.

SOBRA

In laying out Four Hills subdivision, developed by Hicks and Associates in the early 1970s, Ralph Hicks apparently had an extra street with no name; so he chose *Sobra,* Spanish for "excess or surplus," as the name for this tiny street.

SOLANO

In the late 1940s and early 1950s, about the time that this street was created, a number of Solano families were listed in the city directory. As early as 1917, Pieto Solano was a resident of old Albuquerque. He was identified as a musician by profession.

SOLEDAD

In Four Hills subdivision, Ralph Hicks chose street names that created a Western or New Mexican theme. *Soledad,* Spanish for "solitude," is a fitting name for this short street near Four Hills Arroyo, as it provides a quiet area.

SOPLO ROAD

In Four Hills subdivision, this name is a Spanish noun meaning "puff" or "gust." Wind gusts are common in the Albuquerque area.

SPAIN

Dr. Charles R. Spain was a native of Cedar Grove, Tennessee. He earned the Bachelor of Arts degree from Bethel College in McKenzie, Tennessee, in 1936, the Master of Arts from Peabody College, Nashville, Tenneessee, in 1937, and the Doctor of Philosophy from Teachers College of Columbia University in 1941.

Spain taught at Alabama State Teachers College and at the University of Kentucky. He served as president of Moorhead State College in Kentucky, but resigned to come to Albuquerque in 1954 as dean of the College of Education at the University of New Mexico.

In 1956 Spain became superintendent of Albuquerque Public Schools, succeeding John Milne, who had held the post since 1911.

Spain died May 8, 1965.

SPEAKMAN

Frank Speakman, along with his friend William Franklin, created the Albuquerque Airport in 1928. They leased some land on the mesa and proceeded to build a landing field. Both worked for the railroad and created the airport in their spare time.

The street, appropriately situated near what is now Kirtland Air Force Base, honors Frank Speakman and was named by Ralph Hicks of Hicks and Associates.

SPRENGER

Robert Sprenger was a draftsman for M. and Q. Southwest when Loma Del Norte was platted in the early 1970s.

Midge Street, located nearby, was named for Sprenger's wife.

SPRING

Next to Snow Heights Park, the first street to the south is Winter, probably suggested by the name *Snow Heights,* the name of a subdivision developed by Edward H. Snow.

Next to Winter, as a natural progression, are Summer and Spring.

STAGECOACH

In Four Hills subdivision, developed by Hicks and Associates, Ralph Hicks chose names which generally create a Western theme. The stagecoach was crucial as a means of transportation before the advent of the railroad.

STAUBACH AVENUE

Coda Roberson, of Roberson Homes, was a Dallas Cowboys fan. When he created Westwind Subdivision on the West Mesa in 1979, he named two of the streets in the subdivision for Dallas Cowboys—Tom Landry, coach, and Roger Staubach, quarterback.

Staubach played college football at the Naval Academy, winning the Heisman Trophy in 1963. After obligatory service in the Navy, during which he also played for Pensacola Naval Air Station, he played for the Dallas Cowboys from 1969 to 1979.

STOVER

Elias S. Stover came to Albuquerque in 1876. He was a merchant, a former lieutenant governor of Kansas (1872–74), and a Union veteran. He opened a store on *Plaza Vieja* and became quite successful.

He was frequently involved in speculative deals and land transactions. He was an investor in the New Mexico Town Company, which sold the real estate when New Albuquerque was first developing. It was composed of the Santa Fé Railroad and Franz Huning, Elias Stover, and William Hazeldine, three local investors. They had purchased land for the railroad, then transferred title to the New Mexico Town Company for a share of the profits. Merchants who wanted to establish businesses near the railroad had to buy their lots from the railroad.

With the development of New Town, three streets south of Coal were named Stover, Huning, and Hazeldine.

STOVER

Stover was a central figure in many of the events that occurred during the development of Albuquerque. He was one of the founders of the Street Railway Company, which connected New Town to Old Town and Barelas, and he also had a small financial interest in the Huning Highland Addition. He was a member of the Board of Trade, founded in 1881. Also he was one of the founders of the First National Bank of Albuquerque, with Mariano S. Otero as president and Elias S. Stover, Nicolas T. Armijo, and Cristóbal Armijo as directors.

SUMMER

Next to Snow Heights Park, the first street to the south is Winter, a name probably suggested by the name *Snow Heights,* the name of a subdivision developed by Edward H. Snow.

Next to Winter, as a natural progression, are Summer and Spring.

SUMMIT

Located in the hilly area of the East Mesa, Summit Park was given a descriptive name for its location. Summit street lies next to the park.

SUNBIRD ROAD

In Sunset West subdivision, developed by Presley Homes, the street names all begin with *sun.* They include Sunbird Road, Sunbow Avenue, Sunburst Road, Sunridge Avenue, Sunridge Road, Sunrise Court, and Sunspot Road.

SUNDOWN PLACE

In the Ridgecrest Park area, Sundown Place lies on the west side of the addition; Sunrise Place appropriately lies on the east side.

SUNRISE PLACE

See Sundown Place above.

T

TAMARRON

In the eastern portion of Academy Acres, developed in the 1970s, the streets were given descriptive names for their location or for people.

Perhaps this street was named for Bishop Tamarón (spelled with a single *r*), who was bishop of the diocese during the late 1700s.

TAYLOR RANCH ROAD

The street and subdivsion were named for Joel P. and Nina Mae Payne Taylor, who owned about eight hundred acres of land on the west side of the Río Grande, along and on the West Mesa.

After World War I, the United States government gave veterans preferential rights. They could homestead certain property for six months and the property would become theirs. Joel Taylor, one of eleven children and the oldest at home at the time, went to New Mexico to help out with his father's homestead up on the Continental Divide, near Chama, which he claimed in 1920. The family moved there in 1921. Since Joel was the oldest, he

Joel P. and Nina Mae Taylor, owners of Taylor Ranch, for whom Taylor Ranch road was named, pose for a photograph a few days prior to Mr. Taylor's 91st birthday.

went on an immigrant car on the train with the livestock. They had to obtain special permission from the railroad for Joel to take his father's place on the car, however. Joel took the livestock to Albuquerque from Seagraves, Texas.

The elder Mr. Taylor moved his family to Albuquerque, where they lived on Arno Street. They unloaded the railroad car and put the cattle in a corral behind the house on Arno Sreet for awhile. It was hot in Albuquerque, but six inches of snow covered the homestead near Chama. On the homestead, they lived outside at first, but soon built a half-dugout. They built a fireplace in the north end of the dugout, and the dugout served as their housing until they later built a ranch house.

Joel, at the age of eighteen, came back to Albuquerque to finish the eighth grade in the spring of 1922, as he had missed a great deal of school because of work. In an interview in July 1993, a few days before his ninety-first birthday, he remembered that the teacher was Miss Plant, who, he says, was about sixty years old at the time.

After four years, the elder Mr. Taylor went back to Texas, leaving the homestead in Joel's care. When Joel was old enough, he homesteaded also and had about one thousand acres at that point.

In 1925, he went to Texas to farm his father's place near San Angelo, Texas. Apparently that is when he met Nina Mae Payne.

On February 27, 1926, Joel, who was born on July 26, 1902, married Miss Nina Mae Payne, who was born May 19, 1911. They had two children, a son and a daughter.

In 1939 the family felt the need for their son to have a better education than was available in the Chama area. The school was often closed because of snow, and it was several miles away from their home. (Mrs. Taylor said that at one time, she was on the ranch for three years without going into town.) Joel bought eight hundred acres of arid land on the west side of the Río Grande across from Albuquerque so that school would be available for their children. Actually, he leased the property initially, with option to buy. In the meantime he had discovered manganese on his ranch property near Chama, and he used the money from the sale of the manganese to purchase the land near Albuquerque. When they first moved to Albuquerque, they lived in a two-room adobe

house where La Luz subdivision is now located near Montano Place on Coors Road.

In the spring of 1940 they fenced the property down to the Río Grande and moved about 150 head of cattle down to Albuquerque for the winter. This property served as their winter haven; in fact, the street behind Montano Plaza, near their home, is called Winter Haven. (It took eight days to move the cattle from the homestead to Albuquerque.)

The Taylors said that when they first moved there, the area was so grazed out from sheep that there was no vegetation at all. At that time there were only about three trees between what is now La Luz subdivision and the Río Grande. (Their old adobe house is still standing there.) But in the spring of 1941, the Río Grande flooded and washed seeds in. Now there is a *bosque* (grove of trees) all along the west side of the Río Grande.

Also they said that when they moved there, there was nothing on the west side of the river except five houses, which were all homestead houses. There were no roads—only wagon tracks.

The Taylors sold the property on which Taylor ranch subdivision was built. In 1970 they donated the land on which the Albuquerque Children's Home stands. Some years ago, they built a new home behind Montano Plaza, just north of Albuquerque Children's Home.

TERRAZA DRIVE

In Four Hills subdivision, Ralph Hicks generally chose names that develop a Western or Spanish theme. *Terraza* is Spanish for "terrace," but the name seems to have no significance except that it is Spanish.

TESUQUE

The Tesuque Pueblo, Spanish derivation of Tewa *tat' unge'onwi,* "spotted dry place," gave this street its name. Located eight miles north of Santa Fé, the village has been occupied since between A.D. 1250 and A.D. 1300. There are about three hundred residents and 16,813 acres at Tesuque.

TESUQUE

Tesuque played an important role in the Pueblo Revolution of 1680. Two of its members were messengers to the other pueblos, using knotted ropes to coordinate the day for the revolt. When they left Tusuque, they carried with them ropes with knots in them, each knot representing a day. When the last knot was untied, it was the day for the revolt to occur, and all the pueblos were able to strike at the same time.

Tesuque pottery is generally small and brightly painted, though in recent years many of the potters have been returning to the old style.

THAXTON

William C. Thaxton was a real estate agent in the early twentieth century, listed in the 1909–1910 *Worley's Directory of Albuquerque, New Mexico.* He was in business with Lloyd Hunsaker, with an office at 407 S. Walter.

In 1923 Thaxton, who was married to Florence L. Thaxton, maintained an office at 114 W. Gold, with his residence at 410 Luna Boulevard.

Later, Thaxton was president of Albuquerque Mortgage and El Río Lumber Company.

Will Keleher invited Thaxton to take a place on the board of the First National Bank of Albuquerque, which opened for business on October 24, 1933. D.K.B. Sellers and Silvestre Mirabel were also on the board.

THORNTON

In Heritage East subdivision, developed in the early 1970s, the streets were named for governors or heroes of New Mexico.

William T. Thornton served as territorial governor for four years, having been appointed to the position by President McKinley.

Born in Calhoun, Missouri, on February 9, 1843, Thornton received his early education in a private school near Sedalia, Missouri. He was graduated from the law school of the University of Kentucky.

He enlisted in the Confederate army as a private in 1861 and served with General Sterling Price for two years. Captured by Union forces in 1862, he was sent to

Alton, Illinois, where he was kept in confinement for almost a year. He was exchanged and then continued to serve until the end of the war.

He came to Santa Fé in 1877 when his health was failing.

After the nomination of his successor as governor, he left the Territory of New Mexico and moved to Mexico, where he was involved in mining for a time, but by 1912 he was residing once again in Santa Fé.

TIJERAS

This street name honors Tijeras Canyon, which is located a few miles southeast of Albuquerque. Tijeras Canyon was once the site of a number of Indian agricultural villages, possibly as early as A.D. 900. It was the site of the Tijeras Pueblo, inhabited until about 1425, and the canyon was used as a camping place by the Apache in later years.

The name *Tijeras* means "scissors" in Spanish, possibly from the forking of the canyon near the village of Tijeras.

Another name for Tijeras is Carnué or Carnuel, possibly a corruption of a Tiwi Indian word.

TINA DRIVE

When Loma Del Norte was platted in the early 1970s by M. and Q. Southwest, Tom Burlison named this street after the receptionist for the company. Unfortunately, he does not remember Tina's last name.

TINGLEY

Clyde Tingley was born in rural Ohio on January 5, 1881, and spent his early years as a machinist and toolmaker for automobile manufacturers.

He came to Albuquerque almost by accident. Carrie Wooster, the young lady whom he was courting, fell ill with tuberculosis and was on her way to Arizona for a cure. She suffered a severe attack of the illness on her way and had to be taken off the train in Albuquerque.

Tingley soon came to Albuquerque also, and they were married on April 21, 1911.

Tingley was elected alderman in 1916, and he later served as chairman of the City Commission and adopted the *ex officio* title of mayor, which had been discarded in 1917. He did a great deal to clean up the streets of Albuquerque by introducing a city ordinance that regulated billboards.

During the Great Depression of the 1930s, he helped alleviate some of the economic problems that Albuquerque was experiencing. He was elected governor in 1934, and his support of President Roosevelt gave him an advantage through direct contact with the White House. He was responsible for securing for Albuquerque a number of parks, a zoo, an airport terminal, the buildings for a new state fair, the Little Theater, and a railroad overpass at the Central Avenue crossing, as well as a number of improvements at the University of New Mexico, including the Zimmermann Library, a stadium, an administration building, and other structures.

After a second term as governor, Tingley returned to Albuquerque and was re-elected to the City Commission. As chairman of the City Commission, he was *ex officio* mayor once again, and he resumed his rather autocratic behavior of the past. In 1947, however, Tingley lost his seat on the City Commission.

TOBOSO DRIVE

In Thomas Village, developed in the late 1970s and early 1980s by Ed Leslie, the streets were named primarily for Miguel de Cervantes Saavedra's picaresque romance, *Don Quixote de la Mancha.* (See Don Quixote Drive.)

Dulcinea del Toboso was the buxom peasant wench to whom Quixote dedicated his deeds of valor. Her primary claim to fame was her skill in salting pork. She was from the village of Toboso.

TOKAY

In Vineyard addition, platted by Henry G. Coors in 1923, the streets were named for varieties of grapes or vineyard-associated words. (See Vineyard Road.)

TORO

In Four Hills, developed by Hicks and Associates in the early 1970s, Ralph Hicks chose street names that create a Western or New Mexican theme. This street name celebrates the bull used in bullfights. Nearby is Matador, in honor of the bullfighter or the one who kills *el toro.*

TORREON

This street name is a remembrance of El Torreon, a ranch that Don Juan Barela purchased in 1809 in the area that is now south Broadway. The area around the ranch grew into a substantial settlement called Barelas, named for the Barela families who lived there.

The name is Spanish for "tower." Often early settlers in New Mexico built round towers of stone for defense, the entrance to which was from their homes. Probably such a structure existed at this ranch at one time.

TRAILS END

In Quaker Heights, located on the west side of Albuquerque, the street names develop the theme of the peacefulness and friendliness of the Quakers.

The name Trails End suggests a friendly ambiance, the end of struggle, and a place of comfort, warmth, and relaxation.

TRAMWAY BOULEVARD, TRAMWAY COURT, TRAMWAY LANE, TRAMWAY PLACE, TRAMWAY ROAD, TRAMWAY RIDGE DRIVE, TRAMWAY TERRACE LOOP, TRAMWAY VISTA DRIVE, TRAMWAY VISTA LOOP

All of these streets derive their names from the presence of the Sandia Peak Aerial Tramway, which was devel-

The Sandia Peak Aerial Tramway gave its name to a number of streets in Albuquerque.

oped by the Ben Abruzzo family. (Ben Abruzzo was a hot-air ballooning enthusiast and was killed in an airplane accident.)

The Sandia Peak Aerial Tram was constructed between 1964 and 1966, at a cost in 1964 of two million dollars. It operates two cabins, each with a capacity of fifty-five people, and is capable of running four trips per hour, with a maximum capacity of 220 passengers.

The tramway is constructed with a lower terminal, two median towers, and an upper terminal. The lower terminal or beginning of the trip is at an elevation of 6,559 feet; tower one is at 7,010 feet; tower two, at 8,750 feet; and the upper terminal, at 10,378 feet.

The horizontal length of the tram is 14,657 feet, or 2.7 miles; the total vertical rise is 3,819 feet.

From the top of Sandia Peak on a clear day, one can see Santa Fé and even mountain ranges as far away as Colorado. And at the top, one can enjoy top-of-the-line dining.

TRIMBLE

This street lies near the Sandia foothills rather than in the historic section of town; however, it was probably named for W. L. Trimble or one of his descendants. During the pre-automobile days, Trimble owned a livery stable which was located at Second and Copper. He rented coaches and wagons for weekend outings, and ambulances when needed.

TRUCHAS

In the eastern portion of Academy Acres, developed in the 1970s, the streets were named for New Mexico place names.

Truchas is Spanish for "trout." It is the name of a community north of Santa Fé, a name which probably derived from a nearby stream.

TRUJILLO ROAD

Located on the west side of the Río Grande, this street was obviously named for a Trujillo family. The Trujillo name dates back to the early years in Albuquerque's history. Francisco de Trujillo was an early settler who owned a hacienda on the east side of the Río Grande. He died in the 1670s and left his hacienda to his wife, Doña Luisa de Trujillo. The hacienda became the site on which Albuquerque was later founded in 1706.

TRUMBULL

Though the spelling is *Trumbull* with a second *u*, it appears that this street name perhaps should be Trumball.

Walter Trumball was a prominent attorney in Albuquerque during the nineteenth century. He bought the land and built the house at 1211 Roma Avenue N.W. shortly after 1882. In 1892 he sold the property to Goss Military Institute, which remained there until 1902.

Henry Trumball was the legal guardian for Camilla Padilla, who was one of the heirs of Nestor Montoya, who died in 1883. He was one of the early owners of the property on the west side of the *Plaza Vieja* in Old Town, on which the Romero house was later built.

U

UNION

In a portion of Loma Del Norte, the streets were named for towns or counties in New Mexico.

According to *New Mexico Place Names,* Union County was created by the Territorial Legislature on February 13, 1893. It was formed from other counties and was named Union because of "the united desire of the people to establish a county government."

UNIVERSITIES and COLLEGES

See Colleges and Universities.

UNIVERSITY BOULEVARD

University Boulevard runs north-south alongside the west side of the University of New Mexico and, of

Pictured is the east corner of the University of New Mexico, which was founded in 1889.

course, was named because of its proximity to the University of New Mexico, which was founded in 1889.

UNSER BOULEVARD

Unser Boulevard was named for Bobby Unser after he had won his third "Indy 500" championship. The boulevard begins in front of Bobby Unser's house just south of Central/Old U.S. Route 66 on the west side of Albuquerque and runs north alongside Al Unser's land. The boulevard was named in 1981.

By 1984, Bobby Unser had already become a legend in the racing world. He had won the "Indy 500" three times—in 1967, 1975, and 1981. He was a two-time National Champion, in 1968 and 1974, and he had won the Pike's Peak race twelve times. He was also voted one of *Sports Illustrated*'s top five athletes for its first twenty years.

UPTOWN BOULEVARD

Uptown Boulevard is located in the area of Albuquerque known as Uptown, which was created in 1961. Uptown is the area along Menaul Boulevard and south a few blocks, roughly bounded by San Mateo on the west and Wyoming on the east. This is an area of shopping centers, containing Winrock Center, built in 1961, and Coronado Center, built in 1963.

Midtown is located west of Uptown, also along Menaul Boulevard.

Downtown is the area of the court house, city and county buildings, convention center, and old shopping area around and south of Central Avenue and the numbered streets in the lower numbers. The advent of the railroad in Albuquerque brought the development of Downtown in 1880.

Old Town, of course, refers to the plaza area, *la Plaza Vieja*, where Albuquerque was originally founded.

VALENTINO

In Santa Fé Village, the streets were named for actors or actresses of the early twentieth century.

Rudolph (Rodolph Alfonzo Raffaele Pierre Gugliemi) Valentino was born in Castellaneta, Italy, May 6, 1895.

He immigrated to New York in 1913 and worked as a gardener for awhile, ultimately ending up in California, where, for two years, he played bit parts. His success as a star was established with *Four Horsemen of the Apocalypse* in 1921.

A real sex symbol, Valentino attracted women fans and alienated many men. He died at the age of thirty-one of a perforated ulcer.

VALVERDE

Spanish for "green valley," Valverde street may have been named as a remembrance of the Battle of Valverde in February 1862, during the Civil War. Hearing that Confederates were attempting to maintain control of New Mexico, General Henry Hopkins Sibley led troops to the federal stronghold at Fort Craig.

The Union forces collided with the Confederate forces brought from Texas at a Río Grande river crossing. The Union forces retreated, and the Confederates won the battle.

Perhaps, however, the name is merely a description of the Río Grande valley. When one comes into Albuquerque, especially if he flies, he is struck by the band of green which is the Río Grande valley in the midst of the desert.

The street may have been named for a local Valverde family or for Governor Antonio Valverde y Cosio, who was governor of New Mexico in 1717 to 1722.

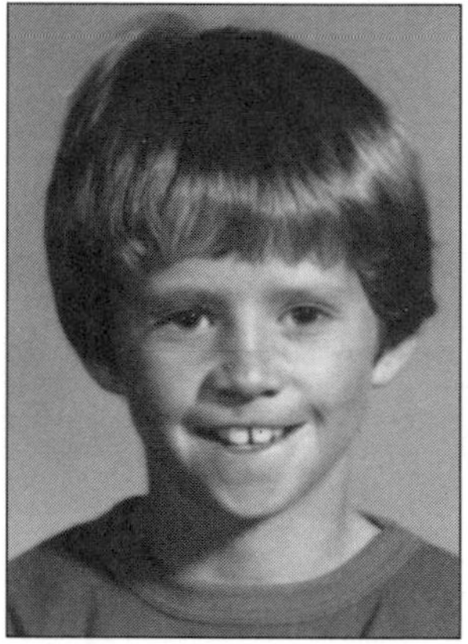

Born in 1972, Van Christopher Pexa lives and works in Albuquerque. He is a Special Olympics International gold medalist and has recently been nominated as Special Olympic Athlete of the Year for the United States. (Photo, 1977, courtesy of Mr. and Mrs. Revi Pexa)

VAN CHRISTOPHER DRIVE

Tom Burlison, employee of Home Planning Corporation in the early 1970s when the company platted Academy Place, named this street for Van Christopher Pexa, youngest son of his friends Revi and Dana Pexa.

Names of nearby streets honor their other two sons, Revi Don and John Thomas.

VENUS

Near Don Juan Onate Park lies a subdivision of streets named for Shakespearean characters.

In Shakespeare's "Venus and Adonis," Venus, the goddess of love, falls in love with Adonis, a handsome mortal youth who goes out to hunt the wild boar. The boar sinks his tusk into the youth's "soft groin," and Adonis dies. Where his blood has spilled upon the earth, a beautiful purple flower checkered with white, the anemone, springs up in Adonis' memory.

VIA POSADA and VIA POSADA COURT

In Four Hills subdivision, developed by Hicks and Associates in the early 1970s, Ralph Hicks chose street names that develop a Western or New Mexican/Spanish theme.

This street name translates from Spanish as "shelter or lodging road." It has a rather attractive sound also.

VINEYARD ROAD

In 1923 Henry G. Coors platted the Vineyard addition and named the streets for varieties of grapes or vineyard-associated names, such as Vineyard Road, Arbor, Mission, Muscatel, Niagara, and Tokay.

VISTA BONITA

Located on the edge of Prospector's Ridge, a subdivision in which most street names develop a theme of prospecting or mining, this street name is Spanish for "pretty view." Unlike the other names, this one does not develop the theme of prospecting.

VISTA CAMPO

In the eastern portion of Academy Acres, developed in the 1970s, the streets were given names descriptive of their locations.

Located across Wyoming Boulevard from Albuquerque Academy, this street provides a "view of the country" with some four hundred acres of the campus of the Albuquerque Academy in sight.

VISTA CEDRO

In the eastern portion of Academy Acres, developed in the 1970s, the streets were given names descriptive of their locations.

From this street, "cedar view," one can see the cedar trees growing on the Sandia Mountains.

VISTA DEL ARROYO

This name, "view of the stream," derives from the proximity of the street to Bear Canyon Arroyo and Arroyo del Oso Park and Golf Course.

VISTA DEL MONTE

Also in the eastern portion of Academy Acres, in which the streets were given names descriptive of their locations, *Vista del Monte,* Spanish for "view of the mountain," is an appropriate name for this street from which the Sandia Mountains provide a splendid view.

VOLCANO ROAD

This street is a remembrance of the volcanoes that once visited their fury upon parts of New Mexico, especially in the west, south, and southwest. West of Albuquerque, over one hundred extinct volcanic cones stand as mute evidence of what once existed.

According to T.M. Pearce (*New Mexico Place Names*), the Laguna Indians refer to "the year of the fire," and many believe that "the fire" was a huge eruption of a volcano.

W

WAGON WHEEL STREET

In Four Hills subdivision, this street name contributes to the Western theme. Alongside Wagon Wheel are Wagon Train, Stage Coach, and others which contribute to the theme.

WAGON TRAIN DRIVE and COURT

In Four Hills, the two Wagon Train streets contribute to the Western theme.

WALLACE

In Heritage East, developed in the early 1970s, the streets were named for governors or heroes of New Mexico.

This street was named for Lew Wallace. In the same subdivision, there is also a street named Lew Wallace.

See Lew Wallace for the story of Governor Wallace.

WALTER

Colonel Walter G. Marmon was the civil engineer employed by the New Mexico Town Company to lay out the townsite of New Albuquerque when the railroad came in 1880. Marmon had worked for the Santa Fé Railroad occasionally. He named two of the streets for his children, Walter and Edith.

Colonel Marmon settled and married at Laguna Pueblo. Lee Marmon, his great nephew, lives in Laguna today and operates the Blue-Eyed Indian Bookshop in New Laguna.

WALTER BAMBROOK PLACE

In Nor Este Manor, Presley Homes named the streets for New Mexico artists who were recommended by the Nor Este Art Association. Many of the artists attended the dedication ceremony and left their hand prints in the concrete of the part fountain near La Cueva High School.

A native of Albuquerque, Walter Bambrook attended the University of New Mexico for several years. He became an apprentice for the Albuquerque *Journal* and began a serious study of art, as he was instructed by Carl von Hassler, a greatly-admired artist.

Bambrook began serious painting in 1934 and studied under Ralph Douglas at the University of New Mexico.

In 1955 he began serving as director of the State Fair Art Gallery. His paintings have been exhibited widely.

WELTON DRIVE and COURT

Wally Welton was a party chief for a surveying crew for Home Planning Corporation, the company that platted Academy Acres in northeast Albuquerque in 1972.

WESTERN TRAIL

In Quaker Heights, located on the west side of Albuquerque, the street names develop the theme of the peacefulness and friendliness of the Quakers.

The name Western Trail calls to mind the traditional friendliness and hospitality of the West.

WESTWARD LANE

Also in Quaker Heights, this name calls to mind the traditional friendliness and hospitality of the West as well.

WHITE CLOUD

In Kachina Hills, this street was named for one of the deities. (See Kachina Hills.)

WHITE STREET

When Loma Del Norte was platted in the early 1970s by M. and Q. Southwest, Tom Burlison named this street for Dorothy White, who was an accountant for the company.

WILLIAM MOYERS AVENUE

In Nor Este Manor, Presley Homes named the streets for New Mexico artists who were recommended by the Nor Este Art Association. Many of the artists attended the dedication ceremony and left their hand prints in the concrete of the park fountain near La Cueva High School.

William Moyers was born in Atlanta, Georgia, in 1916. At age fourteen, he and his family moved to Alamosa, Colorado, where he broke horses, participated in the rodeo circuit, and worked as an all-around cowhand. He received his Bachelor of Arts degree from Adams State University, then attended Otis Art Institute in Los Angeles. For a time, he worked for Walt Disney Studios.

In 1962 he and his family moved to Albuquerque. A Western artist, he is an active member and former president of the prestigious Cowboy Artists of America.

WILSON HURLEY PLACE and WILSON HURLEY STREET

These two streets in Nor Este Manor, a subdivision in which the streets were named for artists, were named for Wilson Hurley.

Hurley was born in 1924. He attended the United States Military Academy at West Point, graduating in 1945. He served in the Air Force and was stationed in the Philippines.

After leaving the service, he attended George Washington University Law School and was granted the L.L.B. degree in 1951. For thirteen years, he practiced law in Albuquerque, but he was not happy with the legal profession. Therefore, he sought a full-time painting career.

A plaque beside one of his paintings in the Museum of Albuquerque suggests that Hurley's interest in broad vistas, mountains, canyons, and clouds is, in part at least, a result of his flying experience.

WIMBLEDON

In Wimbledon West subdivision, developed by Centex Homes in the 1980s, the street names develop a tennis theme.

Wimbledon, a London suburb, is the site of the annual All-England Championships. Men's competition began there in 1877, and women's competition began in 1884.

Other streets in this subdivision include Flushing Meadows and Bjorn Borg.

WINTER

Next to Snow Heights Park, the first street to the south is Winter, probably suggested by the name *Snow Heights,* the name of an area developed by Edward H. Snow.

Next to Winter, as a natural progression, are Summer and Spring.

WINTER HAVEN

Joel and Nina Mae Taylor live on the end of this street, which lies on a small part of the eight hundred acres that they once owned on the west side of the Río Grande.

The Taylors homesteaded near Chama on the Continental Divide, and they used this ranch as their winter haven for wintering their livestock. Also the children and Mrs. Taylor lived on this land so that the children could attend school in Albuquerque. (See Taylor Ranch Drive.)

WOODHAVEN

In a small addition to Loma Del Norte, the *wood* theme was used. Countrywood is the east-west street, and the streets that radiate from it all begin with *wood*—Woodridge, Woodleaf, and Woodhaven.

WOODLEAF

See Woodhaven.

WOODRIDGE

See Woodhaven.

Y

YEAGER DRIVE

Ed Yeager was an engineer with M. and Q. Southwest, the company that platted Loma Del Norte in the early 1970s.

Z

ZEARING

The street was named for the Zearing family, who were prominent during the early twentieth century.

George L., Harry W., and J. M. Zearing owned Star Furniture Store in 1908. The telephone number was 1883-W.

In 1932 Harry W., whose wife was Edna, worked with the Middle Río Grande Conservancy District.

ZIA

Zia Pueblo is a Keresan-speaking pueblo located sixteen miles northwest of Bernalillo. It is the Zia sun symbol that appears on the New Mexican flag, license plates, and other places.

Zia is noted for its pottery, which strictly adheres to tradition. Typically unpolished red ware with a white slip partially overlaid, the pots are painted brown or a muted black.

The population of Zia is about eight hundred, and it contains 112,510 acres of poor land with limited irrigation water.

Zia's mission dates to 1692.

ZIMMERMAN

Obviously named for the Zimmerman family, the street probably was named for Dr. James Fulton Zimmerman or some of his descendants.

Dr. James Fulton Zimmerman was president of the University of New Mexico, being appointed to that position in 1927. Zimmerman Library, pictured, was named for him.

Dr. Zimmerman was a political science professor at the University of New Mexico and was appointed president of the university in 1927.

ZUNI

The street name honors the Zuni Pueblo, which lies forty miles south of Gallup. It was the first pueblo to be seen by the Europeans, but it has resisted most outside forces. The Zuni people speak Keresan. They farm and do really fine inlaid jewelry; also they do some pottery making and weaving.

It is a large pueblo, with a population of near seven thousand people. Zuni includes 408,404 acres of land.

ZURICH

When Academy Place was platted in the early 1970s by Home Planning Corporation and was developed by Ward Brothers, Inc., Tom Burlison named this street for Stan Zurich, an attorney who dealt with many of the property transactions with the homes in the new subdivision.

Santa Fé

Santa Fé was founded in the winter of 1609–1610 by Don Pedro de Peralta, who was third governor of the Province of *Nuevo Méjico.* He founded this town on the bank of the Río Santa Fé at a place that was known to the Pueblo Indians as *Kuapoga,* "place of the shell beads near the water." He named his community *La Villa Real de la Santa Fé de San Francisco* ("Royal Town of the Holy Faith of Saint Francis"). The patron saint of the city is Saint Francis of Assisi, and the cathedral of the city bears that name as well.

In 1609, two years after the founding of Jamestown, Virginia, and eleven years before the Pilgrims arrived in

The Atchison, Topeka, and Santa Fé Railroad played a major role in the development of New Mexico.

Massachusetts, Peralta and a few settlers from San Gabriel selected a site on the north bank of the Río Santa Fé, at the southern end of the *Sangre de Cristo* ("blood of Christ") range of mountains to serve as the site of the new town. During the winter of 1609–1610, work began on the *palacio,* later called the Palace of the Governors. (From the Palace of the Governors, sixty Spanish governors ruled the New Mexico territory for a period of 212 years.) Peralta and his men laid out a plaza and planned a walled city, building a *presidio* and the *palacio.*

Peralta organized a government of four *regidores* (councilmen), two of whom served as *alcaldes ordinarios* (judges) to hear criminal and civil cases within the boundaries of the town. These officers were selected annually.

Each resident of the *villa* or town was given two lots for house and garden, two fields for vegetable gardens, two others for vineyards and olive groves, and about 133 acres of land.

The Ore House, with *ristras* aplenty hanging from the gallery, stands across from the Santa Fé Plaza.

In 1680 Santa Fé was captured by the Indians during the Pueblo Revolt. Angered by the Spaniards, the Pueblo Indians planned a revolt to occur on August 16, 1680. The Tesuque Pueblo played an important role in this revolt. Two men from the Tezuque Pueblo were messengers to the other pueblos, using knotted ropes to coordinate the day for the revolt. When they left Tesuque, they carried with them ropes with knots in them, each knot representing a day. When the last knot was untied, it was the day for the revolt to occur, and all the pueblos were able to strike simultaneously. The *presidio* was besieged by a force of three thousand Indians for five days. With a force of approximately 150 men, Governor Don Antonio Otermín was able to cut his way out of the city and escape. Almost every European in the valley was slain.

It was twelve years before the Spaniards attempted to resettle Santa Fé. In 1692 Don Diego De Vargas Zapata y Lujan Ponce de Léon y Contreras was appointed governor of New Mexico. He took about two hundred men and marched up the Río Grande valley. When they arrived in Santa Fé on September 13, however, he found the village surrounded by walled entrenchments filled with numerous Tano Indians. When his negotiations with the Indians failed, he laid siege, cut off the water supply in the aqueduct, and issued an ultimatum for peaceful surrender. The strategy a success, he and his men entered Sanata Fé, and he proclaimed the city repossessed for King Carlos II of Spain.

Santa Fé has played a major role in the history of New Mexico. In early days, it was the capital, the main city, the end of the Santa Fé Trail. It is still the capital and one of the main cities. And even though it is sixteen miles from the main line of the railroad, a railroad company bears its name. (A group of businessmen underwrote the cost of bringing a railroad spur from the main line to Santa Fé in 1880.)

Though Santa Fé has been the capital of New Mexico for almost four hundred years, the city has remained relatively small, and most Santa Féans seem glad. Tourism is big; and though the money that tourists bring to the city is needed, many residents say that they long for the old days when life was more simple in the small town. In size, Santa Fé has been far outstripped by Albuquerque, its neighbor to the south. It is big enough, but it still maintains a relatively slow pace, especially in the old section. Santa Fé is difficult to describe; it is truly "the city different."

The city has done much to preserve and even add to its Hispanic flavor by imposing the "Santa Fé style" of building for new homes and the use of Spanish words for street names.

From the small, stuggling group of settlers who came with Peralta in 1609 to settle on the bank of the Río Santa Fé, the settlement has now become a city of some fifty thousand people within the city limits and another forty thousand within Santa Fé County.

The street names of Santa Fé reveal much of the history of the city.

A

ABEYTA STREET

The Abeyta family have been prominent in Santa Fé since the early settlement. Don Antonio y A. Abeyta was born in Santa Fé in 1832, the son of Diego Abeyta and Josefita Armijo, whose parents were among the first Spanish settlers in New Mexico.

Don Antonio was educated in Santa Fé. He married Rufina Vigil in 1871.

ACEQUIA MADRE

The *Acequia Madre* ("mother ditch") flows alongside this street that bears its name, and the ditch is still used to water trees and gardens near it. The *Acequia Madre* brought water from the springs or *la cienega* ("the swamp") on the east side of the Plaza. (See La Cienega.)

The *Acequia Madre* is still governed by Spanish law. A *mayordomo de la acequia* and three commissioners supervise the operation of the ditch. Each property owner along the Acequia Madre, if he holds water rights, must pay an annual fee for use of the water. In the spring, all who hold water rights must cooperate to clean it out.

AGUA FRIA

The street was named for a village near Santa Fé. The village was given this Spanish name meaning "cold water" because the wells and springs in the village flow with very cold water.

ALAMEDA STREET

The Spanish word *alameda,* "poplar or cottonwood grove," gave this street its name. Cottonwood trees are common in northern New Mexico, especially in damp areas. This street runs alongside the Santa Fé River.

ALAMO DRIVE, ALAMOSA DRIVE, ALAMOSA PLACE

Alamo is Spanish for "poplar" or "cottonwood," and *Alamosa* is a variant of that word, meaning "cottonwood." Both terms are used widely in northern New Mexico because of the presence of cottonwood trees in areas where any dampness exists.

ALARID STREET

The Alarid family trace their lineage in Santa Fé through much of the city's history. Bautista Vigil y Alarid was acting governor of New Mexico when, on August 18, 1846, General Kearny entered Santa Fé, Governor Manuel Armijo having abandoned the city and headed for Mexico and refuge. Without a fight, Bautista Vigil y Alarid surrendered the Palace of the Governors, and the United States flag was raised in the plaza.

The Alarid family included Don Gaspar Ortiz y Alarid, a trader during the early territorial period. He held a large parcel of land between San Francisco Street and the Santa Fé River. It was for him that Ortiz and Don Gaspar streets were named.

ALL TRADES ROAD

Located in an industrial or commercial park off Cerrillos Road, this street was given its name as a description of the commercial area surrounding it. Nearby are Calle de Comercio, Industrial Road, and Trades West Road.

AMBROSIA STREET

Changed from Montoya Street in 1933, the name of this street was surely given for Ambrosio Ortiz, who owned property adjacent to it as of 1901. Somehow the final *o* became an *a* on the street name.

APACHE AVENUE

The Apache tribes were nomadic invaders who had migrated to the edge of the Pueblo world by around A. D. 1200. Some say that they had come to the Southwest from Canada and Alaska around A. D. 1000. Their presence caused a great deal of friction between them and the Pueblo tribes. They were called Apaches, or "enemies," by the Pueblo people. One tribe of the Apache came to be called *apaches de nabahú,* later known as *Navajo* or *Navaho.*

ARENAL COURT

Many of the streets in Santa Fé were named for Indian tribes or pueblos, and this one is no exception.

Arenal was one of the Tiguex pueblos. After Coronado's arrival, the Tiguex rebelled overtly because of the actions of the Spaniards, who were disliked by the Indians because the Spaniards bothered their women and were gradually taking over more and more of their land.

In the winter of 1541, a war party from Arenal stole a herd of horses from the Spaniards and slaughtered them. As a result, Coronado's troops sacked and burned the Arenal Pueblo. Braves were lanced or taken captive and roasted alive while tied to stakes.

ARMIJO HEIGHTS, ARMIJO STREET, ARMIJO LANE NORTH and SOUTH

The Armijo name is a common name in Santa Fé and in northern New Mexico in general.

George W. Armijo was a part of the Constitutional Convention for New Mexico in 1910. He was named chief clerk of the convention.

The founder of the Armijo family in New Mexico was José Armijo, who was one of the citizens of Zacatecas, Mexico, who had been recruited by De Vargas in 1695 to help resettle the Río Grande valley. Four of his great-grandsons—Francisco, Ambrosio, Juan, and Manuel—played important roles in the history of Albuquerque, serving as *alcalde*, or magistrate, of Albuquerque during the 1820s and 1830s.

In 1837 Mexicans and Indians rebelled against the Mexican government. They executed the governor and seized the Palace of the Governors, installing José Gonzalez, a Taos Indian, as their governor. A month later, General Manuel Armijo, of the Albuquerque Armijo family mentioned above, crushed the rebellion and became governor. He served as governor of New Mexico on three different occasions.

Armijo was governor and the general in charge of Mexican troops in Santa Fé when General Stephen Watts Kearny came to Santa Fé and took possession of New Mexico for the United States. However, when he heard that the United States army was heading for Santa Fé, he led a small army out to Apache Canyon, where they built a few breastworks; but before long, he called off the work and announced that he was giving up the effort. Under threat of being shot by some of his men, he climbed into a carriage and left, driving south to the village of Galisteo. Reports are that he loaded a wagon with some goods and headed for Mexico, leaving Señora Armijo in Albuquerque.

Armijo Heights winds along the hills near Arroyo Saiz, leading off from Armijo Street, which stems from Palace Avenue. Armijo Lane North and South stem from Cerro Gordo Road.

ARNY STREET

Now a portion of present-day Guadalupe Street, Arny Street once existed and was named for W. R. M. Arny, who was chairman of the 1881 street-naming committee. Arny Street later became Griffin Street.

Arny served as secretary of the Territory of New Mexico in 1865 and later as acting governor shortly after the Civil War.

ARROYO CHAMISO ROAD

The road derives its name from Arroyo Chamiso. Chamiso is a type of grayish, narrow-leaved brush that is also called rabbitbrush. Both commonly grow around Santa Fé and Taos.

Also, there is an Old Arroyo Chamiso Road.

AZTEC STREET

This street and Montezuma Avenue were a part of the new subdivision created by Catron, Staab, et al., when the railroad came to Santa Fé in 1880. According to *Santa Fé Historic Neighborhood Study,* the names Aztec and Montezuma "marked the beginning of a romantic fascination with Indian cultures which would lead Santa Fé into Spanish Pueblo Revival architecture in years to come."

The Aztecs were one of the most powerful and civilized groups of ancient America. They inhabited the Valley of Mexico and the surrounding areas until about A. D. 1200, when they were conquered by Hernando Cortes in 1521. The Aztec controlled a large portion of Mexico from their capital city, Tenochtitlán, which is now Mexico City.

A street next to Aztec Street is called Montezuma Avenue, so named in honor of the emperor of Mexico, Montezuma II.

BACA STREET

R. Luciana Baca was the first speaker of the New Mexico House of Representatives in 1912. He was a participant in the House of Representatives as speaker and as a member until the 1930s.

Baca was involved in the development of a subdivision of lots east of the depot, in anticipation of the development of a commercial center around the railroad depot. Baca, Thomas Catron, Abe Staab, Robert Longwill, and Antonio Ortiz y Salazar were involved in the development. Lots were sold by L. Bradford Prince and William Berger.

BANDELIER COURT

This street was named in honor of Adolf Francis Bandelier, an archaeologist who conducted research in New Mexico and Arizona in 1882 to 1892 and who lived in Santa Fé.

He was born in Berne, Switzerland, but later came to the United States.

After doing archaelogical work in Mexico, he went to Santa Fé and did extensive archaelogical and historical work on the New Mexico Indians.

Bandelier died on February 11, 1914, in Seville, Spain. Just before Bandelier's death, however, President Woodrow Wilson proclaimed the ruins of Indian cliff dwellers in Frijoles Canyon the Bandelier National Monument.

BELLAMAH COURT

Dale Bellamah was born in San Juan (now Veguita) in northern Socorro County in 1920, the son of an immigrant Lebanese teacher who opened a grocery store in the Barelas area of Albuquerque. Though his real name was Abdul Hamid Bellamah, "slave of God," he became known as Dale.

In his youth he worked at the Santa Fé Railroad for $3 a day. He went to the University of New Mexico, worked at the railroad, and slept in the fire house at night. He was paid one half-dollar per night for sleeping there and keeping an eye on it.

He married Jeanne Lees of Albuquerque, whom he called Princess Jeanne; and in every town in which he built homes, he named a street Princess Jeanne. In Santa Fé, the equivalent is Calle Princesa Juana. The couple lived in Albuquerque and had no children. Jeanne died in 1970, two years before Dale's death.

Bellamah was a famous builder, one of the top six builders in the United States.

In 1961 Bellamah was the recipient of the American Success Story Award. Beginning with $250, he developed his business into twenty corporations, which were building about one thousand houses a year and which were grossing more than $50 million annually.

Bellamah died on April 19, 1972. He was survived by a niece, Mrs. D. E. Boyle of Albuquerque, and a grand-nephew, Daniel Boyle III.

BEN HUR DRIVE

This Santa Fé street is a remembrance of Lew Wallace's *Ben Hur: A Tale of the Christ,* which was published in 1880.

Lew Wallace was appointed territorial governor by President Rutherford B. Hayes. Wallace was sent to restore order from the havoc that was being created by Billy the Kid and the Tunstall-McSween faction. They were rustling and causing problems in Lincoln County.

While Wallace was governor of the Territory of New Mexico, he wrote *Ben Hur* while living in the Palace of the Governors.

Near Ben Hur Drive lies General Wallace Drive, also named for Lew Wallace, who at one time was the youngest Union general in the Civil War.

BERGER STREET

William Berger and L. Bradford Prince sold the lots in a subdivision of lots developed just east of the railroad depot. Abe Staab, Thomas Catron, Antonio Ortiz y Salazar, Luciana Baca, and Robert Longwill developed the subdivision in anticipation of the development of a commercial center near the depot.

Streets in the subdivision were named for all of these men except Longwill.

The altar in the chapel at *Villa Pintoresca* (Bishop's Lodge) has served as the focal point of religion at the lodge. (Photo, 1942, courtesy New Mexico State Records Center and Archives, Department of Development Collection #34715)

BISHOPS LODGE ROAD

The road was named for the presence of the Bishop's lodge situated along it.

Rt. Rev. Jean Baptiste Lamy was born October 11, 1814, at Lempdes, France. He was educated and ordained in the Diocese of Clermont in France. In 1839 Lamy and his friend Joseph Projectus Macheboeuf came to the United States after having been recruited as missionary priests by J. B. Purcell, the Bishop of Cincinnati. The two priests served in the mission field in Ohio for about ten years or so.

At Bishop's Lodge, developed by Bishop Jean Baptiste Lamy, this was the bishop's chapel, where services have often been performed. (Photo, 1942, courtesy New Mexico State Records Center and Archives, D.O.D. Collection #34718)

Lamy was assigned to Santa Fé and went there in 1850. Accompanied by Father Macheboeuf, Lamy made the trip to Santa Fé from Ohio by horseback. However, although he was well received by the people, the clergy resented him and refused to accept his authority. To deal with the problem, he journeyed into Mexico to gain assistance from his former bishop.

The Diocese of Santa Fé was officially established in 1853, with Lamy as its bishop. He was responsible for bringing the Sisters of Loretto from Kentucky to Santa Fé, where they opened an academy, and he also brought European priests and teaching and preaching orders to serve in the diocese.

One of his main concerns was strengthening the educational system in the territory. When Lamy came to Santa Fé, he brought with him a number of French priests whose job was to help him with church work under his jurisdiction. Their main interest, however, was in establishing educational institutions in which Spanish was a part of the curriculum.

A French priest who expected the utmost in rectitude, apparently, he disciplined those who needed disciplining. It is said that he excommunicated Padre Martínez in Taos, and he once sent Father Macheboeuf to Albuquerque to correct the wandering ways of Father José Manuel Gallegos.

According to Dr. Myra Ellen Jenkins and James R. Thorpe ("From Retreat to Resort"), Bishop Lamy felt the need to have a retreat to which he could occasionally go to be away from the pressures of his job. He found some land along the Little Tesuque stream, located a few miles north of Santa Fé, and he purchased a piece of land for $80 from Natividad Romero and his wife, María Vitalia García.

On a small hill the bishop built his lodge, which he named Villa Pintoresca, apparently for the beautiful view. The lodge consisted of two small rooms, a bedroom and a sitting room, separated by a hallway that led into a small chapel on the east. In the chapel he conducted his devotions and celebrated mass for guests. Around the lodge, Lamy set out shrubs and fruit trees, which flourished because of the irrigation furnished by the *acequia madre.*

It is reported that he had frequent guests when he was at the lodge, always walking three miles over the hills to arrive at the lodge.

Archbishop Lamy died on February 13, 1888, after having contracted a cold, which developed into pneumonia. He was buried under the altar at the Cathedral of Saint Francis in Santa Fé.

With Lamy's death, ownership of the property passed to Archbishop Salpointe. Some problems with the deed existed, but they were finally settled in 1896 after Archbishop Placide Louis Chapelle had succeeded Salpointe. Eventually the issue was settled, and the property included approximately 152 acres.

Over the years, the property changed hands several times, being owned by Carl Stephan, Harper S. Cunningham, and May Woodford. In 1915 the property was deeded by May Woodford to some members of the famous Pulitzer family—William Scoville, Edith Pulitzer Moore, and Constance Pulitzer. They caused to be built two residences, later known as the north and south lodges, and a carriage house. These were later incorporated into the current lodge.

In 1918 the Pulitzer family sold the property to the Bishop's Lodge Corporation, which was headed by James R. Thorpe. The property has remained in the Thorpe family ever since.

The lodge is a modern place that offers all the comforts and conveniences of fine hotels, but it has an atmosphere unlike a hotel. The simple chapel that Lamy built over one hundred years ago offers peace and reflection to those who come to it.

And the road running in front of Bishop's Lodge was named in memory of the retreat created by Archbishop Jean Baptiste Lamy.

BURRO ALLEY

Burro Alley connects Palace Avenue to San Francisco. According to tradition, the alley received its name because burros or donkeys were tied there when vendors of salt from the Galisteo salt basins or of fire wood came to Santa Fé to sell their wares. The word *burro* means "donkey."

Nowadays the alley looks like a normal street except that it has a picture of a burro painted on the wall of a store located there.

Burro Alley, now a street, was given its name because burros were tied there when salt or firewood vendors came to Santa Fé to sell their goods.

CALLE ALVARADO

In the summer of 1540, Captain Hernando de Alvarado led a reconnaissance party sent by Coronado from Coronado's main camp at Zuni Pueblo. Alvarado was in charge of the mule-powered artillery in Coronado's expedition.

CALLE ANAYA

The street name is a remembrance of the Anaya family, possibly descendants of Captain Francisco de Anaya, who was in the army during the Pueblo Revolt of 1680. Two of eight men under his leadership were killed at Santa Clara.

CALLE BARONESA

In the Bellamah addition, Dale Bellamah named one of his streets *Calle Princesa Juana,* "Princess Jeanne Street," for his wife. (See Princesa Juana.) Apparently the royal title of *Princesa* called to mind other royal titles, so three other streets bear royal names—*Calle Baronesa* ("baroness street"), *Calle Condesa* ("countess street"), and *Calle Reina* ("queen street"). Apparently *La Marquesina* was intended to developed this royal theme as well, though the street namer chose *La Marquesina* when he obviously meant *La Marquesa.* (See La Marquesina.)

CALLE CEDRO

Spanish for "cedar street," the name was derived from one of the primary shrubs of the area, the scrub cedar.

CALLE DE COMERCIO

Spanish for "commerce street," this name was given as a description of the surroundings of the street, which is located in a commercial or industrial park. Nearby are All Trades Road, Trades West Road, and Industrial Road.

CALLE DULCINEA

Spanish for "Dulcinea street," this name is a commemoration of the young woman in Miguel de Cervantes Saavedra's picaresque novel, *Don Quixote de la Mancha.* (See Don Quixote.)

Dulcinea del Toboso was the buxom peasant wench to whom Quixote dedicated his deeds of valor. Her primary claim to fame was her skill in salting pork. She was from the village of Toboso in Spain.

CALLE ESTADO

Spanish for "state street," this street is a continuation of Mansion Drive, on which is located the Executive Mansion or Governor's Mansion for the State of New Mexico.

CALLE PRINCESA JUANA

Jeanne Lees Bellamah was the wife of builder Dale Bellamah. In each town in which Bellamah built homes, he named a street for his wife, Princess Jeanne, his pet name for her. In Santa Fé, in order to conform to the Spanish naming of the city, the street is called Calle Princesa Juana.

(See Bellamah Court.)

CALLE REINA

Spanish for "queen street," this name was chosen to fit into the royal theme in the Bellamah addition. See Calle Baronesa, above.

CALLE SANTO NINO

This street name celebrates Christ, the Holy Child. The name is Spanish for "street of the Holy Boy Child."

CALLE TORREON

Spanish for "tower," *torreon* refers to a defense tower that was commonly in use during the early days of New Mexico history. Often a *torreon* would be constructed of stone at the end of a house or *hacienda*. The people would be able to seek refuge in the *torreon* and defend themselves against intruders.

This street lies next to Arroyo Torreon and was obviously named for its proximity to the arroyo. The arroyo probably derives its name from a *torreon* that once existed nearby.

CAMINO ANASAZI

The Anasazi, "the ancient ones," were the Indian culture that existed in northern New Mexico about the time of Christ. Actually, their domain stretched from east of the Río Grande west into Nevada, and from central New Mexico and Arizona north into Colorado and Utah. It was a progressive culture, and its golden age lasted from about A. D. 1000 to A. D. 1500. The Anasazi were noted for their architectural feats.

They were farmers and evolved ingenious water-control devices for the rivers, etc. And even though they had no wheel, they left behind them hundreds of miles of roads.

They built tremendous towns of stone and dirt and lifted themselves in their level of civilization higher than any other people north of Mexico.

Then suddenly the Anasazi left their towns, which lay silently until the nomadic Navajos occupied much of the Anasazi's land. The Navajos called them *Anasazi,* "alien ancient ones." At least 25,000 Anasazi sites have been discovered in New Mexico alone, and it is believed that at least that many exist in Arizona and that thousands more exist in Colorado and Utah.

CAMINO CARLOS REAL

Spanish for "road of royal Carlos," this street name honors King Carlos II, king of Spain during De Vargas' Reconquest in 1692. King Carlos II was succeeded by Philip V.

CAMINO CARLOS REY

Spanish for "road of King Carlos," this street name also honors King Carlos II, king of Spain when De Vargas led the Reconquest of New Mexico in 1692, reclaiming New Mexico in the name of King Carlos II.

CAMINO DE LOS MARQUEZ

This street was named for the Márquez families, several of which have lived in Santa Fé since early times. In Spanish, the use of the masculine article *los* often indicates a family, even though the noun or substantive may be feminine. In this case, the noun is probably a variant of *marques* ("marquis"), but it is already a masculine noun.

See Marques Place for further information.

CAMINO DEL MONTE SOL

This street, which bears a Spanish name meaning "road of sun mount," was the area in which the Santa Fé art colony was first begun. The street was popularly known as Telephone Road at one time.

The art colony was first begun by artist William Penhallow Henderson. Others who settled on this street shortly afterward were Frank Applegate, Will Shuster, J. G. Bakos, Fremont Ellis, Willard Nash, and others. This list includes four of the five artists who were later to call themselves *Los Cinco Pintores* ("the five painters").

CAMINO CRUZ BLANCA

Spanish for "white cross road," this name derives from the presence of the cross at the nearby Seminary of the Immaculate Heart of Mary.

CAMINO ESCONDIDO

This name is Spanish for "hidden road." The street was once called Rose Avenue, in honor of Bill Rose, who built the first house on the street *circa* 1924.

CAMINO REAL

Camino Real, Spanish for "royal road," was the trade route south to Chihuahua and Mexico City. During the Mexican period, the name was changed to Camino National. The *Camino Real* and the Santa Fé Trail met in Santa Fé.

CAMINO ZOZOBRA

Zozobra, or Old Man Gloom, is the name of the effigy that is burned at Fort Marcy Park on the first day of Fiesta. (See Zozobra Street for full story.)

CANDELARIO

The Candelarios were a prominent family in Santa Fé.

Jesus Sito Candelario owned a curio shop that was quite famous. Jesus was born on March 10, 1864, in Santa Fé. He was educated at the Mora, New Mexico, Mission

School and at St. Michael's College in Santa Fé. He graduated from Park College in Missouri in 1888.

Candelario married Estafanita Laumbach of Buena Vista, New Mexico.

He served as city councilman of Santa Fé, 1899–1900, and was city treasurer at one time. He was a large landowner and owner and operator of Candelario Trading Post in Santa Fé, the oldest trading post in the United States.

CANYON ROAD

The road was called Canyon Road because it leads to Apache Canyon, about ten miles east of Santa Fé.

Canyon Road is the major area of art studios and galleries in Santa Fé.

CAPITAL STREET

Stretching in front of the State Capitol to the west lies South Capital Street. The name provides a bit of an enigma, since the spelling is with the second *a* instead of the *o* that should be there.

The name of Capital Street celebrates the fact that Santa Fé is the capital of the State of New Mexico. The street stretches in front of the state capitol building (pictured), a state capitol of non-traditional architecture.

The construction of the capitol was begun with funds allocated by the territorial legislature in 1884, after a long struggle to keep Santa Fé as the capital. Over a period of several years, the Albuquerque people made a concentrated effort to move the capital to Albuquerque.

The first capitol was a towering Victorian structure made of stone, but it burned to the ground in 1892. A new structure was built in 1900.

The present capitol is a round building done in "Santa Fé style."

CATHEDRAL PLACE

Cathedral Place runs in front of St. Francis Cathedral. Construction of the cathedral was begun in 1869 under the auspices of Bishop Jean Baptiste Lamy.

The first church on this site was built by Fray Alonso de Benavides *circa* 1622 (according to one source) or 1628 (according to another), but it was destroyed in the Pueblo Revolt of 1680. *La parroquia* ("parish church") was built in 1712, and it served the people until the cathedral was erected.

When the cathedral was erected, the new walls were constructed around *la parroquia*. The little church was used inside the cathedral until the cathedral was finished; therefore, not a single mass was missed while the cathedral was being erected.

And in the cathedral, to the left of the altar, stands the statue of *La Conquistadora,* which is carried through the streets to the Rosario Chapel during the annual De Vargas procession. (See Paseo de La Conquistadora.)

Cathedral Place runs in front of St. Francis Cathedral, built under the auspices of Bishop Jean Baptiste Lamy and dedicated to St. Francis of Assisi, or *San Francisco de Asis.*

CATRON STREET

Thomas Benton Catron was born in Lafayette County, Missouri, on October 6, 1840. He attended school in Missouri and graduated from the University of Missouri in 1860 with the Bachelor of Arts degree, then with the Master of Arts degree.

He served in the Confederate States of America's Army under General Sterling W. Price and took part in several battles.

After the Civil War, Catron returned to Missouri and studied law. In 1866 he went to Santa Fé and, shortly

Thomas Benton Catron was active in Santa Fé and New Mexico politics. This photograph seems to be an enlargement of a snapshot of Catron, signed Harris and Ewing. (Photo courtesy New Mexico State Records Center and Archives, Olsen Collection #12592)

thereafter, was appointed district attorney for the 3rd Judicial District, though he had not yet been admitted to the New Mexico Bar. He settled in La Mesilla and was admitted to the bar in 1867.

He married Julia A. Walz, of Mankato, Minnesota. They had five children.

In 1869 Catron was appointed district attorney of New Mexico, and in 1872 he was appointed United States attorney by President Grant.

He served as a member of several legislative assemblies, as mayor of Santa Fé, and as president of the school board.

In 1894 he was elected as a delegate to the 54th Congress, and in 1895 he was chosen president of the New Mexico Bar Association.

He served as a member of the constitutional convention in 1910 and was elected United States senator at the first session of the New Mexico state legislature in 1912.

It was partially through his efforts that the state capitol and penitentiary were built in Santa Fé in the late 1800s.

Catron was in partnership in a law firm with Stephen B. Elkins, and he owned the Catron Block in Santa Fé.

He was involved in the development of a new commercial center around the railroad depot. Antonio Ortiz y Salazar, Luciana Baca, Abe Staab, Robert Longwill, and Catron were all involved in this venture. The lots were sold by L. Bradford Prince and William Berger. Streets in this development were named for all of these men except Robert Longwill.

CEDAR STREET

The cedar shrub or small tree is one of the primary flora of the area.

CEDROS CIRCLE, CEDROS LANE, and CEDRO STREET

Spanish for "cedars" circle, this name was derived from one of the primary shrubs of the area, the scrub cedar, which grows on the hills around Santa Fé.

Los Cerrillos ("little hills"), from which turquoise and gold were mined, prompted the name Cerrillos for a nearby community. This photograph, taken south of Santa Fé and looking toward Santa Fé, pictures the little hills that inspired the name.

CERRILLOS ROAD

One of the major thoroughfares of Santa Fé, Cerrillos Road is the old highway to the community of Cerrillos or Los Cerrillos, Spanish for "little hills." This name was applied to a group of haciendas near Turquoise Mountain, southwest of Santa Fé, during the seventeenth and eighteenth centuries.

It was so named because of the many small hills in the vicinity, hills from which turquoise and gold were mined before 1680 by Indians who were enslaved by Spaniards.

The Márquez family hacienda was located at this place (See Marquez Place.)

At the rest area along Interstate 27, just a few miles south of Santa Fé, a highway plaque expresses slight differences from the information given above: "The prominent hills to the east and left are the Cerrillos Hills, site of ancient turquoise mines worked by the Indians centuries before the arrival of the Spanish. The Cerrillos ('little hills') are regarded as the oldest mining district in the United States, and New Mexico is a major turquoise producer."

CHAMA AVENUE

Chama is the Spanish approximation of the Tewa *tzama,* which, according to Pearce (*New Mexico Place Names*), was the name of a pueblo on the Chama River below the

El Rito River. It is believed that the pueblo might have still been occupied when the Spaniards arrived. The name was borrowed and applied first to the general area around the pueblo and then to the river, which rises in southern Colorado and flows south into the Río Ojo Caliente at Española. The name of the town was obviously borrowed from the name of the river.

According to Pearce, some think that *tzama* means "here they have wrestled"; others think that it means "red" in reference to the water of the river.

CHAMISA STREET

The *chamisa* is a wild grayish, narrow-leaved brush which is commonly seen growing along highways and stretches of land in northern New Mexico, especially around Santa Fé and Taos. Called *chamisa* by the Spanish, the brush is also called rabbitbrush.

CHAMISOS COURT

Similar to the *chamisa, chamiso* is another common brush which grows in northern New Mexico. It is commonly called saltbush in English.

CHAPELLE STREET

Once known as Jackson, this street became Chapelle street sometime around 1894 and was named for Placide Louis Chapelle, who served for a time as bishop of Santa Fé, 1894–1897.

After the Spanish-American War, Chapelle was Archbishop of New Orleans. He aided the Dominicans in establishing a chapel in the Lakeview section of New Orleans.

He died on August 9, 1905, during the yellow fever epidemic.

CIENEGA STREET

During the the Spanish Colonial era, the area northeast of the plaza was a marsh or swamp known as *la cienega,*

Spanish for "swamp, marsh." The swamp was fed by several springs, and hay grew there.

The street was once called Flora, but the name was changed to Cienega.

CIRCLE DRIVE

North of Santa Fé, Circle Drive makes an arc or circle of sorts between Bishops Lodge Road and St. Francis Avenue.

CLOSSON STREET

The Closson family owned a livery stable, which was opened in 1903 in the area around Ortiz Street. The street was named for the family.

COCHITI STREET

This street name honors the Cochiti Pueblo, possibly a Spanish derivation of Tewa *Kao Tay-ay*, "stone kiva." A Keresan-speaking pueblo, Cochiti is located about halfway between Albuquerque and Santa Fé. Its population was about nine hundred in 1986, and its land area is 28,779 acres.

Cochiti is noted for its jewelry and its drums, particularly double-headed ones made from aspen or cottonwood.

The Spanish mission, San Buenaventura de Cochiti, was built in the early seventeenth century and is still in use today.

Another street in Santa Fé, Vereda De Cochiti, was also named for this pueblo. That name is Spanish for "Cochiti path," and perhaps it was named because the Cochiti walked in that area going to and from their pueblo located not too far away.

CORONADO LANE and CORONADO ROAD

An early Spanish explorer, Francisco Vásquez de Coronado (1510–1554) led an expedition into the American

Southwest in search of the Seven Cities of Cíbola and Gran Quivira. Indians and other explorers had reported that these cities were rich in gold. With a force of three hundred Spaniards and several hundred Indians, Coronado began his search early in 1540, visiting the area that now includes Arizona and New Mexico. He and his group found Indian pueblos, but no golden cities.

In the spring of 1541, he led his army across *El Llano Estacado* ("The Staked Plains") in the Texas Panhandle, discovering Palo Duro Canyon near present-day Amarillo. Pushing on to central Kansas, the group discovered the Quivira Indians, but no golden cities.

Born in Salamanca, Spain, Coronado went to Mexico in 1535 and became governor of New Galicia, northwest of Mexico City, in 1538.

CRISTO REY STREET

The street was named for Cristo Rey ("Christ the King") Catholic Church, which was built in 1940. According to *Old Santa Fe Today,* the church was designed primarily to serve as a sanctuary for the great stone *reredos,* or altar screen, that originally had been in *La Castrense* on the plaza.

Built in commemoration of the 400th anniversary of Coronado's expedition, Cristo Rey Church is one of the largest adobe structures in existence. It was designed by John Gaw Meem, a famous Santa Fé architect.

The Cross of the Martyrs was erected in honor of the Franciscan priests who were slain in the Pueblo Revolt of August 10, 1680.

CROSS OF THE MARTYRS

The Cross of the Martyrs was erected on a hill in old Fort Marcy Park. Though there is no street by that name, the landmark is a significant part of Santa Fé and of New Mexico in general, as it commemorates the Franciscan priests who were slaughtered in the Pueblo Revolt of 1680. In the Pueblo Revolt, which occurred on August 10, 1680, virtually all Europeans were slain by the Pueblo Indians.

The Franciscans who were slain and to whom this cross is dedicated are the following, with the names of the pueblos that they were serving following their names: Juan Bernal, Galisteo; Juan Domingo De Vera,

Galisteo; Manual Tinoco, San Marcos; Fernando De Velasco, Pecos; Antonio De Mora, Taos; Juan de la Pedrosa, Taos; Matias de Rendon, Picuris; Luis De Morales, San Ildefonso; Tomás De Torres, Nambe; Juan Bautista Pio, Tesuque; Francisco Antonio De Lorenzana, Santo Domingo; Juan De Taleban, Santo Domingo; José Montes De Oca, Santo Domingo; Juan De Jesus, Jemez; Lucas Maldonado, Ácoma; Juan De Val, Zuni; José De Figueroa, Awatobi, Hopi; José De Espeleta, Oraibi, Hopi; Augustin De Santa Marías, Oraibi, Hopi; and José De Trujillo, Shongo Povi, Hopi.

CROSS STREET

George H. Cross was the editor of *The New Mexican,* beginning January 1, 1894, when Max Frost sold the paper. The president of the new corporation was W. T. Thornton.

Cross resigned on January 23, 1897, when the management of The *New Mexican* sold their interests to Max Frost, former editor.

DE VARGAS STREET

See Don Diego Street for story of Don Diego De Vargas.

DELGADO LANE and DELGADO STREET

These streets were named for the Delgado family, whose summer place, El Ranchito, was located nearby.

Ildeberto "Eddie" Delgado was a tinsmith and artist with tin in the early twentieth century.

Felipe S. Delgado was a prominent merchant and freighter on the Santa Fé Trail. He was also a judge. He built a home in Santa Fé in 1890.

Fernando Delgado owned land on the northwest corner of the plaza.

Juan Delgado owned a *placita*-style home and farm buildings at what is now 414 Old Santa Fé Trail.

Simon Delgado was territorial treasurer in 1866 and following. He was a local merchant in the mid-1800s. He purchased *La Castrense,* the Chapel of Our Lady of Light, located on the south side of the plaza.

Governor Francisco Marin del Valle had a military chapel built in 1760. Artisans were brought from Mexico to carve a *reredos*—or altar screen—from stone. It is one of the few examples of such ornamental carving in New Mexico. The chapel was closed in 1835 and was used as a storeroom by the Anglo-Americans. Bishop Lamy sold the chapel called *La Castrense* to Simon Delgado for $2,000 and used the money to make repairs to the parish church. The *reredos* was moved to the parish church during the construction of the cathedral. In 1940 it was installed in the new Church of Cristo Rey, which was designed by John Gaw Meem and was built to house the *reredos.*

Diego De Vargas was the governor of New Mexico who re-conquered the land after the Pueblo Indians had snatched New Mexico back during the Pueblo Revolt of 1680. (Photo taken from a full-length portrait, courtesy New Mexico State Records Center and Archives, Shiskin Collection #31702)

DON CUBERO AVENUE (DON CUBERO PLACE)

Don Pedro Rodriguez Cubero served as governor of New Mexico (1697–1703). He succeeded Don Diego De Vargas. While governor, he was able to achieve a mimimum level of allegiance from the Indians.

DON DIEGO AVENUE

Don Diego De Vargas Zapata y Lujan Ponce de Léon y Contreras was appointed governor of New Mexico and sent there to reconquer the land after the Pueblo Revolt of 1680. As a result of the revolt, the Europeans were virtually wiped out of New Mexico.

De Vargas went to New Mexico in 1691. In August 1692, he took about two hundred men and marched up the Río Grande valley. He met no resistance and found most of the villages deserted. When he arrived in Santa Fé on September 13, however, he found the village surrounded by walled entrenchments, and numerous Indians were present. When his negotiations with the Indians failed, he laid siege, cut off the water supply in the aqueduct, and issued an ultimatum for peaceful surrender. The strategy a success, he and his men entered Santa Fé, and he proclaimed the city repossessed for King Charles II of Spain.

De Vargas served as governor from 1693 to 1697 and again from 1703 to 1704.

DON FERNANDO ROAD

Don Fernando Durán y Chavéz was an early pioneer settler in the Taos area, and a stream in the upper valley, Río de Don Fernando, was named for him. Between 1777 and 1800, Spanish families began moving from near the Taos Pueblo to nearby Río de Don Fernando; they also began calling the Spanish settlement *La Plaza de Don Fernando de Taos.* What is generally known as Taos is really Don Fernando de Taos.

DON GASPAR AVENUE

Don Gaspar Ortiz y Alarid was born in Pojoaque, New Mexico, on March 2, 1834, the son of Don Juan Luis Ortiz and Doña Cruz Alarid.

He was educated in Santa Fé under the tutelage of Don Antonio Sena. In 1842 he was appointed to the *Colegio Militar* of Chapultepec, Mexico. He was commissioned a second lieutenant in the Mexican army and was assigned to Santa Fé, where he served as *aide de camp* to General Manuel Armijo during the invasion of the Americans under Brigadier General Stephen Watts Kearny in 1846 and accompanied General Armijo to Mexico City to report the surrender of New Mexico to the Americans.

Don Gaspar became a wealthy property owner through his trading activities with the Americans, Mexicans, and Indians.

He died in 1882 in Santa Fé.

In addition to Don Gaspar Avenue, Ortiz Avenue was named for him as well.

DON MIGUEL PLACE

Don Miguel A. Otero was born October 17, 1859, in St. Louis, Missouri. He was educated at St. Louis University and Notre Dame University.

He and his wife had one son, Miguel A. Otero, Jr.

Otero was a banker in Las Vegas, 1880–1885, and city treasurer of Las Vegas, 1883–1884. He was governor

of New Mexico, 1897–1906, and was the first governor of Hispanic origin.

Otero was treasurer of New Mexico, 1909–1911, and delegate to the Republican National Convention of 1892, 1900, 1904, and 1908. He was later a member of the Democratic National Convention in 1920.

Otero authored several books.

He died August 7, 1944, in Santa Fé.

DON QUIXOTE

Don Quixote street commemorates the main character of Miguel de Cervantes Saavedra's picaresque novel, *Don Quixote de la Mancha.*

Don Quixote, a retired and impoverished gentleman, loved reading romances of chivalry. He was dubbed knight by a rascally publican at an inn that Quixote had mistaken for a turreted castle.

After his first beating by some traveling merchants, Quixote returned home and was tended by Pedro Perez, the village priest. He later fell in with Sancho Panza, an uncouth rustic who became his squire. And as the mistress to whom he would dedicate his valorous deeds, he chose Dulcinea del Toboso, a buxom peasant wench who was famous only for her skill in salting pork.

DUDROW STREET

Born in Frederick, Maryland, in 1849, Charles W. Dudrow arrived in Santa Fé sometime between 1869 and 1872. He was a driver for the Barlow and Sanderson stage lines.

In 1881 he purchased property that became the site of his lumber company. In 1886 he married Cora Bear, the daughter of his partner, Samuel Bear. They were divorced in 1893.

In 1896 he married Madge Taylor, daughter of Dr. R. Howe Taylor, according to Marion Meyer in "Charles W. Dudrow: A Biographical Sketch," found in the vertical file in the Museum of New Mexico History Library.

Dudrow owned a lumber yard, and Dudrow Street originally served as the entrance to the lumber yard.

DUNLAP STREET

Though the current map lists this street name as Dunl*a*p, it was probably named for Bishop George Kelly Dunl*o*p, Episcopal bishop in Santa Fé in the 1880s and 1890s.

DURAN

In 1912 the José Durán estate was divided among his heirs. In 1919 a subdivision was created and the streets were named.

DURANGO DRIVE

Durango is a state in northwestern Mexico. For many years, the Catholic Church in New Mexico and Colorado was under the Mexican bishop of Durango—until the treaty that brought the Territory of New Mexico to the United States. There is also a town in southwestern Colorado named for the Mexican state.

ENTRE

Entré street serves as the entrance to a small subdivision off West Alameda Road. The name means "entrance."

FEDERAL PLACE

This street was named for the Federal Place, which contains the federal buildings, the court house, and the post office. The area is ovoid and was once used as a race track. The court house was completed in 1889.

FIESTA STREET

Fiesta is a time of light-hearted zaniness during the first two weeks of September. It is held to commemorate the re-entry into Santa Fé by Don Diego De Vargas in 1692.

Fiesta begins on a Friday morning with religious services. Then on Friday night, with the burning in effigy of Zozobra, or Old Man Gloom, the fun begins in earnest.

People are to have no serious thoughts during this time, only light-heartedness and fun.

"Que vivan las Fiestas!" is the traditional form of greeting during this time.

FORT UNION DRIVE

Fort Union was established in 1851 near Las Vegas, New Mexico. The fort was erected at a cost of three hundred dollars, including buildings required for a four-company post, for depot stores, and for a magazine.

Fort Union served during the Civil War and was a vital force in the winning of the Southwest.

The fort was abandoned on May 15, 1891, and the detachment there was transferred to Fort Wingate.

G

GALISTEO STREET (COURT, LANE, and PARKWAY)

One of the oldest streets of Santa Fé, Galisteo Street was named for the road that led to the old village of Galisteo, which was originally a pueblo located twenty-two miles south of Santa Fé. The pueblo was first mentioned by the Fray Rodriguez exploration party of 1581.

According to T.M. Pearce (*New Mexico Place Names*), the name is an old term for a native of Galicia, but it may have been transferred from a town in Estre Madura in Spain. A Spanish community has existed at that place off and on through many years.

The old salt lakes of the region have provided salt to the area for hundreds of years.

GARCIA STREET

Once called Camino de los Garcias, for the Garcia families who lived on the south side of *Acequia Madre*, the street was later given the English name Garcia Street.

GARFIELD STREET

Located in the subdivision developed by Thomas Catron, Abe Staab, Antonio Ortiz y Salazar, Luciana Baca, and Robert Longwill in the early 1880s, this street was named for President James A. Garfield, who was assassinated shortly thereafter. Garfield was in office at the time that the railroad spur was built from the main line to Santa Fé, opening on February 9, 1880.

GENERAL SAGE DRIVE

This street was named for Charles G. Sage, who was a colonel in command of the famous 200th Regiment, which was in the thick of the fighting on the Bataan Peninsula in 1941–1942. This was the regiment that was forced to make the "March of Death" and that spent more than three years in enemy prison camps, suffering starvation and torture. Almost eight thousand prisoners were captured by the Japanese after American General Edward P. King, Jr., surrendered the Bataan Peninsula. The War Department estimates that eight hundred to twelve hundred died or were killed on the march. And another eighteen hundred prisoners died during the first five weeks of confinement.

The Bataan Building in Santa Fé commemorates this regiment and the suffering of the men.

GENERAL WALLACE DRIVE

Lew Wallace was once the youngest Union general in the Civil War. He arrived in New Mexico during the turbulent times of land and mining speculation and railroad building. President Hayes appointed him governor of the Territory of New Mexico in 1878 and sent him to the territory to clean it up.

Lew Wallace, Union general and territorial governor of New Mexico, 1878–1881, wrote *Ben Hur: A Tale of the Christ* while he was living in Santa Fé and serving as governor. (Photo, copy of a *Harper's Weekly* portrait, courtesy New Mexico State Records Center and Archives, Shiskin Collection #22721)

Wallace is best remembered as the author of *Ben Hur: A Tale of the Christ*, which was written in Santa Fé while Wallace was serving as governor, 1878 to 1881. A street located near General Wallace Drive is called Ben Hur Drive.

Wallace was born in Brookville, Indiana, in 1827. He worked as a court and legislative reporter and studied law. During the Mexican War, he served as a volunteer in the Army. After the war, he practiced law and participated in politics.

When the Civil War began, he became adjutant general of Indiana, and he quickly won promotion to the rank of major general of volunteers. In 1864 he temporarily stopped a Confederate offensive at the Battle of Monocacy, probably saving Washington, D.C., from capture.

After the Civil War, he served as governor of the Territory of New Mexico (1878–1881) and as minister to Turkey (1881–1885).

Wallace died in 1905.

GOVERNOR DEMPSEY DRIVE

John J. Dempsey was born on June 22, 1879, in Whitehaven, Pennsylvania. He married, and the couple lived in Santa Fé. They had three children.

Dempsey worked as a water boy with a railroad crew at age thirteen. He worked in various positions with Brooklyn Union Elevator Company and served as vice-president of Brooklyn Rapid Transit Company, then as vice-president of Continental Oil and Asphalt Company, 1919–1920. He was an oil operator, 1920–1928, and president of United States Asphalt Corporation from 1928.

He was a member of the 74th Congress, elected at large in New Mexico, and he was re-elected in 1936.

He was a Democrat, and he served as governor of New Mexico for two terms, 1943–1947.

GRAN QUIVIRA

In April 1541 Coronado led his Spanish soldiers east to the Staked Plains of the Texas Panhandle in search of the golden cities that had been rumored to exist. Disappointed at finding no golden cities, he sent the main expedition back to New Mexico under the command of Captain Alvarado. He and thirty of his soldiers went on to Quivira, which was the home of the Wichita Indians in central Kansas. Greeted by the poverty of this group, he and his men realized that the cities of gold apparently did not exist.

GRANT AVENUE

Ulysses Simpson Grant, general of the United States Army during the Civil War and eighteenth president of the United States (1868–1877), is remembered in this street name.

Grant's connection to Santa Fé is that he and his family visited Santa Fé in 1880 and stayed at one of the officers' residences at Fort Marcy.

After graduating from West Point, he was assigned to the frontier in the Southwest; then he was in Zachary Taylor's 4th Infantry Regiment. He fought in the major battles of Mexico during the Mexican War.

During the Civil War, of course, he commanded the Union forces and accepted Lee's surrender at Appomattox.

GRIFFIN and GRIFFIN STREET

Born in Clarksburg, Virginia, in 1830, William W. Griffin came to New Mexico as a federal land surveyor. He was a businessman in Santa Fé, and he served on the first board of directors of the First National Bank of Santa Fé in 1871.

Griffin Street was once called Arny. (See Arny.)

GUADALUPE STREET

The street was named for the *Santuario de Guadalupe,* a chapel or sanctuary that was built in 1795–96. It was remodeled in 1880 or so and again in 1922, after a fire.

Santuario de Guadalupe was built in 1795–96 and gave its name to Guadalupe Street.

The church was dedicated to the Virgin of Guadalupe, the patroness of Mexico. It is said that she appeared miraculously to an Indian named Juan Diego near Mexico City in 1531.

HANCOCK

According to *Santa Fé Historic Neighborhood Study,* this street was named for John Hancock, one of the signers of the Declaration of Independence. The street was developed in the new subdivision created by Catron, Staab, et al., near the depot when the railroad came to Santa Fé in 1880.

HOPI ROAD

The Hopi Indians live about one hundred miles west of Gallup in the northern part of Arizona, in the land called Tusayan. The Hopi villages were built on three mesas, including the villages of Hano, Sichomovi, Walpi (the oldest of the Hopi towns), Mishongnovi, Shipaulovi, Shimopovi, Hotevila, and Bacabi.

The word *Hopi* is derived from the word *Hopitu,* which means "peaceful people." These people are home-loving, agricultural, and peaceful. Their silver jewelry work is distinctively different from the work of other tribes and is particularly attractive.

The Hopi believe in a number of kachinas or spirits, and they make replicas of these spirits, which they call kachina dolls.

HOUGHTON STREET

The roots of the Houghton family go far back in Santa Fé history. Joab Houghton was on the editorial committee, along with T. S. Johnson and publisher Céran St. Vrain, of an early issue of *The New Mexican* on May 5, 1850.

HYDE PARK ROAD

Benjamin Talbot Babbitt Hyde was born in New York City on November 23, 1872. He grew up in New York and married Helen Chauncey Bronson in 1918.

Always interested in the welfare of boys, he was a scoutmaster in New York before moving to Santa Fé in 1927. He continued scouting work in Santa Fé as well.

Hyde was a pioneer southwestern explorer and archaeologist. He and his brother first excavated the ruins at Chaco Canyon and owned the Pueblo Bonita ruin.

Because of his enthusiasm in working with boys, Hyde was loved by all and was fondly called "Uncle Benny."

He founded a nature center and Children's Nature Foundation in Santa Fé on the old Pinson ranch. He also worked in scouting for Indian boys.

Hyde died in an automobile accident on July 22, 1933. At his funeral, Boy Scouts served as the Guard of Honor.

This road was named for Hyde Park, which was named for Benjamin Hyde and which is located in the mountains a few miles out of Santa Fé.

INDUSTRIAL ROAD

In an industrial park off Cerrillos Road, this street was given a name that is descriptive of its surroundings. Nearby are All Trades Road, Trades West Road, and Calle de Comercia.

IRVINE STREET

A subdivision of small lots was platted by Alexander Irvine, who bought the land sometime between 1879 and 1881.

Irvine arrived in Santa Fé in 1871. He was a tinner by trade, and in 1872 he built a tin roof on the J. L. Johnson building, one of the first tin roofs of the city.

Irvine married Catherine McKenzie, daughter of Henry McKenzie.

ISLETA AVENUE

The street was named in honor of the Isleta Pueblo. The name is Spanish, meaning "little island." Located thirteen miles south of Albuquerque, Isleta is the largest of the Tiwa-speaking pueblos. It has about three thousand residents and 210,948 acres of land.

This avenue was named for Isleta Pueblo. St. Augustine Church is one of the oldest mission churches in the United States, having been established in 1613. Originally called St. Anthony, the church was destroyed during the Pueblo Revolt of 1680, though the walls remained. It was rebuilt in 1716 on the original walls and was renamed St. Augustine.

Isleta has occupied the same site since before Coronado explored the area in 1540. It was the only pueblo that did not join in the Pueblo Revolt of 1680.

J

JEFFERSON

Thomas Jefferson (1743–1826), third president of the United States (1801–1809) and first secretary of state, is commemorated in this street name, apparently given because of his important influence on the development of the Southwest.

During Jefferson's presidency, he acquired for the United States the huge Louisiana Purchase from France in 1803, thus moving United States-owned territory ever closer to New Mexico and the Spanish territories.

JIMENEZ

Jimenez street was a private lane originally, but it became a city street after World War II. It was probably named for the Jimenez family.

JOHNSON STREET

In 1879–1880, James L. Johnson, who owned property north of Johnson Street, had his property surveyed and subdivided into thirty-three building lots called the Choice Building Lots. Buyers of these lots included Alexander Irvine and Henry McKenzie. (See also Irvine and McKenzie streets.)

Johnson came to New Mexico in 1852 from Maryland and became a prominent merchant through trading on the Santa Fé Trail. He originally owned what is now called the Catron Block, but lost it through bankruptcy.

JOSE

José street was developed on the land once owned by José Durán. In 1912 the José Durán estate was subdivided among his heirs. In 1919 they made a subdivision and named this street.

KEARNEY AVENUE

This street was named for Brigadier General Stephen Watts Kearny. Somehow the name was misspelled with the second *e*, and that spelling has become the official name.

General Kearny led United States Army troops to claim New Mexico for the United States in 1846. He and his men marched on Santa Fé, where Mexican Governor Manuel Armijo capitulated without a fight.

KIVA ROAD

This street name honors a vital part of every permanent pueblo, the kiva or ceremonial room. *Kiva* comes from the Tusayan language.

KIVA ROAD

The Pueblo Indians believe that in past ages, their home was in a dim underground world and they had not yet become fully human. They believe that they emerged from some sacred spot. For many, this sacred spot is the sipapu, the hole in the kiva. Because of the belief that they came from underground, the kiva is always partially underground.

L

LA CONDESA

In the Bellamah addition, Dale Bellamah named one of his streets *Calle Princesa Juana,* Spanish for "Princess Jeanne," for his wife. (See Calle Princesa Juana.) Apparently the royal title of *Princesa* called to mind other royal titles, so three other streets bear royal names—*Calle Baronesa* ("baroness street"), *Calle Condesa* ("countess street"), and *Calle Reina* ("queen street"). Apparently it was intended to use a fifth royal name as well in order to develop the royal theme with the name *La Marquesina.* (See La Marquesina below.)

LA MARQUESINA

Apparently the street namer—whether it was Dale Bellamah or one of his employees—made a slight mistake in using his Spanish dictionary when choosing the name for one of the streets in the Bellamah addition. *Calle Princesa Juana, Calle Baronesa, Calle Condesa, Calle Reina,* and *La Condesa* all develop the theme of royalty by their being royal titles. Apparently, *La Marquesina* was intended to contribute to that theme as well. However, *La Marquesina* means "a glass canopy or porch." Obviously, the namer wanted the word for a marchioness or wife of a marquis, but that Spanish word is *la marquesa,* not *la marquesina.* So forever, it is presumed, the Bellamah addition will have a "glass canopy" through which the female royal names can be displayed.

LAGUNA STREET

After the Pueblo Revolt of 1680 and the Reconquest of 1692, Keresan-speaking refugees from Santo Domingo,

Laguna Street was named for Laguna Pueblo, located on a hilltop west of Albuquerque.

Ácoma, Cochiti, and other pueblos founded the Pueblo of Laguna. The Spaniards named the pueblo for a marshy lake located to the west. *Laguna* means "a pool or lagoon." The pueblo still occupies its original hilltop site. Laguna is the only pueblo which was created after the Spanish came to New Mexico.

LINCOLN AVENUE

Constructed in 1866 as a passage to the federal building, Lincoln Avenue was named in honor of the late President Abraham Lincoln, who had been assassinated just one year prior to the construction of this street.

LOS LOVATOS DRIVE

This street was named for the Lovato families who lived in the north part of Santa Fé. One of the Lovatos was Roque Lovato, who lived near Paseo de Peralta and Bishops Lodge Road.

LOVATO LANE

(See Los Lovatos Drive above.)

LUJAN STREET

Manuel Lujan was born in 1893 at San Ildefonso on property that his father had homesteaded. His parents—

Martin Lujan and Zenaida Sanchez—were native New Mexicans, born of parents who were native to the area.

He attended St. Michael's High School in Santa Fé, earning a diploma in 1911. He had a teaching career in the public schools and later became a clerk in the Santa Fé post office. He married Lorenzito Romero in 1915. His wife was a teacher, and he became a principal in Santa Cruz.

Lujan went into the insurance business and served as school superintendent of Santa Fé County for two terms.

In 1948 he ran for the office of governor but lost to Mabry. He was later chosen as commissioner of revenue, serving from November 1951 to December 1954.

He was active in the Sierra Club and was one of the founders and first president of the Santa Fé Boys Club.

M

MADRID LANE, MADRID PLACE, and MADRID ROAD

The Madrid family have been present in the Santa Fé area for much of the European history of the area. According to T. M. Pearce (*New Mexico Place Names*), Francisco de Madrid came to New Mexico shortly after the Oñate conquest, and he is the ancestor of the Madrid family which returned with the De Vargas Reconquest in 1692. One of De Vargas' captains, Roque Madrid, was interested in lead mines in the general area of the coal mines where the community of Madrid is presently located.

The community, located about twenty-four miles southwest of Santa Fé, was settled sometime around 1869. Its name probably commemorates the Madrid family as well as the capital city of Spain. The name of the community is pronounced *Mad'rid* instead of the usual *Ma-drid'*.

The community of Madrid was owned and operated by the Albuquerque and Cerillos Coal Company. Coal was discovered in Madrid in 1835, but it was not until 1869 that production really began. The Madrid mines produced coal steadily for some time following 1869.

Today, with little demand for coal, the mines are no longer producing. In the 1970s, Madrid was reborn when

artists appropriated the tiny shacks that had belonged to the miners. Now many of them house gift stores and antiques stores.

These streets in Santa Fé probably were named for a Madrid family.

MANSION DRIVE

The Executive Mansion or Governor's Mansion is located just off Mansion Drive. The new Executive Mansion was built on the north outskirts of Santa Fé in 1955. Previously, governors had lived in the Palace of the Governors on the plaza. Now the Palace of the Governors is the Museum of New Mexico.

The Executive Mansion was built on the northern outskirts of Santa Fé in 1955 and serves as home to the governor of New Mexico and his family.

MANSION RIDGE ROAD

Mansion Ridge Road connects with Mansion Drive and runs north through a hilly subdivision, along a ridge. Thus, it derives its name from its location.

MARCY STREET

When Brigadier General Stephen Watts Kearny took possession of Santa Fé and New Mexico on August 18, 1846, he ordered a fort built in Santa Fé.

MARCY STREET

During the early colonial days of Santa Fé, the area north of the plaza had been established as a *presidio* or military post. (The military barracks were mentioned in the Dominguez report on Santa Fé in 1776.) The *presidio* was rebuilt between 1789 and 1791, according to plans made by Governor Fernando de la Concha in 1787.

The United States Army reorganized and rebuilt various parts of the post for Kearny.

The fort was named, in 1891, for William L. Marcy, who had been United States Secretary of War.

In 1891 seventeen acres of the old Fort Marcy reservation were sold at public auction to L. Bradford Prince. The ruins of the fort and the lands surrounding the fort were sold to the city of Santa Fé in 1969.

MARQUEZ PLACE

The Márquez family are an old family of the area. *Sargento Mayor* Bernabé Márquez led a group of soldiers in attempting to protect the nearby town of Los Cerrillos during the Pueblo Revolt of 1680. They were forced to leave the Márquez hacienda and seek refuge in Santa Fé.

Lorenzo Márquez was living in Santa Fé at the time that he appealed to Governor Fernando Chacón for a land grant, along with fifty-one other people, at El Vado, near Pecos Pueblo. It was granted.

Chacón was governor in the 1790s.

McKENZIE STREET

The *Santa Fé Historic Neighborhood Study* says that the street was named for Henry McKenzie, father-in-law of Alexander Irvine, who platted a small subdivision on what became Irvine Street. McKenzie purchased a portion of the land in that subdivision.

According to Rosina Ransom Rodriguez ("My Name is Santa Fe . . ."), the street was named for William A. McKenzie, who came from Peoria, Illinois. He was in partnership with Irvine in a hardware business and occupied the only living quarters on that street, at 313 McKenzie.

MEDIO

In a small subdivision just off West Alameda Road, there are three parallel streets—Calle Don José, Medio, and Santa Fé River Road. *Medio,* Spanish for "middle," interestingly enough, lies in the middle between Calle Don José and Santa Fé River Road. Entré, "entrance," leads into the subdivision.

MEEM COURT

John Gaw Meem was born November 17, 1894, in Pelotas, Brazil. He married Faith Bemis of Boston, Massachusetts, and went to New Mexico in 1920 from New York.

He was educated at Virginia Military Institute, from which he received the Bachelor of Science degree in civil engineering. He also earned a Master of Fine Arts degree.

During World War I, he was a captain of infantry. He began practicing architecture in 1924, specializing in Spanish Pueblo styles. He designed La Fonda Hotel and the Laboratory of Anthropology in Santa Fé and the Fine Art Center in Colorado Springs. He was supervising architect for the University of New Mexico.

In 1930 Meem won a $400 prize for the best plans to remodel the buildings around the Santa Fé plaza in the "Santa Fé style."

Meem served in several professional organizations.

MESA VERDE STREET

The street remembers Mesa Verde, fittingly named because it is a large plateau that is covered with greenery of cedar, piñon, spruce, and yellow pine. The name is Spanish for "green table."

Located just over the state line in Colorado, the site was the home of the Mesa Verde culture. Large caves in the sandstone on the sides of the mesa sheltered entire villages, and quite an extensive culture existed at this site.

MIGUEL CHAVEZ ROAD

Miguel Chavez was a Santa Fé resident for whom the Miguel Chavez Parochial School was named. The school had been built by 1933 on the corner of Agua Fria and Guadalupe streets. Later the school building became the Mercado del Norte.

MONTEZUMA AVENUE

This street, along with Aztec Avenue, was named when Catron, Staab, et al., opened a subdivision near the depot when the railroad was brought to Santa Fé in 1880. (See Aztec Avenue.)

Montezuma II (*c.* 1480 to 1520) was the great-grandson of Montezuma I. Montezuma II, who ruled from 1502 to 1520, was Emperor of Mexico when the Spaniards came.

At first Montezuma II believed that Cortes was the White God of the Aztecs, and he welcomed the Spaniards with gifts. Later he attempted to keep Cortes out of his capital city, Tenochtitlán, but Cortes captured the city and Montezuma.

MOUNT CARMEL ROAD

This road lies in front of the Carmelite Monastery in the east part of the city and draws its name from the monastery.

N

NAMBE STREET

The name of this pueblo derives from Tewa *namby-ongwee,* meaning "people of the roundish earth." It is located about sixteen miles north of Santa Fé. The population is about 420, and the pueblo has 19,076 acres of land.

Nambe has been continuously occupied since about A.D. 1,300. It was active during the Pueblo Revolt of 1680, and the people there murdered their priest and destroyed their church.

Nambe is making a comeback in weaving and pottery making. Their pottery is black-on-black or white-on-red in style.

In 1951 the Nambe Pueblo created and began producing Nambe ware, beautiful and rather expensive designer-like serving pieces made of a pewter-like metal.

NAVAJO DRIVE

This street was named for the Navajo tribe of Indians, the largest tribe of Indians in the United States. The Navajo reservation, which consists of approximately fourteen million acres, is the nation's largest reservation. It is located in parts of New Mexico, Arizona, and Utah.

The ancestors of the Navajo migrated to the southwestern United States from what is now Alaska and Canada sometime around A. D. 1000, and by around A. D. 1200 they had migrated to the edge of the Pueblo world, causing a great deal of friction between themselves and the Pueblo people. The Pueblo Indians called them Apaches, or "enemies." One tribe of the Apache came to be called *apaches de nabahú*, later known as *Navajo* or *Navaho.*

The Pueblo people taught them to raise crops and to weave, though the women instead of the men in the Navajo tribe do the weaving.

NUSBAUM STREET

According to Rosina Rodriguez ("My Name Is Santa Fé . . ."), the street was named for Simon Nusbaum, one of the early Jewish settlers in New Mexico. Nusbaum worked in the surveyor general's office and became territorial treasurer. Later he served as postmaster.

He married Dora Rogers Rutledge in 1902, and they lived in a house on the corner of Washington and the street that was later to be Nusbaum.

According to La Farge (*Santa Fé*), Jacob Nusbaum apparently arrived in Santa Fé before Simon and worked as a clerk in Spiegleberg's store. He later became postmaster also. Perhaps Jacob and Simon were brothers.

Simon was born in Harrisburg, Pennsylvania, in 1844, and died in Santa Fé in 1921.

OLD PECOS TRAIL

Both the Old Pecos Trail and the Old Santa Fé Trail follow parts of the present-day Las Vegas Highway. Located some twenty-eight or so miles southeast of Santa

Fé, the Pecos area was the site of the Pecos Pueblo, which was the strongest pueblo in the fourteenth century and the easternmost inhabited village in the days of the Spanish Conquest. It served as the trading point between the Pueblo Indians and the Plains Indians. The old trail to Santa Fé from the Pecos Pueblo wound along what is now Old Pecos Trail.

The Pecos Pueblo was a huge quadrangular structure built sometime around 1348 (based on tree-ring dating). It consisted of two huge communal dwellings of four stories each. One contained 585 rooms, and the other contained 517 rooms.

Coronado conquered the Pecos Pueblo in 1540, and Fray Luis de Escalona remained there as a missionary in 1541.

It is believed that Pecos Pueblo was abandoned in August 1838 because of sickness and Comanche raids on the pueblo.

The Indians have an interesting story that explains the abandonment of the pueblo. According to pagan tradition, a huge snake lived in the *kiva* at Pecos Pueblo, and regular offerings were made to it, including human sacrifices of young childen. As the Indians embraced Christianity and drifted away from their religion, the sacred fire in the *kiva* went out and fewer human sacrifices of small children were made to the great snake deity that lived in the *kiva*. At one point, an epidemic had killed off most of the small children. The medicine man or *cacique* called for a sacrificial child and chose the son of his war captain. But the war captain had already given one of his children and had only one left. So he gave his son to the priest, who hid him and substituted a kid goat for the sacrifice. The sacred snake was not deceived, and he crawled out of the *kiva* into the Río Grande, followed it to its mouth, and disappeared into the Gulf of Mexico. The Indians say that the Galisteo River is the path that the snake made as he crawled away.

The Santa Fé Trail ended at the Plaza in Santa Fé.

OLD SANTA FE TRAIL

The Santa Fé Trail was opened in 1821 by William Becknell, an American trader, to transport goods from Missouri to New Mexico. The trail ended at the plaza in

Santa Fé, where now a plaque commemorates this bit of history.

ONATE PLACE

Don Juan de Oñate, after much preparation and waiting, led a group of settlers and priests to New Mexico in 1598. When he arrived at the Río Grande, he took possession of New Mexico in an elaborate ceremony, claiming it for the Spanish king.

They settled at the Pueblo of Ohke in July, at a place where the Río Grande and the Río Chama meet and renamed the site Don Juan Bautista. They erected a church building and dedicated it on September 8, 1598.

Oñate's expedition was a private one, one he had proposed, and he was governor.

Having fallen into disfavor with the Spanish government and with the prospect of removal from his position as governor, he resigned his post on August 24, 1607. Investigation into his conduct was begun in 1612, and in 1614 he was convicted of a number of charges. But later he filed appeals, and in 1622 his petition for leniency and restoration of his titles apparently was granted by the king.

ORTIZ STREET

The street was named in honor of Don Gaspar Ortiz y Alarid, a Santa Fé probate judge and wealthy land owner.

Don Gaspar Avenue also was named for him. (See story under Don Gaspar Avenue.)

OTERO STREET

Don Miguel A. Otero was the first New Mexico governor of Hispanic origin.

He was born October 17, 1859, in St. Louis, Missouri. He was educated at St. Louis University and at Notre Dame University.

He and his wife had one son, Miguel A. Otero, Jr.

Otero was a banker in Las Vegas, 1880–1885, and city treasurer of Las Vegas, 1883–1884. He served as governor of New Mexico, 1887–1906.

Miguel Otero was the first New Mexico governor of Hispanic origin, serving 1887–1906. (Photo courtesy New Mexico State Records Center and Archives, SRC Misc. Collection #54946)

PALACE AVENUE

The street was named for the Palace of the Governors, which stands on the north side of the Santa Fé plaza. It is an adobe structure that has stood at this place since the winter of 1609–1610, when Governor Don Pedro de Peralta founded *La Villa Real de la Santa Fé de San Francisco.*

According to *New Mexico,* a book prepared by the New Mexico Writers Project, the Palace has undergone a number of renovations but was finally restored in 1909 according to some old plans that had been found in the British Museum.

Originally, the Palace was the most important part of the *presidio,* which was the fortress built by the followers of Peralta. It extended east and west along the north side of the plaza for about four hundred feet and north and south more than eight hundred feet. The entire area was enclosed by an adobe wall, and all the buildings within the enclosed area were known as *Casas Reales,* or Royal Houses.

A *portal,* or covered porch, extended the entire length of the building. From this *portal,* many a prisoner of war was hanged. Presently Indians arrive each day and display their jewelry and pottery for sale along the *portal*. In mid-1993 a young boy took his mother's auto-

The Palace of the Governors was built in 1609–1610 and served as the seat of government for many governors. It is now the Museum of New Mexico. Pictured above, members of area Indian tribes display their jewelry and pottery for sale to tourists.

mobile without her permission and, in an alleged "joy ride," lost control of the car and hit the *portal*, doing substantial damage to it and requiring extensive repair.

The Palace of the Governors, now the Museum of New Mexico, has served as the home of six governments: The Spanish Empire, 1610–1680; The Pueblo Indians (following the Pueblo Revolt of 1680), 1680–1692; The Spanish Reconquest, 1692–1821; The Empire of Mexico, 1821–1822; The Republic of Mexico, 1823–1846; United States Territory of New Mexico, 1846–1907. The new executive mansion was built in 1907; so the governor no longer lived in the Palace of the Governors.

New Mexico became the forty-seventh state in 1912, but the Palace of the Governors was never the seat of government for the State of New Mexico.

In 1909 the New Mexico Legislature established the Museum of New Mexico and located it in the Palace of the Governors.

PASEO DE LA CONQUISTADORA

Spanish for "walk of the female conqueror," this name was borrowed from the name of the patroness of Santa Fé. De Vargas brought the statue of the patroness, *La Conquistadora*, with him when he arrived for the Reconquest of 1692. While the soldiers fought the Indians who maintained control of the Palace of the Governors, the women and children were praying to *La Conquistadora*. After the reconquest, De Vargas made a vow to repeat the procession annually on the first Sunday after the Feast of Corpus Christi, in thanksgiving for her making his mission a success. On this day, the statue is taken to the Rosario Chapel for a novena of masses and then returned to the cathedral.

PASEO DE LA SERNA

The Serna name has been of significance in northern New Mexico for many years. The first permanent Spanish settlement in the Taos Valley was established in 1725. It was originally called Las Trampas de Taos, but later became known as Los Ranchos de Taos. The settlement was developed on the Cristóbal de la Serna land grant, which was first granted to Fernando Durán y Chávez and his son, Cristóbal, who were the only Spaniards in the area to escape the Taos Valley during the Pueblo Revolt of 1680. However, they did not return to the Taos Valley after the Reconquest of 1692. Finally, in 1710, Governor José Chacón Vallaseñor awarded the land grant to Cristóbal de la Serna, a soldier.

Apparently his descendants also live in Santa Fé.

PASEO DE PERALTA

Don Pedro de Peralta was appointed governor of New Mexico in 1609, succeeding Governor Don Juan Oñate. Peralta was the founder of Santa Fé, and in recent years Paseo de Peralta, a sort of loop through Old Town Santa Fé, has been created. Paseo de Peralta was created in 1983 and following.

Peralta and a few settlers from San Gabriel selected a site on the north bank of the Río Santa Fé, at the southern end of the *Sangre de Cristo* ("blood of Christ") range of mountains. They called the town *La Villa Real de la Santa Fé de San Francisco* ("Royal Town of the Holy Faith of St. Francis").

They laid out the town in the spring of 1610. Peralta set up a government of four *regidores* (councilmen), two of whom served as *alcaldes ordinarios* (judges) to hear criminal and civil cases within the boundary of the villa. These officers were selected annually.

Each resident of the town was given two lots for house and garden, two fields for vegetable gardens, two others for vineyards and olive groves, and about 133 acres of land.

Peralta is commemorated in this street name.

PENA PLACE

Obviously the street was named for the Peña family, possibly for Sergeant Francisco de la Peña, who purchased the house at 831 El Caminoto in May 1845. When Peña died in 1887, his wife and eight children inherited the property. When his wife died in 1909, each of the six surviving children inherited a portion of the property.

PINO ROAD

Though *Pino* means "pine" in Spanish, this street was probably named for the Pino family. Miguel E. Pino is mentioned in an article about Santa Fé's reaction to Abraham Lincoln's assassination. He was listed as one of the vice-presidents of a huge meeting held in the plaza, in front of the Palace of the Governors.

PRINCE AVENUE

Le Baron Bradford Prince was born in Flushing, New York, in July 1840. He was a graduate of Columbia College School of Law.

Prince moved to New Mexico when he was appointed chief justice. He left for New Mexico on February 1, 1879, and opened a court at Santa Fé upon his arrival.

He was elected president of the University of New Mexico in 1881, and he served as governor of the territory, 1889–1893. During his term as territorial court justice, he was involved in some real estate transactions when Thomas B. Catron, Abe Staab, Robert Longwill, Luciana Baca, and Antonio Ortiz y Salazar developed a subdivision of lots east of the depot. Prince and William Berger sold the lots for the group.

In Santa Fé, streets were named for all of these men except Robert Longwill.

PROCTOR COURT

The street was obviously named for the Proctor family, probably for the Francis Proctor family. An article in *The New Mexican* mentions Mrs. Francis Proctor as treasurer of an Indian welfare benefit in August 1930.

QUEMADO STREET

The word *quemado* is Spanish for "burned." The word may have been applied to this street because of a burning off of brush. It could, however, have been named in honor of the town in north-central Catron County.

According to T.M. Pearce's *New Mexico Place Names,* José Antonio Padilla and his family moved from Belen in

1880 to a place which they called Rito Quemado because the *chamiso* or rabbitbrush had been burned on both sides of the creek. Later, the name was shortened to Quemado.

Another explanation is that the town is situated in the area of an extinct volcano, and the land around it appears to have been scorched.

Rito is Spanish for "ceremony."

QUINTANA

Captain Luis Quintana led the settlers at La Cañada (now Santa Cruz) to protect their settlements during the Pueblo Revolt of 1680.

The name was in the Santa Fé area during the 1600s, and the street obviously commemorates the family name.

Martin Quintana resided in Santa Fé during the mid to late 1800s. He was descended from pure old Mexican ancestry, according to Helen Haines in *History of New Mexico.*

Also, a Quintana family purchased a parcel of land in the 1920s, extending from W. San Francisco Street to the river, and built several houses there.

R

RANCHO SIRINGO DRIVE

Literally "Siringo Ranch" Drive, this street was named for the Siringo family, on whose property the subdivision was developed.

See Siringo Drive.

READ

Benjamin M. Read was a resident of Santa Fé during the early 1890s, owning a house at 309 Read Street. The street on which he lived was named for him.

A direct descendant of George Read, of Delaware, one of the signers of the Declaration of Independence, Read was a long-time member of the territorial legislature, a historian, and a prominent lawyer.

Originally Metropolitan Avenue, this street name was changed to Read Street sometime between 1912 and 1924.

RIO GRANDE AVENUE

Though the Río Grande does not actually flow through Santa Fé, the city does have a street named after the river that gives life to much of New Mexico.

The Río Grande stretches some 1,885 miles from its source to its mouth in the Gulf of Mexico. During the summers, the river is usually almost dry, if not totally dry, partially because much of its water is diverted into irrigation canals and partially because so little rain falls during the summer and fall. In the late spring, however, when the snow begins to melt in the high mountains, the river can become a raging torrent.

RIO VISTA PLACE and RIO VISTA STREET

Located in the Río Vista subdivision, these streets and the subdivision were so named because of their proximity to the Río de Santa Fé. Spanish for "river view," the names are descriptive.

RODEO PARK WEST and RODEO PARK EAST

These two streets form a circle of sorts in the small Rodeo Park subdivision, which derived its name from its location almost across the street from the rodeo grounds.

RODEO ROAD

Rodeo Road received its name because the Santa Fé Rodeo Grounds are situated along it, in the southwestern part of Santa Fe. The annual Rodeo de Santa Fé is held there during the early part of July. The annual Rodeo de Santa Fé was begun in 1950 and has continued since that time.

ROSARIO STREET (ROSARIO BOULEVARD and ROSARIO HILL)

The Rosario Chapel and Cemetery are located on this street. The chapel was built in 1806 and was intended to receive the statue of *La Conquistadora* when it was taken from the St. Francis Cathedral (and originally from *la parroquia,* the little church that once was on the site of the cathedral) to the site where De Vargas and the people involved in the Reconquest of 1692 had been camped while they were negotiating with the Indians for the surrender of Santa Fé.

De Vargas brought the statue of the patroness, *La Conquistadora,* with him when he arrived for the Reconquest of 1692. While the soldiers fought the Indians who maintained control of the Palace of the Governors, the women and children were praying to *La Conquistadora.* After the reconquest, De Vargas made a vow to repeat the procession annually on the first Sunday after the Feast of Corpus Christi, in thanksgiving for her making his mission a success. On this day, the statue is taken to Rosario Chapel for a novena of masses and then returned to the cathedral.

Spanish for "rosary," the name is a part of the name of the chapel, Our Lady of the Rosary.

ROYBAL STREET

The Roybal family have resided in Santa Fé for many generations. According to John Sherman (*Santa Fé: A Pictorial History*), a Roybal was a soldier from Spain who remained in Santa Fé after De Vargas and his men reconquered Santa Fé in 1692.

S

SALAZAR STREET

In anticipation of the development of a new commercial center around the railroad depot, Antonio Ortiz y Salazar, Luciana Baca, Abe Staab, Thomas B. Catron, and Robert Longwill developed a subdivision east of the depot. The lots were sold by L. Bradford Prince and Wiliam Berger.

Streets in the development were named for all of these men except Longwill.

SAN ANTONIO STREET

San Antonio Street, which lies next to San Pasqual Street, commemorates Saint Anthony. Although there were two

saints named Anthony, this one probably is Saint Anthony of Padua (1195–1231), who was a noted Franciscan scholar and teacher of theology. The priests who came to New Mexico to christianize the Indians were Franciscans.

Born in Lisbon, Portugal, of noble parents, Anthony was a great orator and reformer. He is reputed to have performed miracles.

SAN FELIPE AVENUE and CIRCLE

San Felipe, or Saint Phillip Neri, was a sixteenth-century priest of the city of Rome, and he is the patron saint of the first church in Albuquerque. Located on the *Plaza Vieja,* San Felipe de Neri Church was founded in 1706, and it has been in continuous service since its founding. It is claimed that mass has been said in this church every day since 1706.

Inside, the choir-loft stairway winds its way around the trunk of a spruce tree.

SAN FRANCISCO STREET

San Francisco Street runs beside the plaza and leads to St. Francis Cathedral. *San Francisco* is Spanish for "Saint Francis."

Saint Francis of Assisi (1181?–1226) founded the Franciscan religious order of the Roman Catholic Church. His simple life of poverty has inspired many, and many people admire him because of his respect for all living creatures.

Born in Italy, he was the son of a prosperous textile manufacturer. In 1202, after seeing a vision of Christ, he changed his way of life, disowning his father, rejecting his inheritance, and devoting his life to rebuilding churches and helping the poor. He adopted absolute poverty as his ideal and tried to pattern his life after the life of Christ by preaching the Gospel and healing the sick.

Pope Innocent III approved the formation of the Franciscan order by Francis in 1209 or 1210. Many of his followers became priests, but Francis remained a layman.

When the Spanish came to Mexico and to New Mexico to convert the Indians, they were accompanied

San Francisco Street leads to San Francisco (St. Francis) Cathedral. Photo was taken *circa* 1910. Note wood-laden burros, cathedral in background, and sign for Seligman's store. (See Seligman street in Albuquerque.) (Photo courtesy New Mexico State Records Center and Archives, R. H. Martin Collection #10206)

by Franciscan priests. In the Pueblo Revolt of 1680, many Franciscan priests were slain by the Pueblo Indians. (See Cross of the Martyrs.) Saint Francis is the patron saint of Santa Fé.

SAN ILDEFONSO ROAD

This road was named for the pueblo of the same name. The Tewa name is *pok-wo ghay ongwee,* "place where the water cuts through." The Spanish named the pueblo for St. Ildephonse, a seventh-century Archbishop of Toledo.

The pueblo is located twenty miles northwest of Santa Fé. A small pueblo, it has a population of only about 450; it is situated on 28,000 acres of land.

Noted for its pottery and the friendliness of its people, San Ildefonso is primarily an agricultural community, but many of the residents drive to Los Alamos for work.

SAN JUAN DRIVE

San Juan, the largest of the Tewa Pueblos, provided the name for this street. The name is Spanish for "Saint John the Baptist." The pueblo had a population of 1,700 in 1986 and consisted of 12,238 acres.

The Spanish established the first capital of New Mexico in San Juan in 1598, across the river from the present site. It was called San Gabriel at first, but later the name was changed to San Juan de los Caballeros.

SAN PASQUAL

San Pasqual (Saint Paschal) was pope of the Roman Catholic Church (817–824). He and Emperor Louis the Pious agreed to have free papal elections.

San Pasqual is the patron saint of kitchens.

The name *paschal* comes from the Greek name for the Jewish Passover, the season of the first Easter.

SANDIA STREET

Sandia is Spanish, meaning "watermelon." It is said that the name was given because, particularly when the evening sun shines on the reddish granite on the western face of the mountain, it resembles a slice of watermelon. Near the ridge or crest line at the summit, the thin layers

The Sandia Mountains, Spanish for "watermelon," stand sentinel just east and southeast of Albuquerque.

of pale limestone and a cover of dark-looking timber suggest a green rind, according to Marc Simmons.

The Pueblo Indians, however, perceived something different. They called the mountain *Oku Piñ,* "Turtle Mountain," as they saw the outline of the mountain as a turtle's shell. They believed the mountain holy and the home of many deities.

According to Erna Fergusson, granddaughter of Franz Huning, who was the developer of Huning's Highland Addition in Albuquerque, the mountains were referred to as *la Sierra de la Santilla,* "the mountain of the little saint." Other records give *Santo Dia,* "holy day"; and in the Spanish language, it is possible that *Sandia* could have derived from that phrase.

ST. FRANCIS DRIVE

St. Francis Drive was named for the patron saint of Santa Fé, Saint Francis of Assisi. (See San Francisco Street for story of Saint Francis.)

Saint Michael's Drive was named for San Miguel, the saint for whom San Miguel Chapel was named. The *Colegio de San Miguel* (Saint Michael's College) was originally located next to San Miguel Chapel (pictured). The original adobe walls and altar were built by Tlaxcala Indians from Mexico under the direction of Franciscan *padres, circa* 1610.

ST. MICHAEL'S DRIVE

St. Michael's College, *Colegio de San Miguel,* was founded by the Christian Brothers, who were brought to Santa Fé in 1859 by Archbishop Lamy. Originally this college for boys was adjacent to San Miguel Church.

In 1947 the college was divided into two campuses. The post secondary school moved to what is now St. Michael's Drive, and now it is known as College of Santa Fé.

Known as the oldest church in continuous use in the United States, San Miguel Church was built in 1626 for the use of the Spaniards' servants, the Tlaxcalan Indians. It was destroyed during the Pueblo Revolt of 1680. The present chapel was built in 1710, and the church has been maintained by the Christian Brothers since 1859.

SANDOVAL STREET

Anastacio Sandoval was a nineteenth-century resident of Santa Fé. He owned a large section of property in Santa

Fé and was a trader on the Santa Fé Trail. Sandoval died March 31, 1886.

SANGRE DE CRISTO

Located in the northern portion of Santa Fé, this street winds through the foothills of the Sangre de Cristo range of the Rocky Mountains. *Sangre de Cristo,* a Spanish name meaning "blood of Christ," is the name given to the mountains by early Spaniards because of the reddish cast of the mountains, especially at sunset.

SANTA FE RIVER ROAD

In a small subdivision just off West Alameda Road, Santa Fé River Road runs parallel with the Santa Fé River. Homes on that street back on the river.

SENA STREET

The Seña family is an old and prominent family in Santa Fé. Don Juan Seña owned a home on Palace Avenue, near the Palace of the Governors. It was built in 1840.

His son, José D. Seña, inherited the house in the mid-1800s. It was he who expanded the house to thirty-

Though the street is located several blocks from Seña Plaza, the street remembers the family of Don Juan Seña, who built the first part of the house in 1840.

three rooms to accommodate his twenty-three children. Though the street is located several blocks away, it was probably named for the same family.

Seña Plaza, on Palace Avenue, now is home to many shops.

SHELBY STREET

Colonel Valentine S. Shelby, born in Tennessee in 1827, moved to Santa Fé in 1869. He had been a colonel in the Union Army.

While in Santa Fé, Shelby was involved in a variety of financial endeavors. He was a partner in the famous Aztec mine with Governor William Thornton and Thomas Benton Catron. He was managing owner of the Palace Hotel, which was built in 1880 but later burned. And he was a director of the First National Bank.

Shelby died on December 3, 1896, in El Paso, Texas.

SHERIDAN AVENUE

According to Size and Spears (*Santa Fé Historic Neighborhood Study*), this street was named for Philip H. Sheridan, a Civil War hero who was later appointed chief-in-command of the United States Army and was made a full general.

Sheridan was born in Albany, New York, on March 6, 1831, and died August 5, 1888.

A famous cavalry officer, he was instrumental in defeating the Confederate army.

SIRINGO COURT (LANE, ROAD)

These three streets were named for the Siringo family of Santa Fé. Charley A. Siringo was a rather famous author of the early 1900s, publishing *A Cowboy Detective* in 1912 and *History of Billy the Kid* in 1920.

SIRINGO RONDO

Apparently *Rondo* is used here to mean "a circle road," though that word perhaps should be the feminine form *la ronda*. Nevertheless, the name describes a circular road in a subdivision developed on land once belonging to the Siringo family.

See Siringo Court.

SPARKS STREET

Ishmael Sparks introduced the telephone to Santa Fé in 1910. The street later became Alameda Street.

STAAB STREET

In anticipation of the development of a new commercial center around the railroad depot, Abe Staab, Thomas Benton Catron, Antonio Ortiz y Salazar, Luciana Baca, and Robert Longwill developed a subdivision east of the depot. The lots were sold by L. Bradford Prince and William Berger.

Streets in the subdivision were named for all of these men except Longwill.

T

TAOS STREET

Located in an area of streets named for Indian pueblos, this street commemorates the Taos Pueblo near Don Fernando de Taos.

According to T. M. Pearce (*New Mexico Place Names*), the word is a Spanish approximation of Tewa Indian words *tu-o-ta,* meaning "red willow place," or *tua-tah,* "down at the village." Most Taoseños seem to lean toward the "red willow place" meaning. Red willows do, indeed, grow in the area.

The pueblo is known as San Gerónimo de Taos. This is the pueblo that is the prototype, so to speak, of pueblos, the pueblo that most people see in their mind's eye when they think of pueblos.

The original old church built by Fray Pedro Miranda in 1617 was destroyed in 1680 during the Pueblo Revolt. A small church was built near the pueblo entrance in 1848.

Approximately two hundred people currently live at Taos Pueblo, without electricity or plumbing. They carry their water from a creek that flows nearby.

TESUQUE DRIVE

The Tesuque Pueblo gave this street its name. The *Tesuque* is a derivation of Tewa *tat' unge'onwi,* "spotted dry place." Located eight miles north of Santa Fé, the village has been occupied since A.D. 1250 to A.D. 1300. There are about three thousand residents and 16,813 acres of land at Tesuque.

Tesuque played an important role in the Pueblo Revolution of 1680. Two of its members were messengers to the other pueblos, using knotted ropes to coordinate the day for the revolt. When they left Tesuque, they carried with them ropes with knots in them, each knot representing a day. When the last knot was untied, it was the day for the revolt to occur, and all the pueblos were able to strike at the same time.

Tesuque pottery is generally small and brightly painted, though in recent years many of the potters have been returning to the old style.

TEWA ROAD

Tewa is one of the Tanowan group of tribes. The Tewa maintained a number of towns and villages in New Mexico.

TIJERAS ROAD

This street name honors Tijeras Canyon, which is located a few miles southeast of Albuquerque. Tijeras Canyon was once the site of a number of Indian agricultural villages, possibly as early as A.D. 900. It was the site of the Tijeras Pueblo, inhabited until about A. D. 1425, and the canyon was used as a camping place by the Apache in later years.

The name *Tijeras* means "scissors" in Spanish, possibly from the forking of the canyon near the village of Tijeras.

Another name for Tijeras is Carnué or Carnuel, possibly a corruption of a Tiwi Indian word.

TRADES WEST ROAD

Located in an industrial park off Cerrillos Road, this street was given a name that contributes to its surround-

ings. Nearby are All Trades Road, Industrial Road, and Calle de Comercio.

VEREDA DE COCHITI

Spanish for "path of the Cochiti," the name was given to honor the Cochiti Pueblo Indians. With the pueblo located about halfway between Albuquerque and Santa Fé, possibly the name was so given because this was once the walking trail of the Cochiti to and from their pueblo.

VIA ROBLES

In a subdivision of streets named for trees—Alder, Oak, Spruce, and Cedar—this street was given the Spanish name for "strong oak." *Via Robles* is Spanish for "road or way of the oaks."

VIGIL LANE

Donanciana Vigil was in the Santa Fé area in the early 1800s. He was a soldier of the Mexican period and was a prominent territorial politician, serving as territorial governor, 1847–1848.

In 1856 Vigil sold his property, which included a mill, to Vicente Garcia.

Vigil was custodian of land records in Santa Fé at one time. He managed to save many of the old papers of state records of property, ownership, etc., that had been carelessly handled or used to wrap meat.

WASHINGTON AVENUE

Colonel John M. Washington (born 1791 in Stafford County, Virginia) served as military and civil governor of New Mexico from October 11, 1846, to October 23, 1849. He was appointed to this position when the United States gained possession of New Mexico in 1846. (It was not until 1850 that New Mexico was organized as a territory and James C. Calhoun became the first territorial governor.)

Washington died with three officers and 178 enlisted men in a storm off the mouth of the Delaware River when he was washed overboard.

He was a distant relative of George Washington, his father being a second cousin of our nation's first president.

WATER STREET

Originally called Río Chiquito Street, this street was renamed Water Street in 1881. According to *Santa Fé Historic Neighborhood Study,* the street was so named because of waste water that collected there. The presence of waste water was a frequent source of complaints at City Council meetings during the late 1800s. The problem was not fully corrected until a modern public sewer was laid beneath Water Street.

Z

ZIA ROAD

Zia Pueblo is a Keresan-speaking pueblo located sixteen miles northwest of Bernalillo. It is the Zia sun symbol that appears on the New Mexico flag, license plates, and other places.

Zia is noted for its pottery, which strictly adheres to tradition. Typically unpolished red ware with a white slip partially overlaid, the pots are painted brown or a muted black.

The population of Zia is about eight hundred, and it contains 112,510 acres of poor land with limited irrigation water.

Zia's mission dates to 1692 with the Reconquest by De Vargas.

ZOZOBRA LANE

Zozobra is Spanish for "worry, anxiety."

The traditional burning of Zozobra, or Old Man Gloom, begins Fiesta in Santa Fé. (Technically, the word should be *Fiestas,* but most people refer to the time as Fiesta.) Fiesta takes place during the first two weeks of September and is held to commemorate the re-entry into Santa Fé by Don Diego De Vargas in 1692.

Zozobra, a huge effigy created originally by artist Will Shuster, is burned at Fort Marcy Park on Friday night, the first day of Fiesta, and the next few days are filled with religious and pagan activities. Fiesta resembles somewhat the frenzied period of activities of Mardi Gras in New Orleans.

"Que Vivan las Fiestas!"

ZUNI ROAD

This street name honors the Zuni Pueblo, which lies forty miles south of Gallup. It was the first pueblo to be seen by the Europeans, but it has resisted most outside forces. The Zuni people speak Keresan. They farm and do really fine inlaid jewelry; also they do some pottery making and weaving.

It is a large pueblo, with a population of near seven thousand people. Zuni includes 408,404 acres of land.

Taos

Though not incorporated as a village until 1932, the town of Taos has a history that dates back long before. The Taos Pueblo, of course, has been in existence for hundreds of years. It was already ancient when Alvarado and his men first saw it during the Coronado expedition in 1540–1542. European settlement of the Taos area was begun in 1617 when Fray Pedro de Miranda built a mission there.

Prior to the Pueblo Revolt or Rebellion of 1680, a settler named Don Fernando Durán y Chavéz was an important landowner in the area. His family was slain during the Pueblo Revolt, and he and his son, Cristóbal, were the only Europeans to escape the Taos Valley. Following the Reconquest of New Mexico by De Vargas in 1692, however, Don Fernando did not return. Finally, in 1710, Cristóbal de la Serna petitioned for a grant of land, referring to the previous owner of the land as Don Fernando.

Even though the Spaniards and the Indians had lived in close proximity, the church having been built near the pueblo, there was often bad blood between the Spaniards and the Indians. Finally, the Indians grew displeased with the frequency of intermarriages between the Spaniards and their children, and they asked the Spaniards to move away from the Taos Pueblo. They moved approximately two miles over to the Río de Don Fernando, and the village known as Don Fernando de Taos was established. This move apparently occurred sometime between 1777 and 1800.

The Taos Indians owned the *plaza* and the streets. In fact, it was reported that only in recent years have the

Indians given ownership of the streets to the town; they have retained ownership of the *plaza,* which at one time was the site of the trading fairs for Indians from all around the area, especially for the Plains Indians. The northernmost of the pueblos, Taos Pueblo today is home to approximately nine hundred people.

Gradually French trappers began arriving in Taos, originally to attend the Taos fairs and trade days. Eventually, however, many of them began settling in Taos. Following 1803 and the Louisiana Purchase, which was brought about by President Thomas Jefferson, the so-called "Mountain Men" began arriving in Taos. Usually these men were brave, hardy, and bewhiskered. And the Mountain Men did much for Taos. Some common names of the Mountain Men include Christopher "Kit" Carson, Céran St. Vrain, the Bent brothers, and many others.

The post office was established in 1852.

Over the years Taos has become an art colony, and it owes its position as an art colony primarily to Joseph Henry Sharp, a young painter who was sketching in New Mexico in 1880, and to an accident. Sharp had reported

San Francisco de Asis church in Ranchos de Taos is one of the most photographed churches in the United States.

North side of Taos Plaza, *circa* 1912. (Photo courtesy Kit Carson Memorial Museum, Taos)

to his friends Bert Phillips and Ernest L. Blemenschein so enthusiastically what he had heard about Taos that they decided to visit the little village. They took a train to Denver and set out in a wagon and camping outfit, painting as they proceeded south. About thirty miles from Fernando de Taos, a wheel on their wagon broke; Blumenschein was chosen by the flip of a coin to make the ride into Taos to have the wheel repaired. After a three-day trip into Taos for the repair, Blumenschein returned, convinced that Taos was the place where they should remain. So thanks to a broken wagon wheel, the Taos art colony was established. Over the years, the colony has continued to develop and has played a major role in the art of North America.

Ranchos de Taos, about four miles to the southwest of Fernando de Taos, is a part of Taos. It is the home of the famous Saint Francis of Assisi Church, one of the most-photographed and most-painted churches in the United States.

Taos is a resort in the summer and a ski resort in the winter, with excellent skiing nearby. Though it is busy in all seasons, it is still a small town. Allen Vigil, Town Planning Commissioner, reports that it has been just in the past ten years or so that signs with street names on them have been installed. Until that time, people did not really need street signs; they just knew the names of the streets, most of which were given for people who lived on those streets or for landmarks, such as spruce trees.

For many years, the blinking yellow light at the intersection of U. S. Highway 64 and New Mexico Highway 522 was *the* local landmark; now the town of Taos sports five traffic lights. And Rev. Norman Hollen, who lives near Kit Carson Memorial Cemetery and voluntarily tends Kit Carson's grave, reported that his gas bill still says, "Last house on Dragoon Street." Such is a part of the charm of Don Fernando de Taos.

A

ÁCOMA STREET

This street was named by the Randall family when Elisha P. Randall (1896–1971) developed Randall subdivision. The family chose American Indian names—Ácoma, Apache, Sipapu, Tewa, Toalne, Zia, and Zuni. According to John Randall, son of Elisha, "It was just something different [for Taos], I think."

Ácoma, "Sky City," is one of the desert pueblos of New Mexico, like the Zuni. Though first reported by Hernando de Alvarado in 1540, Ácoma was possibly founded before A. D. 1400 and is, therefore, one of the oldest continuously occupied towns in the United States. Located on a 357-foot-high mesa, approximately fifty-six miles west of Albuquerque, Ácoma was originally accessible only by a staircase cut into stone. Now the pueblo residents conduct tours by bus, with access by road.

The name comes from the Keres Indian language—*aki*, meaning "white rock," and *ma*, meaning "people." The name, then, means "people of the white rock."

ADOBE LANE and ADOBE ROAD

In Ranch Park subdivsion, created *circa* 1981, Wallace Chatwin and Rod Thomas chose Spanish surnames or Spanish generic terms for street names.

Adobe, of course, is a mixture of mud and straw traditionally used as building material in the southwest.

ALAMO LANE

This street name is a remembrance of the *alamo*, "poplar or cottonwood tree," that grows in areas where there is sufficient water throughout much of New Mexico.

ALBRIGHT STREET

The Albright family have long been in Taos. In the 1930s, Paul Albright and Ben Randall owned clay tennis courts where mostly Anglo children had tennis matches. Reportedly, the street was named by Melvin Weimer when he developed the area.

ALEXANDER STREET

Melvin Weimer owns a great deal of property around Taos. He developed a small addition of three streets in southwest Taos and named the streets for his daughter, Dea, and his two sons, Alexander and Reed.

ANAYA ROAD

According to Fayne Lutz, of the local historical society, this is a family name that has been in New Mexico for a long time.

There was an Anaya family in the Bernalillo area before the Pueblo Revolt of 1680, but all members of that family were slain during the Revolt.

ANGLADA LANE

The Anglada family have been in northern New Mexico for three hundred years or so, and this lane is named for some of that family.

APACHE STREET

This street was given an Indian name by the Randall family when Elisha P. Randall (1896–1971) developed the Randall subdivision. (See Ácoma.)

APACHE STREET

The Apache tribes were nomadic invaders who had migrated to the edge of the Pueblo world by around A. D. 1200, causing a great deal of friction between themselves and the Pueblo tribes. They were called Apaches, or "enemies," by the Pueblo people. One tribe of the Apache came to be called *apaches de nabahú*, later known as *Navajo* or *Navaho.*

There are Apache reservations in two parts of New Mexico.

ARCHULETA DRIVE

This drive was named for the prominent Archuleta family. Fayne Lutz of the local historical society says that the Archuleta family have been in New Mexico for probably 350 years, going back to the *conquistadores.* Even today there are two pages of Archuleta families in the telephone directory.

Juan de Archuleta is cited in Taos history as early as *circa* 1650. According to Twitchell (*The Leading Facts of New Mexico History*), some trouble had occurred at Taos; as a result, certain prominent families had migrated eastward. Juan de Archuleta was sent by Governor Peñalosa to take them back to Taos.

ARROYO COYOTES DRIVE

This street was named for Arroyo Coyotes, which it borders. An arroyo is a stream, brook, or watercourse, which is usually dry in New Mexico except after rains. Apparently the watercourse was given its name because of the presence of coyotes in the area, though it is interesting to note that in northern New Mexico Spanish, *coyote* is a word that refers to a person who has one Indian parent and one Hispanic or Anglo parent.

B

BACA LANE

The Baca family have been prominent in Taos for many years. Fernando "Fred" Baca served as mayor of Taos from 1940 to 1942 and 1952 to 1954, and Fred Baca Park is named for him.

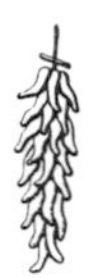

BARELA LANE

Patrociño Barela was born in Bisbee, Arizona, in 1902. He moved to Taos in 1911, and it is believed that he was in and out of Taos for a time. It is known for sure that he was a resident of Taos between 1930 and 1964, the year that he died.

Barela was a renowned woodcarver; and in the view of many art scholars, Barela was one of the greatest artists ever to have worked in New Mexico.

A self-taught artist, he was something of a primitive who happened to work in a stylistically modernist way.

It is said that he was often given to hard drink and that he sometimes would trade one of his now-almost-priceless woodcarvings for a bottle of liquor.

This street in historical Taos remembers Patrociño Barela, woodcarver.

BEIMER STREET

According to Gary Beimer, the street was named for his grandfather, Benjamin J. ("B.J.") Beimer (1854–1950). Beimer came to Taos in the early 1920s from Eagle Nest, where he had served as justice of the peace and as marshal.

A plasterer and contractor, he built and plastered a large percentage of the homes in Taos.

Charles Bent, acting governor of New Mexico, was slain in the Taos Indian Revolt of 1847. Having been scalped alive and with arrows protruding from his body, Bent was attempting to crawl through a hole in an adobe wall. (From a full-length portrait of Charles Bent in formal clothing, painted by Lotave in 1910, presented to be hung in the council chamber of the state capitol. Photo courtesy New Mexico State Records Center and Archives, SRC Misc. Collection, #9467)

BENT STREET

With the coming of the Americans, Indians and many Spanish alike were displeased, and plans were made for a revolt in December of 1846. Tomás Ortiz, Colonel Diego Archuleta, members of the Pino family, some of the Armijos from Albuquerque, and several clergymen, including Padre Antonio José Martínez were involved. Originally, the plot was to kill acting governor Charles Bent and Colonel Price on December 19, but it was postponed to Christmas Eve. The plot was discovered, but nothing happened. Governor Bent journeyed from Santa Fé to Taos to spend Christmas at home, thinking that nothing would happen. However, on January 19,

1847, an uprising in Taos occurred, and Governor Bent and five other men of importance were slain.

Bent reportedly was attempting to crawl though a hole in the adobe wall of his home, with arrows protruding from his body and after having been scalped while still alive. According to his daughter, Teresina Scheurich, the women had dug through the adobe wall of the house with a poker and an iron spoon. Mrs. Bent and their daughters escaped through the hole into an adjoining building.

Bent Street recalls the memory of Governor Charles Bent, and nearby Martyrs' Lane honors Bent and the others who were slain in the Taos Revolt. Others slain with him were Louis Lee, acting sheriff of Taos; Cornelio Vigil, prefect; J. W. Leal, district attorney; Pablo Jaramillo, a brother of Mrs. Bent; and Narcisco Beaubien, a son of Don Carlos Beaubien, circuit judge.

A native of Virginia, Charles Bent was born in 1797 in Charlestown. He graduated from the United States Military Academy at West Point and served in the Army for a time. He resigned from the Army and operated a mercantile business in St. Louis.

In 1832 Bent went to Santa Fé and, with his brother William, opened a general merchandising store in Santa Fé. He also was a business partner with Céran St. Vrain.

Bent was married to María Ignacio Jaramillo.

When he was killed, he was buried in the National Cemetery in Santa Fé.

BROOKS STREET

Frank Brooks operated a slaughterhouse at the end of this street in the 1920s and 1930s. His descendants still live in the Taos area.

BUENA VISTA DRIVE

This short residential street in the southeast part of town affords a beautiful view of the Sangre de Cristo mountains, and its Spanish name, which means "good view," was aptly chosen.

BURCH STREET

There was a Burch who was a merchant in Taos in the 1870s or 1880s and who was a member of a prominent Spanish family. The original Burch settler may have been one of the mountain men from the early part of the nineteenth century. In Kit Carson Cemetery there are graves for Sarah B. Burch (1874–1927) and Juneth Burch (1914–1926).

C

CALLE ALVARADO

Captain Hernando de Alvarado was with Coronado's expedition when he came to New Mexico in 1540. Coronado's main camp was at Zuni, and Coronado sent a reconnaissance party under Alvarado's leadership.

Alvarado was in charge of the mule-powered artillery in Coronado's expedition. He was one of the first Europeans to see Taos Pueblo.

CALLE CONQUISTADOR

In a small addition just off Cruz Alta Road, the streets were named for New Mexico history, including Camino Coronado, Camino Cortez, Calle Alvarado, and Ledesma Lane.

This street was named for the Spanish conquerors, especially Hernando Cortes.

CALLE DE ORO

Builder Rod Thomas developed this subdivision which includes streets with names somewhat on the order of those that Colonel Walter Marmon gave some of the streets of Albuquerque—names of minerals which have been exported from New Mexico. These minerals include *oro,* "gold," *plata,* "silver," and *cobre,* "copper."

CALLE DEL LLANO

Spanish for "street of the plain or flatland," this name is descriptive of the area around it.

CALLE DEL MONTE

Next to Calle del Llano lies Calle del Monte, Spanish for "street of the mount." From this subdivision, the mountains on the south side of Taos are clearly visible.

CALLE DEL SOL

In the same subdivsion with Calle del Llano and Calle del Monte, Calle del Sol, Spanish for "street of the sun," bears a descriptive and attractive name.

CAMINO CORONADO

In a small addition just off Cruz Alta Road, the streets were named for New Mexican history, including Camino Cortez, Calle Conquistador, Calle Alvarado, and Ledesma Lane.

In 1540 Francisco Vásquez de Coronado led an expedition into the Southwest in search of the Seven Cities of Cíbola and Gran Quivira, which had been reported to be rich in gold. He visited what are now Arizona and New Mexico and found no golden cities, only Indian pueblos.

CAMINO CORTEZ

In the same small addition, this street honors another character from Spanish and Southwest history.

Hernando Cortes (Cortez) was a Spanish adventurer (1485–1547) who conquered Mexico. He governed Mexico (New Spain) for a time, and the king of Spain titled him Marquis of the Valley.

Eventually Cortes fell out of favor with the king and returned to Spain in 1540 to defend himself. His rights were not restored, however.

CAMINO DE LA PLACITA

One of the main thoroughfares through Taos, this street derives its name from *La Placita,* Spanish for "little place or plaza," which is a small community located about two miles north of the Taos plaza. The name means "road to (of) the little plaza."

CAMINO DE LA SERNA

The Serna family provided this street name.

The first permanent Spanish settlement in the Taos Valley was established in 1725. It was originally called Las Trampas de Taos, but later became known as Los Ranchos de Taos. The settlement was developed on the Cristóbal de la Serna land grant, first granted to Fernando Durán y Chávez and his son, Cristóbal, who were the only Spaniards in the area to escape the Taos Valley during the Pueblo Revolt of 1680. However, they did not return to the Taos Valley after the Reconquest of 1692. In 1710 Governor José Chacón Villaseñor awarded the land grant to Cristóbal de la Serna, a soldier.

CAMINO DE SANTIAGO

In Rancho Park subdivision, developers Wally Chatwin and Rod Thomas named the road for Saint Santiago, for whom Saint Santiago Episcopal Church was named.

Santiago liberated Spain from the Moors. In New Mexico he is the protector of the settlers on the frontier. He is believed to have been seen in several battles with the Indians. And he symbolizes the introduction of the horse and its powerful attributes to the pueblos.

Santiago is St. James. According to Marc Simmons ("Santiago: The Saint of Conquest"), the wagon train of settlers belonging to the colonizing effort of Don Juan de Oñate was led by a page carrying a banner on which were emblazoned Oñate's coat of arms and a picture of Santiago riding his charger.

CAVALRY ROAD and CAVALRY COURT

This street name is a remembrance of the cavalry that was stationed at nearby Fort Burgwin, which is now a research center on State Road 3. Fort Burgwin was built during the post-Civil War period for protection of the Taos Valley. It was occupied by United States forces for only about ten years. It was designed to protect the people of the area from marauding Indians, especially those from the eastern plains.

CHAPEL LANE

The Chapel of Our Lady of Sorrows (*Nuestra Capilla de la Señora de Dolores*) is located on this lane off Witt Road near Kit Carson Lane.

CHARLOTTE LANE

This street was named about 1988 for Charlotte Sanchez, descendant of an old Taos family.

CHATWIN LANE

Wallace Chatwin and Rod Thomas created this street in 1981 and named it for Wallace "Wally" Chatwin.

CIVIC PLAZA DRIVE

Once known as Armory Drive because the armory was situated there, the street has been renamed Civic Place Drive since the armory was converted into an auditorium. The Civic Plaza consists of a swimming pool, auditorium, and other halls.

COBRE STREET

This street lies in a subdivision developed by builder Rod Thomas. He named three of the streets for minerals that have been exported from New Mexico over the years. Much as Colonel Walter Marmon named streets in Albuquerque for native minerals, Rod Thomas chose a similar tactic in Taos. *Cobre* is Spanish for "copper," and it lies next to *Calle de Oro*, "street of gold," and *Plata* "silver" Street.

CONRAD LANE

The Conrad family lived along this lane.

CORDILLERA ROAD

La Cordillera is Spanish for "mountain chain or range." A community near Taos is called Cordilleras, in the plural form, though the road uses the singular form. The road may have been named for the community, though certainly it could have been named for the mountain ranges that are prominent around Taos.

CORDOBA

The lane was named for the Cordoba family who live in Taos. Dalio Cordoba once operated a grocery store in the town.

CORTEZ ROAD

It is believed that Cortez Road was named for a Cortez family who lived there rather than for Hernando Cortes, the explorer.

D

DE TEVES LANE

Though the street is De Teves, the name of the man for whom it was named is De Tevis, with an *i* instead of a second *e*.

Peter Joseph De Tevis was born in St. Michael, in the Azores Islands, in 1814. He established a trading post in Taos in 1840 and participated in overcoming the insurrectionists of the Taos Rebellion in 1847. He was a close friend of Kit Carson, and he served on Carson's behalf as an Indian agent on three of Carson's appointments in 1854, 1857, and 1858. De Tevis died in Fernando de Taos on January 21, 1862.

DEA LANE

Melvin Weimer owns a great deal of property around Taos. In a small addition consisting of three streets, he named the streets after his daughter, Dea, and his two sons, Alexander and Reed.

DEL NORTE

(See Thomas Trail.)

DES GEORGES PLACE

The prominent Des Georges family came to Taos from Germany shortly after the Civil War. Esteban Des Georges (1847–1921) and his wife, Soledad (1856–1928), were buried in Kit Carson Cemetery.

Joseph A. Des Georges served as mayor of Taos from 1954 to 1956.

DOLAN STREET

In the late 1800s and early 1900s, Pete Dolan owned a grocery store, which was bought by Rudolph Liebert, Dolan's brother-in-law, upon Dolan's death. The grocery store was located on Pueblo Road North.

Next door to Pete Dolan's store, Dr. Dolan and Dr. Bergman shared an office.

Descendants of the Dolans are still active in Taos life.

DON FERNANDO STREET

Don Fernando Durán y Chavéz was an early pioneer settler, and a stream in the upper valley, Río de Don Fernando, was also named for him. Between 1777 and 1800, Spanish families began moving from near the Taos Pueblo to nearby Río de Don Fernando; they also began calling the Spanish settlement *La Plaza de Don Fernando de Taos*. What is generally known as Taos is really Don Fernando de Taos, and this is a street in the town.

DOÑA ANA DRIVE

A popular place name in New Mexico is Doña Ana. Apparently the name memorializes Doña Ana Robledo, who, according to *New Mexico Place Names*, was a legendary woman who was reputed to have lived in this

place a few miles north of Las Cruces during the seventeenth century. She was outstanding for her charity and good deeds and for opening her home to soldiers.

Also the governor of Chihuahua issued a land grant that was known as *El Anco de Doña Ana.*

DOÑA LUZ STREET

Doña Luz Martínez y Lucero lived on Kit Carson Road. The site of her home is now La Doña de Taos. El Rincón ("the corner") was the first trading post in Taos, located next to present-day La Doña de Taos.

DRAGOON LANE

Lying between the Kit Carson Cemetery and Kit Carson Road, this street was named in honor of the soldiers who were killed or who served in the campaigns of the First United States Dragoons against the Mexicans and Indians near Taos in 1847 and 1854.

(See Bent Street.)

The First Dragoons were led by Zachary Taylor and Brigadier General Stephen Watts Kearny in 1846.

DUANE STREET

The street was named for Duane Van Vechten Lineberry, wife of Ed Lineberry. According to one source, she was an Armor Meat Packing heiress who married Ed Lineberry in 1941, and they moved to Taos. For a time, Ed operated the Mariposa Supermarket on North Pueblo Road, and Duane built the Kachina Lodge in Taos. They lived on an eighteen-acre estate called *El Rancho de la Mariposa de Taos.*

ESPINOSA ROAD

According to Fayne Lutz of the local historical society, this road was named for the Espinosa family who lived there.

FAUSTIN ROAD

The street remembers Faustin Gonzales, who operates school buses in Taos.

FERNANDEZ LANE

Often the name Don Fernando de Taos has been mistakenly called Don Fernandez de Taos. (See story at Don Fernando Street.) This lane may have been named for the Fernandez family, however.

FRESQUEZ ROAD

Fayne Lutz, of the local historical society, reports that this street was named for a local Fresquez family.

FRONTIER ROAD

Frontier Oil Company came to Taos in the 1920s and built a motel by that name. The street beside the motel is called Frontier Road.

G

GARCIA LANE

The lane was named for the Garcia family in north Taos.

GERONIMO LANE

The lane was named in honor of the patron saint of the church at the Taos Pueblo, San Geronimo or St. Jerome. Some say that the church was a mission, but Fayne Lutz of the local historical society maintains that it was never a mission church. The church was founded by the Franciscans in 1598.

During the Rebellion of 1847, the church was destroyed by United States troops when the rebelling Indians sought refuge in the church.

On September 30 every year, the Taos Pueblo celebrates San Geronimo Day. Originally it was a fall trading day held at the plaza in Taos (The Indians still own the plaza and, until recently, owned the streets of the town);

then it was moved to the Pueblo. It was a time when neighboring tribes would gather for trading.

After colonization by the Spanish, San Geronimo Day became an institution, and the original rituals became incorporated with the rituals of the church. Races are held in the morning, and in the afternoon the pole climb is a popular event. In general, it is a day of fun and activities nowadays.

GUSDORF ROAD

Alex Gusdorf was the first Gusdorf to operate a store in the area. According to John Sherman (*Taos: A Pictorial History*), he built a three-story, steam-operated flour mill on the Ranchos de Taos plaza in 1879, the first in the territory. In 1895 his flour mill burned, and he moved to Don Fernando de Taos and opened a general merchandise store, located on the plaza where the Plaza Food Store was later operated. Alex sold his store to his younger brother, Gerson, Frank Bond, and John H. McCarthy in 1905, but Gerson left the partnership that same year and opened his own store. Alex also served as the president and chairman of the board of First State Bank of Taos. He died in 1923.

Alex Gusdorf's steam-operated mill was built on the Ranchos de Taos Plaza in 1879. It was the first steam-operated mill in the territory. (Photo courtesy Kit Carson Memorial Museum, Taos)

GUSDORF ROAD

The Gusdorf family came from Westphalia, near Hanover, Germany; Alex and Gerson were the sons of Joseph and Sophia. Gerson Gusdorf was born in 1869 and died in 1951.

According to Rebecca Salsbury James in "Allow Me to Present . . . ," Gerson had heard about life in New Mexico from his older brother, Alex. In 1885 he decided to come to the United States. He arrived in New York in 1885, where he remained for six months while he learned English; then he set out for New Mexico.

He worked in Ranchos de Taos for Alex for three years; then he became a traveling salesman for his uncles, A. and Z. Staab, of Santa Fé. With a wagon loaded with merchandise, he traveled from place to place throughout northern New Mexico and southern Colorado, selling clothing and fabric in small communities to people who had little opportunity to purchase goods elsewhere.

After three years on the road, he opened a store in Amizett, a small mining community located seventeen miles from Taos. Then he followed the gold boom to Red River, where he was proprietor of another store until that gold boom collapsed. He then became sheep and wool buyer for the Bond Brothers of Española until 1905 when he became part owner of his brother's former store.

When he left Alex's store, he opened his own store, called "The Largest Store in the World away from a Railroad." Later that store was converted into a huge, elaborate hotel, complete with paintings by Taos artists in the lobby. The hotel burned in 1933.

Gerson was married to Emma in 1907. She was the daughter of a Bavarian merchant who had settled in Mora, New Mexico.

Gusdorf Road honors the Gusdorf family.

GUYORA LANE

Guy and Ora Lund created a small subdivision in the 1950s, and this street name is a combination of their given names. (See also Lund Street.)

HACIENDA ROAD

This road leads from Lower Ranchitos Road to the Martínez Hacienda, built by Severino Martínez, the father of

Padre Antonio José Martínez. Work on the hacienda was begun in 1804. The hacienda was constructed as a fortress, as Indian raids were still common during that time.

The Martínez Hacienda is now a museum and national historic landmark.

HATCHERY ROAD

The road was named for the fish hatchery which was operated by the Siler family at this site near the springs just off Ranchitos Road. (See Ojitos Road and Siler Road.)

HILL DRIVE

Buford Hill developed some homes in Villa View Estates, and the street name is reminiscent of his family name.

HINDE PLACE

In the 1920s or so, according to Fayne Lutz of the local historical society, this street was named for the Hinde family. No one by that name currently resides in Taos, however.

J

JARAMILLO LANE

A family of writers and musicians, the Jaramillo family have long lived in Taos. Kit Carson married Josefa Jaramillo in the early 1800s, and Governor Charles Bent was married to her sister, María Ignacio Jaramillo.

Many Jaramillo families still live in Taos and in the valley surrounding Taos.

JOSEPH STREET

It was reported that this street was named for Pete Joseph of Cañon.

JUAN LARGO LANE

Juan Largo is Spanish for "Long John," and the name is reminiscent of "Long" John Dunn, one of the more

colorful personages of Taos. Born in Texas in 1867, John Dunn was dubbed "long" because of his stature and general looks. He was six-feet-four-inches tall and had long arms, a long nose, and long ears.

Long John Dunn ran afoul of the law when he was involved in a fight with his brother-in-law, who frequently beat Dunn's sister. In the fight, Dunn accidentally killed the brother-in-law. He was sentenced to life imprisonment, but escaped after having served only six months. He stole some guns and a horse and headed for Mexico, where he became involved in smuggling, but he gave up smuggling when his partner was killed by an assailant one night.

Returning to Texas, Dunn discovered that he was still wanted by the law; so he went to New Mexico, eventually ending up in Taos in 1889.

While in the Taos area, he saw a bridge that crossed the gorge at the junction with Taos Creek. He wanted to buy the bridge and set up a stage coach line to connect with the Chili Line (the railroad from the Taos area northward to Colorado). However, the owner wanted $15,000 for the bridge, an amount that Long John did not have.

In an effort to raise that much money, he first went to Red River, which was experiencing a gold boom, and tried to earn money at gambling. From there, he went to Montana and Wyoming and drifted on out to California and Nevada before returning to Taos.

Back in Taos, he met Myers, the owner of the bridge, again and found the price much lower—$2,200.

Larry Lopez (*Taos Valley*) recounts the anecdote that Long John made a deal with Myers that if Long John could find a buyer for the bridge, Myers would give him $100 commission. The next day he bought the bridge for $2,200 but received a refund of $100. Myers had been duped.

Long John began a stage coach line that connected Taos to the Chili Line, through the use of his bridge. He also charged tolls for use of the bridge.

Upriver a few miles, another bridge had been built, and Long John bought that right-of-way as well.

And at the site where the Río Grande and Arroyo Hondo confluence, he built another bridge at Servilleta. He convinced the railroad to build an additional siding there. Dunn built a hotel at that site, and he created roads that switched back and forth in hairpin curves down the sides of the gorge.

Perhaps he was the first big tourism operator in Taos.

Dunn died on May 21, 1953, at the age of ninety-five. His body was buried in Kit Carson Memorial Cemetery in Taos.

K

KARAVAS ROAD

The Greek Karavas family once lived along this road, but no one by that name currently resides in Taos. In the 1920s John Karavas was a resident of Taos; and during the oil boom in Borger, Texas, he moved there and operated a cafe for a time before returning to Taos.

KIT CARSON ROAD

Famous in Taos and in northern New Mexico in general, Kit Carson was one of the mountain men who came to Taos in the early 1800s. (Photo courtesy Kit Carson Memorial Museum, Taos)

Christopher "Kit" Carson was the most famous of the mountain men in Taos, arriving there in 1826. He had been a runaway apprentice saddler from Missouri when he went to the mountains.

Carson was first married to an Arapaho woman named Waa-nike, but later married a Taoseña named Josefa Jaramillo. They had eight children.

He served as John Fremont's guide on the trip to California and was an Indian fighter. He spoke several Indian languages and served as Jicarilla Apache Indian Agent on three appointments, in 1854, 1857, and 1858.

Carson died of an aneurism in 1868, just a month after Josefa had died of complications in childbirth. They died near Fort Lyons in Colorado and were buried there, but their remains were returned, within the year, to Taos, where they were buried in Kit Carson Memorial Cemetery. The Kit Carson house is now a museum on Kit Carson Road.

KKIT LANE

This street was named for KKIT radio staion, 1340 AM, which is located on this street. According to Stuart Jones, an employee, they thought of naming the street Memory Lane because frequently they play "oldies," but they

decided on KKIT Lane. The station was founded in 1961, but the street was named in the early 1970s.

L

LA LOMA ROAD

La Loma, Spanish for "the hill," is the name given to this street because the area around the Plaza and this street is situated on a hill. The name was given as a description of the surroundings.

LA LUZ DRIVE

The La Luz family name goes far back in the history of Taos. Padre Martínez (See Padre Martínez Lane) married María de la Luz Martín. This street lies adjacent to Padre Martínez Lane and obviously was named for Padre Martínez's wife's family.

LAS CRUCES ROAD

This road was named in honor of the crosses associated with *La Morada,* which is located at the end of Las Cruces road, off in a field. The nearby cemetery also contains

The crosses in the cemetery of Jesus the Nazarene gave Las Cruces Road its name.

many crosses; and, of course, the *Calvario* associated with *La Morada* utilizes the crosses. (See Morada Road for story of *La Morada*.) Thus, the name, which means "the crosses," is significant.

LAVADIE ROAD

According to F. R. Bob Romero ("A Brief History of Taos"), the original Lavadie was a mountain man, a trapper who, when the fur trade declined in 1830, settled in Taos. Even today, several Lavadie families live in Taos and in the valley.

LEATHERMAN AVENUE

When Guy and Ora Lund created a small subdivsion off Lund Street in the 1950s, they named one of their streets for the Leatherman family who lived on the avenue.

LEDESMA LANE

José de Ledesma was attorney for Captain Valverde, who was appointed captain of the El Paso presidio. He was a friend of De Vargas, and he lived in Santa Fé for some time. Governor Cubero did not want him in that position because of the friendship of Valverde and De Vargas.

Perhaps this street in Taos was named for José de Ledesma or for some of his descendants in later years.

In 1993 Angel Ledesma lived on nearby Calle Conquistador but refused an interview regarding the name.

LEDOUX STREET

According to F. R. Bob Romero ("A Brief History of Taos"), the original Le Doux was a mountain man, a trapper who, when the fur trade declined in 1830, settled in Taos.

Skip Miller, Curator of Kit Carson Memorial Museum, says that Julian, Antoine, and Abram are LeDoux names that have surfaced frequently in the history of Taos and that the *d* occurs as both a capital letter and a lower-case letter.

Today, several LeDoux families reside in the Taos valley.

LIEBERT STREET

The street was named for the Liebert family, who were merchants. Aloys A. Liebert was born June 11, 1846, in Baden, Germany. Liebert married María Piedad Ledoux de Liebert (1857–1906). Aloys died on May 22, 1905. Only one Liebert still lives in Taos in 1993.

In 1882, Aloys Liebert built the Liebert Hotel; later, the name was changed to the Columbia Hotel.

LINDA VISTA LANE

The Spanish name *Linda Vista* means "pretty view." It is a generic, descriptive name, but one would have difficulty finding in Taos a place that does not provide a pretty view.

LOVATO PLACE

Several Lovato families live in Taos and the valley today. Phil Lovato was mayor of Taos from 1978 to 1986.

LUCERO ROAD

Several Lucero families live in Taos nowadays, but none lives on Lucero Road. The name, however, is a popular one and probably traces back to the pioneer settler Juan Lucero de Godoy, for whom Río Lucero, a stream in the upper valley, was named. The road runs alongside Río Lucero and was obviously named for the stream.

The word *Lucero* means "star."

LUND STREET

Fletcher M. Lund (1863–1943) came to Taos from St. Louis in the 1920s. He owned and operated a livery stable at the corner of Paseo del Pueblo Norte and Armory (now Civic Plaza Drive). The street name honors the

Lund family and was probably named by Guy Lund, who built some homes in the 1950s.

MABEL DODGE LANE

Mabel Dodge (1879–1962) was a wealthy socialite from the east coast who married Tony Luhan, a Taos Pueblo Indian. When she came to Taos after they married, she built a home called *Las Palomas,* "the doves or pigeons," and entertained lavishly the art colony and intellectuals who flocked to Taos in the early twentieth century. These included such people as artists Ernest Blumenschein, Bert Phillips, and Georgia O'Keeffe, writer D. H. Lawrence, photographers Ansel Adams and Paul Strand, psychoanalyst Carl Jung, and others.

Las Palomas was once owned by Dennis Hopper, who purchased it after he had stayed in Taos while filming *Easy Rider* in 1969.

The home is now a conference center and a bed and breakfast.

Pictured is the entrance to *Las Palomas,* the former home of the late Mabel Dodge Luhan, who married Tony Luhan and moved to Taos, where she entertained celebrities. (Photo courtesy Kit Carson Memorial Museum, Taos)

MAESTAS ROAD

The Maestas family was honored in this street name. Today, Taos has many families named Maestas.

MARES LANE

The name of this lane is a remembrance of the Mares family which has lived in Taos for many years. In Kit Carson Memorial Cemetery, the graves of José Julian Mares (1836–1925) and Manuelita R. Mares (1850–1930) serve as evidence of the early habitation of the family, and even today several families of Mareses still reside in Taos.

MARTINEZ LANE

This lane was named for the Manuel C. Martínez family who settled here in the 1890s. Their heirs still live there.

MARTYRS' LANE

The name of this street honors Governor Charles Bent and the other men who were slain in the Taos Revolt of 1847. In addition to Governor Bent, others who were slain were Louis Lee, acting sheriff of Taos; Cornelio Vigil, prefect; J. W. Leal, district attorney; Narcisco Beaubien, a son of Don Carlos Beaubien, circuit judge; and Pablo Jaramillo, a brother of Mrs. Bent.

(See Bent Street for full story.)

Wealthy socialite Millicent Rogers visited Taos and fell in love with the town. While living in Taos, she began a collection of native arts and crafts. After her death, the Millicent Rogers Museum was established.

MILLICENT ROGERS ROAD

The Millicent Rogers Museum is located just off this road; and the name, of course, honors Millicent Rogers, who was born in New York in 1902, the grand-daughter of Henry Huttleston Rogers. Rogers was a partner with John D. Rockefeller in Standard Oil and a founder of Anaconda Copper and U. S. Steel.

A striking beauty and a woman of high fashion in clothing and jewelry, Millicent Rogers led a glamorous life. She was married and divorced three times, and she

came to Taos in 1947 after having ended a relationship with Clark Gable that had lasted for three years.

She fell in love with Taos and moved there. While doing research for the renovation of an adobe house, she became interested in the art and design of the area and began collecting rugs, blankets, jewelry, santos, and kachinas.

On January 1, 1954, she died of a massive stroke caused by a fall in her bathroom. By that time, she had amassed, in a short period, one of the nation's most important collections of Southwest Indian art.

Paul Peralta Ramos, her son, purchased the collection from the estate, and he and other family members founded the Millicent Rogers Museum, which was opened three years later in the Manby-Thorne House Stables, adjacent to the Taos Inn. In 1968 it moved to its present quarters about four miles from the heart of town, about a mile from the blinking yellow light, (which for years, according to Allen Vigil, Town Planning Commissioner, was Taos' one landmark).

MIMBRES CIRCLE

The word is Spanish, meaning "willow trees." The Spaniards gave the name *Mimbreños* to an early Indian tribe who built pit houses and lived near the river that is called Mimbres River.

MONDRAGON STREET

The Mondragón family name is a popular one in Taos and in the valley.

Sebastián de Monroy Mondragón came to New Mexico with De Vargas during the Reconquest of 1692.

MONTANER STREET

According to Fayne Lutz of the local historical society, this street was named for a Montaner family, though no one by that name is currently listed in the telephone directory.

MONTANO LANE

Mrs. Lutz reports that this lane was named in honor of the Montaño family, a number of whom currently reside in Taos.

MONTECITO LANE

On the north side of Taos, near the mountains, Montecito Lane, Spanish for "little mountain," is aptly named.

MONTOYA STREET

The Montoya family was honored in this street name. Montoya is a very common name in Taos and in the Taos valley.

MORA LANE

The Spanish word *la mora* means "mulberry," and it is possible that the lane was named for the mulberry tree. Howwever, there is a legend that links the name to Taos.

According to T. M. Pearce (*New Mexico Place Names*), Céran St. Vrain found a dead man in 1823 on the banks of the Río de la Casa and called the place *L'Eau de Mort*, "the water of the dead." This story suggests that a misunderstanding of the French may have provided the name.

Another legend says that the Spaniards supplemented their diets with *moras* or mulberries growing on the mountainsides. And thus the name came to apply.

Also there are a town, a river, and a county in New Mexico by that name. The entire Mora Grant was designated as *Lo de Mora* or *De Lo Mora*. Pearce says that the Spanish neuter article *lo* means "thing, that which belongs to" and is used in other names as well. He suggests that the Mora surname comes from one or more individuals, such as Mora Pineda and Garcia de la Mora, who came to New Mexico after the Reconquest of 1692. People by this name were living on the frontier by the end of the eighteenth centruy.

Possibly the street name remembers Father Mora, who was killed (along with Fr. Pedrosa) in 1680 at Taos Pueblo when the pueblo Indians rebelled.

In 1993 there were Mora families in nearby Angel Fire and Penasco.

MORADA ROAD

This street was named for *La Morada,* which is located on nearby Las Cruces Street. From Spanish *morada,* "abode or home," the name applied to the home of the *Penitentes,* a lay order of Saint Francis. The *Penitentes* functioned as priests when there was no church with a priest available. They could perform marriages, rosaries, funerals, baptisms, and other rites.

A young man could be initiated into the *Penitentes* at age fifteen, and all rites were secretive.

The *Penitentes* were a group of penitents, and a part of their penitence included flagellating themselves, as is evidenced even today by the blood-spattered beams in the living area of the edifice.

During Holy Week, they seemed to associate more with the Passion of Christ than with the Resurrection. They carried huge crosses, and sometimes they would crucify one of their group. Usually, however, the person being crucified would survive.

Just outside *La Morada* stands a very large cross; and about a quarter of a mile down their land, stand another large cross (about ten to twelve feet high) and a smaller cross (eight to nine feet) on either side of the large one.

The *Penitentes* lived at *La Morada*, practicing penitence, austerity, and flagellation. Pictured is one of the crosses that the group used for crucifixion on occasion.

This particular *morada* was known as *Morada Centro,* and it served New Mexico and Colorado. The oldest part of the structure was built prior to 1830. It is the largest *morada* in existence and possibly the largest one ever constructed. The structure as it now appears was completed in 1911. It lies on Indian land, which the Indians deeded to the *Penitentes.* The land is a long, narrow strip which includes the nearby cemetery called *Composanto de Nuestro Padre Jesus Nazareno.*

La Morada was abandoned earlier in the twentieth century and was vandalized severely, including destruction of records of two hundred years or so. It now serves as the archives of the Kit Carson Memorial Museum, which is doing some restoration work, including restoration of the seven-hole outdoor privy.

MORGAN ROAD

Melvin Weimer, builder and developer, named this street, presumably for a relative.

MURRAY LANE

This little street was named for the Murray family, presumably for Curly Murray, who was quite a personality in Taos.

According to Rebecca Salsbury James in "Allow Me to Present . . . ," Curly was born near Wichita, Kansas, in 1888, the son of Thomas L. Murray and Martha Burger Murray. When he was eight years old, the family moved to a ranch in Oklahoma, where he learned to love and ride horses. In time, he became a jockey, and he won often, especially at the tracks at fairs. When he became overweight and could no longer be a jockey, he began a gambling career, with dice and cards.

He used money gained from gambling to buy oil leases in some of the Oklahoma boom towns, but the leases went bad, and he went broke. For a time, he bought legal whiskey in Missouri and distributed it in other states by use of a fleet of taxicabs.

He enlisted in the Army in 1917 but was assigned as an ambulance driver because of his hand, which had been broken. When he was mustered out of the army in

1918, he married Florence Williams, of Blackwell, Oklahoma. Within three months of the marriage, she contracted tuberculosis and died within four years.

He headed for Borger, Texas, when it became a boom town in 1925. He firmly established his gambling and bootlegging in Borger, then, growing restless, went to Europe, visiting Monte Carlo, where he won big and everyone in the place was gathered around watching him.

In later years he returned to the race track, following his own horses at the races.

O

OAKELEY LANE

This street was named for Edward Oakeley (1900–1986), according to Betty Saiz, his daughter. Oakeley worked in construction and built two homes on this street. His father, Richard Oakeley, came from England sometime before 1900.

OJITOS ROAD

Ojitos, Spanish for "the springs," refers to the springs which are located below the old fish hatchery, which was operated by the Siler family until the 1940s. The fish hatchery was located just off Ranchitos Road.

ORINDA LANE

Truly a small lane, this street leads to the Orinda Bed and Breakfast, located at 461 Orinda Lane. Created in 1988 by David and Karol Dondero, the bed and breakfast was named in honor of Orinda, California, from whence they had come.

The name derives from an Indian language and means "for a bountiful grain harvest."

In 1992 Cary and George Pratt, from Chicago, purchased the establishment and continue to operate it today.

ORTIZ LANE

The Ortiz family are a promient family in the town and area. The street was named for E. B. Ortiz during the 1960s.

P

PADRE MARTINEZ LANE

The street has been known officially as Padre Martínez Lane; but because of some confusion with Martínez Lane, the town is changing the name to Padre Lane.

It was named for Padre Antonio José Martínez, who was born in Abiquiú, New Mexico, in 1793. His father, Severino Martínez, moved his family from Abiquiú to Taos early in the 1800s and had begun construction of the Martínez Hacienda in 1804. The hacienda was constructed as a fortress (it is now a museum and national historic landmark).

After the deaths of his wife and child when he was twenty-three, Antonio José entered the seminary in Durango, Mexico, and began a life of laborious study and religious scholarship. He returned to Taos in 1826 to become parish priest after having served in that position in his native Abiquiú.

In Taos he established the first co-educational school in New Mexico and published several textbooks, religious materials, political documents, and the first newspaper in the area, *El Crepusculo de Liberdad* ("The Dawn of Liberty"), with his own printing press, the first one west of the Mississippi. According to Campa (*Hispanic Culture in the Southwest*), some writers say that Josiah Gregg brought that printing press to the Southwest, but Campa indicates that Antonio Barreiro actually brought the press from Mexico City and sold it to Ramón Abreu, who passed it on to Padre Martínez.

The street name remembers Padre Antonio José Martínez, whose remains were buried in Kit Carson Memorial Cemetery in Taos.

Padre Martínez opposed mandatory tithing and charging for the sacraments. His liberal views brought him into conflict with Bishop Lamy, and he was supposedly excommunicated by Lamy. One source says that the excommunication occurred in 1856; others say it happened in 1862. Regardless, if he was, indeed, excommunicated, the action apparently was recorded only in the church in Arroyo Hondo, and Lamy's superiors were not notified. Martínez continued to serve as parish priest and then as a minister of a schismatic protestant church until his death on July 28, 1867. He was buried by his Penitente brothers.

Martínez was also politically active, serving in the assembly that helped organize the New Mexico Territory in 1848, although he was said to have been involved in

the revolt of the Taos Indians the previous year. In 1851 and 1862, he was a deputy in the Territorial Legislature.

PASEO DEL CANON EAST and WEST

The primary east-west road through Taos is Paseo del Cañon, with *East* or *West* added, depending on which side of Paseo del Pueblo it is located. The Spanish name means "avenue of (from) the canyon," and it leads to the Cañon community east of Taos.

PASEO DEL PUEBLO NORTE and PASEO DEL PUEBLO SUD

Spanish for "Avenue to (from) the Pueblo," this is the principal street of the town. It lies north-south, and the Taos Pueblo is about two miles off Paseo del Pueblo Norte.

The main through street in Taos, Paseo del Pueblo was named for the Taos Pueblo, which is located on the north side of Taos. (Photo courtesy Kit Carson Memorial Museum, Taos)

PERALTA STREET

Although Peralta is a common name in northern New Mexico, this particular Peralta family immigrated to New Mexico around 1820, according to Fayne Lutz of the local historical society. In Spain, Peralta had been a wine maker for the king of Spain before coming to the United States.

Of course, Don Pedro de Peralta was the second governor of New Mexico, succeeding Governor Oñate in 1609. He was the founder of Santa Fé. (See Paseo de Peralta in Santa Fé.)

PIEDMONT ROAD

This road is aptly named, as it curves along the foot or base of the mountain on the east side of Taos. This street name comes from Piedmont, Italy, and literally means "foot or base of the mountain." The name has become an eponym, a generic term which refers to land or a stream at the base of a mountain.

PLATA STREET

Builder Rod Thomas developed the subdivision in which *Plata* "silver" Street lies near *Calle de Oro,* "street of gold," and *Cobre* "copper" Street. Much as Colonel Walter Marmon chose names of minerals native to New Mexico for street names of Albuquerque, so Rod Thomas chose a similar tactic for Taos.

PLAZA GARCIA

This street was named for Leroy Garcia, who owns a compound or "plaza" of buildings situated there. His father, Rumaldo Garcia, served as mayor of Taos from 1968 to 1972.

QUINTANA ROAD

The Quintana name is a popular one in Taos and the valley. Though there are currently many Quintana families in Taos, the telephone directory shows no evidence of a Quintana family's currently living on Quintana Road.

In the early history of the area, Captain Luis Quintana led the settlers at La Cañada (now Santa Cruz) to protect their settlements during the Pueblo Revolt of 1680.

The name was in the Santa Fé and Taos area as early as the 1600s, and the street obviously commemorates the family's name.

RANCHITOS ROAD

The *ranchitos* or "little ranches" are the small acreages on the western outskirts of Taos. Ranchitos Road leads from the downtown area out west to where it splits into Lower Ranchitos Road and Upper Ranchitos Road.

RANDALL LANE

Charles Howard Randall (1867–1943) owned property on either side of this street, and the street was named for him. His son, Elisha P. Randall (1896–1971), developed some property in Taos. (See Ácoma.) His grandsons still operate Taos Lumber Company.

REED STREET

Builder Melvin Weimer, who owns a great deal of property around Taos, developed a small addition in southwest Taos. He named the three streets for his daughter, Dea, and for his two sons, Alexander and Reed.

RIBAK LANE

According to David Witt at the Harson Library. Louis Ribak (1903–1979) moved to Taos in 1944. A moderately well-known artist in New York before moving to Taos, Ribak became known as one of the painters involved in social realism. During the 1950s in Taos, he converted to abstract expressionism. While in Taos, he was one of the artists most highly regarded and respected by other artists.

RIBAK LANE

During the 1950s, the art community of Taos basically re-invented itself and became an outpost of postwar modernism, and Louis Ribak was one of the leaders of this movement.

His wife, Beatrice Ribak, whose professional name is Beatrice Mandelman, is a significant abstract artist.

Their home is located on the street named for them.

RIO CHIQUITO ROAD

The street was named for the nearby Río Chiquito, "little river," a fork of the Río Grande that exits the mountains northeast of Ranchos de Taos.

ROY ROAD

Reportedly, Roy Road was named by Melvin Weimer, builder and developer, for one of his family members.

S

SAAVEDRA STREET

The Saavedra family were prominent in Taos during the early twentieth century. For many years, Norberto Saavedra operated Río Grande Rexall, the first Hispanic-owned drug store in the area. He was also a builder.

Today only one Saavedra is listed in the telephone directory.

SALAZAR STREET

The street was named for the Salazar family. Arturo Salazar was a builder during the 1930s and 1940s.

SANGRE DE CRISTO ROAD

This road lies near the Sangre de Cristo ("blood of Christ") Mountains and is named in their honor. This mountain range, particularly when the sun hits them in the late afternoon just before sunset, are blood red, thus calling to mind the blood of Christ.

SANTISTEVAN

The street remembers the Santistevan family who were early settlers in the region. Don Juan Santistevan (1883–1908) was a member of this well-known family who were owners of large parcels of land in the valley and in the village of Taos. Don Juan established the first bank in Taos and owned the property surrounding the Kit Carson Cemetery until it was acquired by Arthur Manby. The Santistevan family also operated a blacksmith shop in the early twentieth century.

There are several families of Santistevans still in Taos today.

According to Wally Chatwin, he and Rod Thomas, with their company known as Wally-Rod, named this street for the Santistevan who owned the property.

SARSON COURT

According to William Sarson, the street was named for him because he was the first resident on the street, moving there in 1968. A real estate agent, Sarson came to Taos in 1963 and married a local girl. He is a real estate appraiser.

SCHEURICH LANE

Aloysius Scheurich, a native of Germany, arrived in New Mexico in 1854. He married Teresina Bent (1841–1920), daughter of Governor Charles Bent. Teresina was one of the daughters who escaped through the hole in the adobe wall. (See Bent Street and Martyrs' Street.)

The couple had three children—Lena, who apparently remained single; Mercedes, who married Frank Ellis; and Dora, who married John Royal Berry.

Scheurich earned his living as a teamster.

SECO LANE

Located in the northern portion of Taos, this street was probably named for Arroyo Seco, Spanish for "dry stream," a community located seven miles north of Taos.

SECO LANE

Settlement of Arroyo Seco was begun in 1804 when Cristóbal Martínez and José Gregario Martínez, from Río Arriba County, planted crops there. Later, they built their homes there in 1807.

SIERRA VISTA LANE

Spanish for "view of the mountain," this street is fittingly named, as the mountains around Taos are in full view.

SILER ROAD

The Siler family owned quite a bit of property in the area and operated a fish hatchery on Hatchery Road near the springs until the 1940s.

SIMPSON STREET

This street name honors Captain Smith H. Simpson (1832–1916) and the Simpson family. Captain Simpson is famous in Taos from Civil War days.

The United States flag had flown over the Taos plaza from a short flagpole since 1846. In 1861 Confederate sympathizers kept tearing Old Glory down from the pole. So Captain Simpson and a group of men went to Taos Canyon and found a tall, slender cottonwood tree, cut it, trimmed it, and brought it back to the Taos plaza. With the help of Kit Carson, Céran St. Vrain, Thomas Boggs, and others, Simpson nailed the flag to the tree and raised it above the plaza. Simpson spread the word around the plaza and the town that anyone who dared to bother the flag would be shot. He and the others went to a nearby store and guarded the flag. Because it was nailed to the "pole," it was impossible to lower the flag except by taking down the pole; so the flag flew twenty-four hours a day. When military officials in Santa Fé heard of the courageous act, they permitted Taos to fly the flag twenty-four hours a day. Later, Congress granted permission for the continuous flying of the flag twenty-four hours a day.

When they died, Captain Simpson and his wife, Josefa, were buried in Kit Carson Memorial Cemetery.

SIPAPU STREET

This street was given an Indian name by the Randall family when Elisha P. Randall (1896–1971) developed the Randall Subdivision. (See Ácoma.)

In a pueblo kiva, the sipapu is a shallow hole covered by a plank or stone, located in front of the fire. It represents the entrance to the underworld or place of beginning, where man first arrived at self-conscious existence. According to Indian mythology, when they climbed out of the dark, dreary underworld, the entrance never completely closed; therefore, the slab covering the symbolic sipapu has a round hole in it. According to Ickes (*Mesa Land*), the unclosed band frequently found on pueblo pottery and the plugged hole found in the center of ceremonial baskets symbolize the unclosed hole into the sipapu.

Skip Miller of the Kit Carson Memorial Museum in Taos says that the Indian myth of the emergence of man from the sipapu is an allegory to the birth process and man's emergence into consciousness.

SPRUCE STREET

When one turns off Kit Carson Road onto Spruce Street, one immediately sees a very large, tall, blue spruce tree on the left at the first house. Just beyond that point, on the right, the next house has five huge blue spruce trees in the front yard.

SUNSHINE ROAD

Apparently selected by whim, this name may be an optimistic moniker. However, in an interview, Fayne Lutz quipped, "No trees, maybe that's why the name was chosen."

TERESINA LANE

This street connects to Scheurich Lane and was named for Teresina Bent Scheurich, daughter of Governor Charles Bent, who was murdered during the Taos Rebellion of 1849. Bent's name is remembered just one street away, on Bent Street.

TEWA STREET

This street was given an Indian name by the Randall family when Elisha P. Randall (1896–1971) developed the Randall Subdivision. (See Ácoma.)

One of the Tanowan group of tribes, the Tewa maintained a number of towns and villages in New Mexico.

THOMAS COURT

Located near Thomas Trail, this street was created by and named for Rod Thomas, a building contractor, during the 1980s.

THOMAS TRAIL

In the mid-1980s, builder Rod Thomas constructed four units on this short street and named it Thomas Trail. In early 1993, according to Allen Vigil, Town Planning Commissioner, the residents of the street petitioned the Planning Commission to change the name to Del Norte, and the new name was granted.

TRUJILLO LANE and TRUJILLO ROAD

The Trujillo family provided the names for these two streets. Trujillo is a common name in Taos, and there are many families by that name, including a mayor of Taos, Eloy D. Trujillo, who served from 1942 to 1944.

TOALNE STREET

This street was given an Indian name by the Randall family when Elisha P. Randall (1896–1971) developed the Randall Subdivision. (See Ácoma.)

According to John Randall, son of Elisha, the name is a Zuni word that means "corn mountain," and the family liked it because it was different.

VEGAS DE TAOS WEST, VEGAS DE TAOS CIRCLE, and VEGAS DE TAOS LOOP

These streets derived their names from Spanish *vegas*, "meadows," and the name was applied because of the meadow area on which the subdivision was developed.

VALDEZ

The Valdez family have long been residents of Taos. Records show that in 1856 Antonio José Valdez was a resident of the town.

VALVERDE STREET

Spanish for "green valley," the name may be a description, but probably the street was named for a family by that name. The family may be descendants of Captain Don Antonio Valverde y Cosia, who was acting governor of New Mexico from 1717 to 1722. Pearce (*New Mexico Place Names*) says that even though his only mode of transportation was by foot, he visited all the Indian pueblos.

VIGIL STREET

Nelson and Rudy Vigil are the contractors who built the Vigil Subdivision in the 1980s and named the street for their surname.

The Vigil name is an old one in Taos.

Donanciano Vigil was appointed governor after Governor Bent's death. He was born in Santa Fé in 1802, the son of Juan Cristobál Vigil and Doña María Antonia Marin. His father was a descendant of Francisco Montes Vigil, who had been a soldier and had arrived in New Mexico during the seventeenth century shortly after De Vargas' Reconquest of 1692.

Jesse Vigil served as mayor of Taos, 1964–1966.

And an early reference says that the José Vigil family lived in Taos just after the Reconquest of 1692. His family lived outside the walls of the pueblo, and a Vigil

built a *torreon,* a defense tower, which survived until 1910, according to John Sherman in *Taos: A Pictorial History.*

W

WEIMER ROAD

Melvin Weimer owns a great deal of land around Taos and has done a considerable amount of building and developing of subdivisions. This street in southeast Taos was named for him.

WITT ROAD

The Witt family were early inhabitants of Taos. They settled in Eagle Nest, from Oklahoma, in the early 1800s, according to Fayne Lutz, then came to Taos and built a lodge and a planing mill. Simeon Witt established a sawmill in the Taos area in the early 1850s, the first in northern New Mexico.

In the Kit Carson Cemetery are the graves of William Simeon Witt (1843–1917) and probably his son, Walter S. Witt (1885–1949). One Witt family still lives in Taos in 1993.

Y

YOUNG-HUNTER ROAD

Born in Glasgow, Scotland, in 1874, John Young-Hunter was a resident of Taos during most of the time between 1917 and 1955, when he died. Best known as an oil painter, he made his living mostly as a portrait painter.

Young-Hunter was very much a follower of John Singer Sargent, whom he knew even as a boy, as their families were friends.

The road on which Young-Hunter resided was named for him.

Z

ZIA DRIVE and ZIA STREET

These two streets were named by the Randall family when Elisha P. Randall (1896–1971) developed the Randall Subdivision. The family chose American Indian names—Ácoma, Apache, Sipapu, Tewa, Zia, and Zuni. (See Ácoma.)

Zia Pueblo, located sixteen miles northwest of Bernalillo, is honored in this street name. From the native word *Tsia,* the name appears variously as *Zia, Chia,* and *Sia*. The pueblo is mentioned in Castañeda's account of the Coronado expedition in 1540–1541, according to T. M. Pearce (*New Mexico Place Names*).

ZUNI STREET

This street also was named by the Randall family when Elisha Randall developed Randall Subdivision. (See Zia and Ácoma.)

Zuni Pueblo is located five miles east of Gallup. According to T. M. Pearce (*New Mexico Place Names*), the word is a Spanish adaptation of the Keresan *sunyi 'tsi* or *su'nyitsa,* of unknown meaning. It is one of the New Mexico desert pueblos with Ácoma and Laguna.

Bibliography

Abousleman, Michel D., ed. *Who's Who in New Mexico.* Albuquerque: The Abousleman Company, 1937.

Alberts, Don E. *Balloons to Bombers: Aviation in Albuquerque 1882–1945.* Albuquerque: The Albuquerque Museum, 1987.

An Illustrated History of New Mexico. Chicago: The Lewis Publishing Company, 1895.

Beach, Rev. Robert M. "*Ayer y Hoy-Taos, N.M.*" Los Lunas, New Mexico: Saint Clement's Church, 1976.

Beck, Warren A. *New Mexico: A History of Four Centuries.* Norman: University of Oklahoma Press, 1962.

Biebel, Charles D. *Making the Most of It.* Albuquerque: The Albuquerque Museum, 1975.

Brewer, Steve. "The Picks on Route 66," Albuquerque *Journal* (July 4, 1993), C 1.

Campa, Arthur L. *Hispanic Culture in the Southwest.* Norman: University of Oklahoma Press, 1979.

Canby, Thomas Y. "The Anasazi Riddles in the Ruins," *National Geographic* (November 1982), 562–592.

Casaus, Phill. "Street Stories: Developer Showed Devotion to Dallas," The Albuquerque *Journal* (January 31, 1993), G 4.

Cassidy, Ina Sizer. "Art and Artists of New Mexico," *New Mexico Magazine* (January 1932), 10, 44.

Chamberlain, T. H. and Editors of *Newsweek. The Generals and the Admirals.* New York: The Devin-Adair Company, 1945.

Chilton, Lance, et al. *New Mexico: A New Guide to the Colorful State.* Albuquerque: University of New Mexico Press, 1984.

Clark, Willard F. *Recuerdos de Santa Fé 1928–1943.* Santa Fé: Clarks' Studio, 1990.

Cordel, Linda S., ed. *Tijeras Canyon.* Albuquerque: University of New Mexico Press, 1980.

Davis, Mary P., and Michael J. Roch. "Huning Highland Neighborhood Walking Tour." No date, no publisher listed.

Delgado, N. and D. *Guide to the Historical Markers of New Mexico.* Albuquerque: Ward Anderson Printing Company, 1968.

"Dr. Charles R. Spain, Head of City Schools, Dies of Heart Attack," Albuquerque *Journal* (May 9, 1965).

Duffus, R. L. *The Santa Fé Trail.* New York: Longmans, Green and Company, 1931. Republished by Scholarly Press, St. Clair Shores, Michigan, 1971.

Edelman, Sandra. *Summer People Winter People.* Santa Fé: Sunstone, 1986.

Ellis, Bruce. *Bishop Lamy's Santa Fé Cathedral.* Albuquerque: University of New Mexico Press, 1985.

Ellis, Richard N. *New Mexico Past and Present.* Albuquerque: University of New Mexico Press, 1971.

Emmett, Chris. *Fort Union and the Winning of the Southwest.* Norman: University of Oklahoma Press, 1965.

Espinosa, J. Manuel. *Crusaders of the Río Grande.* Salisbury, North Carolina: Documentary Publications, 1977.

Ferguson, Erna. *Albuquerque.* Albuquerque: Merle Armitage Editions, 1941.

______. *New Mexico: A Pageant of Three People.* New York: Alfred A. Knopf, 1951.

Fitzpatrick, George, and Harry Caplin. *Albuquerque: 100 Years in Pictures.* Albuquerque: Modern Press, 1976.

"Former Justice Henry G. Coors Is Dead at 75," Albuquerque *Journal* (January 2, 1961).

Galbraith, Den. *Turbulent Taos.* Santa Fé: Sunstone Press, 1983.

González, Nancie L. *The Spanish-Americans of New Mexico: A Heritage of Pride.* Albuquerque: University of New Mexico Press, 1967.

Haines, Helen. *History of New Mexico 1530–1890.* New York: New Mexico Historical Publishing Company, 1891.

Hakin, Besim S. *Historic Old Town: Albuquerque, New Mexico.* Unpublished report for Department of Community and Economic Development, City of Albuquerque, New Mexico, March 1983.

Harrington, Eldred. *An Engineer Writes.* Albuquerque: Calvin Horn, Publisher, 1967.

Harvey, Fred, ed. *Enchantorama 250th Anniversary of Albuquerque 1706–1956.* Albuquerque: Chamber of Commerce, 1956.

Hening, H. B., and E. Dana Johnson. "Albuquerque, New Mexico," Albuquerque *Morning Journal*, 1908.

Higgins, Philip. "Some Street Names Obvious, But Others Are Misleading," The *New Mexican* (April 4, 1956), no page given in vertical file.

History of New Mexico. 2 vol. Los Angeles: Pacific States Publishing Company, 1907.

Horgan, Paul. *Conquistadors in North American History.* New York: Farrar, Straus and Company, 1963.

______. *Lamy of Santa Fé.* New York: Farrar, Straus and Giroux, 1975.

______. *The Centuries of Santa Fé.* New York: E. P. Dutton and Company, Inc. 1956.

Hudspeth's *Albuquerque City Directory 1959.* El Paso: Hudspeth Directory Company, 1960.

Ickes, Anna Wilmarth. *Mesa Land.* Boston: Houghton Mifflin Company, 1933.

James, Rebecca Salsburg. "Allow Me to Present 18 Ladies and Gentlemen and Taos, N. M. 1885–1939." Taos: El Crepúsculo, 1953.

Jamison, Bill. *The Insider's Guide to Santa Fé.* Boston: The Harvard Common Press, 1987.

Jenkins, Dr. Myra Ellen, and James R. Thorpe, III. "From Retreat to Resort." Albuquerque: McLeod Printing Company, no date.

Johnson, Bryon A. *Old Town, Albuquerque, New Mexico: A Guide to Its History and Architecture.* Albuquerque: City of Albuquerque, 1980.

Johnson, Byron A., and Robert K. Dauner. *Early Albuquerque: A Photographic History 1870–1918.* Albuquerque: Albuquerque *Journal*, 1981.

Jones, Oakah L., Jr. *Pueblo Warriors and Spanish Conquest.* Norman: University of Oklahoma Press, 1966.

Kalloch, Eunice, and Ruth K. Hall. *The First Ladies of New Mexico.* Santa Fé: The Lightning Tree, 1982.

Keegan, John, ed. *Who Was Who in World War II.* New York: Thomas J. Crowell, 1978.

Keleher, William A. *Memoirs: 1892–1969.* Santa Fé: The Rydal Press, 1969.

______. *The Fabulous Frontier.* Albuquerque: University of New Mexico Press, 1962.

Kenner, Charles L. *A History of New Mexican-Plains Indian Relations.* Norman: University of Oklahoma Press, 1969.

Kessell, John L. *Kiva, Cross, and Crown.* Washington, D. C.: National Park Service, 1979.

LaFarge, Oliver. *Santa Fé.* Norman: University of Oklahoma Press, 1959.

Lamar, Howard Roberts. *The Far Southwest 1846–1912: A Territorial History.* New Haven: Yale University Press, 1966.

LeViness, W. Thetford. "Disney Films Legend of New Mexico Honored," The Denver *Post* (July 25, 1958).

Lopez, Larry. *Taos Valley: A Historical Survey.* Santa Fé: New Mexico Bureau of Land Management, 1975.

McMullen, Thomas A., and David Walker. *Biographical Dictionary of American Territorial Governors.* No city listed: Meckler Publishing Company, 1984.

Meyer, Marian. "Charles W. Dudrow: A Biographical Sketch," found in vertical file in Museum of New Mexico History Library.

Monaco, James, and the editors of BASELINE. *The Encyclopedia of Film.* New York: Putnam Publishing Company, 1991.

Natella, Arthur A., Jr., ed. *The Spanish in America 1513–1974.* Dobbs Ferry, New York: Oceana Publications, Inc., 1975.

New Mexico Writers Project, *New Mexico: A Guide to the Colorful State.* New York: Hastings House, 1940.

Noble, David Grant, ed. *Santa Fé: History of an Ancient City.* Santa Fé: School of American Research Press, 1989.

Nusbaum, Rosemary. *Tierra Dulce.* Santa Fé: The Sunstone Press, 1980.

"100 Years from Founding of Menaul School 1881–1981," published for the Menaul School Centennial by a special committee. Albuquerque: Menaul Historical Library, 1981.

Overbeck, Joy, and Wolfgang Pogzeba. *Ranchos de Taos: San Francisco de Asis Church.* Kansas City: Lowell Press, 1981.

Pearce, T. M., ed. *New Mexico Place Names.* Albuquerque: University of New Mexico Press, 1965.

Perrigo, Lynn S. *Our Spanish Southwest.* Dallas: Banks Upshaw and Company, 1960.

Pinkerton, Elaine. *Santa Fé on Foot.* Santa Fé: Ocean Tree Services, 1986.

Plaisance, Vana J. "Bataan Death March Survivor Recalls War Atrocities," The Lafayette, Louisiana, *Daily Advertiser* (September 24, 1993), B 1.

"Prominent Builder Dale Bellamah Dies," Albuquerque *Journal* (April 20, 1972), 1.

Rebord, Bernice Ann. *A Social History of Albuquerque 1880–1885.* Unpublished M.A. thesis, University of New Mexico, 1947.

Reeve, Frank D. *History of New Mexico.* New York: Lewis Historical Publishing Company, 1961.

Rodriguez, Rosina Ransom. "My Name Is Santa Fé and they call me the City Different." Santa Fé: Rosina, 1991.

Romero, F. R. Bob, and Neil Poese. "A Brief History of Taos." Taos: Kit Carson Museums, 1992.

Sánchez, Joseph. "The Peralta-Ordóñez Affair and the Founding of Santa Fé," *Santa Fé: History of An Ancient City.*

David Grant Nobel, ed. Santa Fé: School of American Research Press, 1989.

______. "Twelve Days in August," *Santa Fé: History of An Ancient City*. David Grant Nobel, ed. Santa Fé: School of American Research Press, 1989.

Santa Fé Mirror. Santa Fé: Piñon Publishing Company, 1961.

Sargeant, Kathryn, and Mary Davis. *Shining River Precious Land*. Albuquerque: The Albuquerque Museum, 1986.

Segale, Sr. Blandina. *At the End of the Santa Fé Trail*. Milwaukee: The Bruce Publishing Company, 1948.

Severson, Jack. "Museum Hidden Among Typical Taos Tourist Site," Albuquerque *Journal* (July 14, 1991), 6C.

Sherman, John. *Santa Fé: A Pictorial History*. Norfolk, Virginia: Donning Company, 1983.

______. *Taos: A Pictorial History*. Santa Fé: William Gannon, 1990.

Simmons, Eve. "Grant County Loop," Silver City *Daily Press* (July 16, 1966).

Simmons, Marc. *Albuquerque: A Narrative History*. Albuquerque: University of New Mexico Press, 1982.

______. *New Mexico: An Interpretive History*. Albuquerque: University of New Mexico Press, 1988.

______. "Santiago: The Saint of Conquest," *New Mexico Magazine* (January 1992), 24–31.

______. *Spanish Government in New Mexico*. Albuquerque: University of New Mexico Press, 1968.

______. *Yesterday in Santa Fé*. Santa Fé: Sunstone Press, 1989.

Size, Corinne P., and Beverley Spears. *Santa Fé Historic Neighborhood Study*. Santa Fé: City of Santa Fé, 1988.

Stanley, F. *The Duke City: The Story of Albuquerque, New Mexico 1706–1956*. Pampa, Texas: Pampa Print Shop, 1963.

"Taos' Golden Years: 1934–1984: 50th Anniversary of Incorporation of the Town of Taos," The Taos *News*, 1984.

The Historic Santa Fé Foundation. *Old Santa Fé Today*. Albuquerque: University of New Mexico, 1991.

Thomas, Alfred Barnaby, ed. *After Coronado: Spanish Exploration Northeast of New Mexico, 1696–1727*. Norman: University of Oklahoma, 1935.

Threinen, Ellen. *Historic Architecture of Albuquerque's Central Corridor*. Copy. October 1977.

Tryk, Sheila. "Somber Colors, Sunny Outlook," *New Mexico Magazine* (March 1981), 48.

Twitchell, Ralph Emerson. *The Leading Facts of New Mexico History*. Albuquerque: Horn and Wallace, 1963.

Umansky, Diane. "New Mexico Allure," *First for Women* (September 1993), 102–104.

"Uncle Benny Hyde Dies," The Santa Fé *New Mexican* (July 27, 1933), 1.

VanNess, John R. *Hispanos in Northern New Mexico.* New York: AMS Press, 1991.

Vigil, Maurilio E. *Los Patrones: Profiles of Hispanic Political Leaders in New Mexico History.* Washington, D.C.: University Press of America, 1980.

Wallace, David. "Signature in Silver," Los Angeles *Times* (May 17, 1991), E 10.

Warren, Jill. "Fremont Ellis: Always a Ray of Sunlight," *New Mexico Magazine* (July 1984), 28–32.

Weigle, Marta. *New Mexico in Cameo and Camera.* Albuquerque: University of New Mexico Press, 1985.

Weigle, Marta, and Peter White. *The Lore of New Mexico.* Albuquerque: University of New Mexico Press, 1988.

West Point Alumni Foundation, *Register of Graduates and Former Cadets of the United States Military Academy.* West Point, New York: West Point Alumni Foundation, 1967.

Wilson, Chris. *University Neighborhoods Handbook.* Albuquerque: no publisher listed, 1986.

Worley, John F. *Worley's Directory of Albuquerque, New Mexico.* Dallas: John F. Worley Directory Company, 1910.

Index

Index

C

D

E

F

Index

G

H

I

J

Index

N

O

Index

S

Y-Z